Emerson's Pragmatic Vision

Literature & Philosophy

A. J. Cascardi, General Editor

This new series will publish books in a wide range of subjects in philosophy and literature, including studies of the social and historical issues that relate these two fields. Drawing on the resources of the Anglo-American and Continental traditions, the series will be open to philosophically informed scholarship covering the entire range of contemporary critical thought.

Already published:

J. M. Bernstein, *The Fate of Art: Aesthetic Alienation from Kant to Derrida and Adorno*
Peter Bürger, *The Decline of Modernism*
Mary Finn, *Writing the Incommensurable: Kierkegaard, Rossetti, and Hopkins*
Robert Steiner, *Toward a Grammar of Abstraction: Modernity, Wittgenstein, and the Paintings of Jackson Pollock*

Emerson's Pragmatic Vision

The Dance *of* the Eye

David Jacobson

The Pennsylvania State University Press
University Park, Pennsylvania

Library of Congress Cataloging-in-Publication Data

Jacobson, David, 1953–
 Emerson's pragmatic vision : the dance of the eye / David Jacobson.
  p.   cm.
 Includes bibliographical references and index.
 ISBN (invalid) 0-271-00986-2 (alk. paper)
  1. Emerson, Ralph Waldo, 1803–1882—Philosophy. 2. Pragmatism in literature. I. Title.
 PS1642.P5J33   1993
 814′ .3—dc20   92-14266
                                                                                  CIP

Copyright © 1993 David Jacobson
All rights reserved
Printed in the United States of America

Published by The Pennsylvania State University Press, Suite C, Barbara Building, University Park, PA 16802-1003

It is the policy of The Pennsylvania State University Press to use acid-free paper for the first printing of all clothbound books. Publications on uncoated stock satisfy the minimum requirements of American National Standard for Information Sciences—Permanence of Paper for Printed Library Materials, ANSI Z39.48–1984.

Contents

Acknowledgments	vii
Introduction: The Joyous Science of Power	1
Part I: Standing	27
1 Vision and Thought	31
2 Culture and Ownership	63
Part II: Falling	85
3 The Falling Away of Man	91
4 Experience Joy or Power	115
Part III: Whirling	165
5 The Fatal Event and the Birth of Agency	171
Conclusion: The Art of Power	199
Index	205

For Alexander and Brendan

Acknowledgments

I have completed this project with the help of a number of people and programs, whom it is now my pleasure to acknowledge. The Department of English at the University of Rochester provided me much appreciated aid as their Andrew W. Mellon Postdoctoral Fellow in 1987–88. During that year of research and writing I formulated the basic argument of the book. I have profited as well from the generous release time policies of the Department of English and the Campus Research Board at the University of Illinois, Urbana-Champaign. A number of my colleagues at the University of Illinois kindly read and commented on part or all of the book. I am grateful to Nina Baym, Peter Garrett, Bruce Michelson, Robert Parker, and Emily Watts. Leon Chai was particularly helpful at the late stages of revision. Among my teachers at the University of Washington I remember with gratitude the encouragement of Robert Abrams, Ann Kibbey, Raimonda Modiano, Hazard Adams, and, most of all, Charles Altieri. Portions of Chapter 1 first appeared as "'Compensation': Exteriority beyond the Spirit of Revenge," in *ESQ*, and "Vision's Imperative: 'Self-Reliance' and the Command to See Things As They Are," in *Studies in Romanticism*. I gratefully acknowledge the editors' permission to reprint them here. Finally, I want to thank Bunita Berg, without whose support I could not have written this book.

Ah ye old ghosts! ye builders of dungeons in the air! why do I ever allow you to encroach on me a moment; a moment to win me to your hapless company? In every week there is some hour when I read my commission in every cipher of nature, and know that I was made for another office, a professor of the Joyous Science, a detector & delineator of occult harmonies & unpublished beauties, a herald of civility, nobility, learning, & wisdom; an affirmer of the One Law, yet as one who should affirm it in music or dancing, a priest of the Soul yet one who would better love to celebrate it through the beauty of health & harmonious power.
  —Emerson, *The Journals and Miscellaneous Notebooks*

[Philosophy] wants . . . a Dionysian affirmation of the world as it is, without subtraction, exception, or selection—it wants the eternal circulation:—the same things, the same logic and illogic of entanglements. The highest state a philosopher can attain: to stand in a Dionysian relationship to existence—my formula for this is *amor fati*.
  —Nietzsche, *The Will to Power*

Introduction:
The Joyous Science of Power

When Emerson stood before the Society of the Adelphi in Waterville College, Maine, and said, "That man shall be learned who reduceth his learning to practice," he expressed the pivotal sentiment in his lifelong meditation on the relation between Man and nature. The statement, and the lecture "The Method of Nature" in which it is found, indicates and inaugurates the practical foundation of his later theory and sets it in sharp contrast to his writings before 1841.[1] To be sure, Emerson recognized the practical application of thought as elemental to the idea of self-reliance developed in the 1830s. Under the concept of self-reliance he repeated, and one could say summarized, the premise of humanism, the intrinsic relation between thought and action and the legislative power of the former over the latter. Always the seer is a sayer, Emerson had put it; visionary insight predicts its application, and the thoughtful individual stands self-reliant at the center of his or her world. The extremes to which Emerson took this premise in his early period, beginning with *Nature* and including *Essays: First Series* and the great lectures of the 1830s, justify the characterization of him as a radical humanist. But the state-

---

1. Ralph Waldo Emerson, *The Collected Works of Ralph Waldo Emerson*, ed. Alfred R. Ferguson et al. (Cambridge, Mass.: Harvard University Press, 1971), 1: 136. Hereafter cited as *CW*.

ment in "The Method of Nature" invites an even more extreme, and contrary, interpretation. It suggests, not the reciprocity of thought and action that sponsor Central Man, but the "reduction" of thought, or learning, to practice, and accordingly the priority of practice over thought, or, to put it in terms Emerson used, the obedience of thought to practice. The practical philosophy of obedience this entails is the substance of Emerson's later doctrine of fate. Understanding how he moved from a spiritualist faith in the creative thought of the individual to a philosophy of obedience at odds with a customary understanding of Emersonian self-reliance is the topic of this book.

Such a discussion of the development of Emerson's thought requires, I believe, a philosophical interpretation of his writings, for the distinctions that he uses to characterize his thinking in each of its phases are philosophical in nature, and they are presented by drawing on the fundamental terms and concepts of his philosophical tradition, which is narrowly modern philosophy and broadly the Western metaphysical tradition emanating from Plato's works. It is unfortunate that Emerson critics have until recently been reluctant to read his essays and lectures within a philosophical frame of reference.[2] If this has been because of his own insistence that he was not a philosopher but a poet, then it is worthwhile recalling that early on he abolished the distinction between the philosopher and the poet, a convergence of discourses that many are now prepared to accept without reservation. Emerson's writings in fact reflect the complementarity of philosophical and poetic discourse, and they give their full meaning to an interpretation sensi-

---

2. A notable exception to this tendency is Stanley Cavell, who in many recent essays has Emerson stand for philosophy, and who overtly criticizes what he calls "the most widely shared, fixated critical gesture toward Emerson . . . namely the gesture of denying to Emerson the title of philosopher" ("Finding as Founding: Taking Steps in Emerson's 'Experience,'" in *This New Yet Unapproachable America* [Albuquerque, N. Mex.: Living Batch Press, 1989], 77–78). See also by Cavell "Thinking of Emerson" and "An Emerson Mood," in *The Senses of Walden* (San Francisco: North Point Press, 1981); "Being Odd, Getting Even: Threats to Individuality," in *Reconstructing Individualism: Individuality and the Self in Western Thought*, ed. Thomas C. Heller, Morton Sasna, and David E. Wellbery (Stanford, Calif.: Stanford University Press, 1986); *In Quest of the Ordinary* (Chicago: University of Chicago Press, 1988); and *Conditions Handsome and Unhandsome: The Constitution of Emersonian Perfectionism* (Chicago: University of Chicago Press, 1990). Other recent philosophical interpretations of Emerson include David Van Leer, *Emerson's Epistemology: The Argument of the Essays* (New York: Cambridge University Press, 1986); John Michael, *Emerson and Skepticism: The Cipher of the World* (Baltimore: Johns Hopkins University Press, 1988); Cornel West, *The American Evasion of Philosophy: A Genealogy of Pragmatism* (Madison: University of Wisconsin Press, 1989); Russell B. Goodman, *American Philosophy and the Romantic Tradition* (Cambridge, Eng.: Cambridge University Press, 1990).

tive to his use, abuse, and reuse of the terms and concepts of the philosophical tradition. A philosophical reading of Emerson has significant value, then, but only its first value, in this respect; it is useful as an explanatory tool that retrieves themes and arguments from the essays that other methodologies do not illuminate. But along with clarifying Emerson's thought and revealing the trajectory it contains, a philosophical approach to his writings emphasizes how important the question of Being, and therefore of philosophy, was to him. Reading Emerson's essays, lectures, and journals for their philosophical content puts one in position to draw out this concern in his writings and to reveal, thereby, that his development of a philosophy rooted in practice is tied up with his recognition of the threats posed to this discourse and in its final form is intended to preserve and guard philosophy itself.

The province of philosophy is the discourse of truth and reason, and this discourse never left Emerson's mind. But his identification of truth with eloquence, or the emergent efficacy of "highest reason," as he puts it in *Nature* and elsewhere, indicates he was no dogmatist. Emerson defined truth contextually, as the power of gathering the accumulated variables of a scene under a unified explanation. For instance, in his description of the genealogy of will in the "Reality" section of "Experience," he writes, "Bear with these distractions, they will one day be *members*, and obey one will" (*CW* 3:41). Truth for Emerson was the power of will, which he eventually understood as "the power of statement."[3] Statement is his final name for what is "so commanding that we find pleasure and honor in obeying" (*CW* 1:85). His faith in the eloquence of truth did not depend on the hypostatization of the concept but rather on its contested status and its consequent fluidity within and across contexts. Truth and reason are gauged by the capaciousness of a thought, its intrinsic effective power. That is why he never doubted that a higher reason would find its audience and would move it. It would do so because its ideational structure explained more, gathered more variables, was, in short, more eloquent than other statements.[4]

---

3. Ralph Waldo Emerson, *Emerson's Complete Works*, ed. Edward W. Emerson (Boston: Houghton Mifflin & Co., 1883), 8:126. Hereafter cited as *C*.

4. I am not unaware of the dangers of "ignoring the performative aspects of [Emerson's] compositions" and the potential narcissism of his oratorical posture that recent critics have noted (Jeffrey Steele, *The Representation of the Self in the American Renaissance* [Chapel Hill: University of North Carolina Press, 1987], 3). But there is a greater danger of misunderstanding Emerson's overall purpose if one ignores the primarily ideational nature of his conception of eloquence and its relation to his understanding of reason and truth. Thus, I find Gertrude Reif Hughes convincing when she asserts, "Emerson is preeminently an interior

The continuity, not to say stasis, of Emerson's thought, rests here, in his conviction in the identity of truth and eloquence and in his confidence that this identity can survive any skepticism. This conviction is the ground of his well-known "vast affirmative," an affirmative capacity that he retained even during the most abysmal period of his intellectual life, the early 1840s. It is the conviction that returns him in *Conduct of Life* to confidence that nature does "meliorate." That is to say, reason grows (nature follows reason in Emerson's nomadic idealism), becoming increasingly complicated, increasingly capacious, and thus increasingly eloquent. But strikingly, reason and nature became for him also increasingly irrespective of Man.[5]

The development in Emerson's thought, what does change, respects this growing disregard of Man. The decisive change in theory that Emerson experienced in the early 1840s, the turn from freedom to fate

---

orator and therefore not primarily concerned with the techniques or dynamics of persuasion" (*Emerson's Demanding Optimism* [Baton Rouge: Louisiana State University Press, 1984], 73–74). And I find further, if more qualified, support for this position in Julie Ellison's remark that "Emerson pictures himself both as the source of inspiration and as its recipient . . . [and] is from the start both humble and narcissistic" (*Emerson's Romantic Style* [Princeton, N.J.: Princeton University Press, 1984], 24). If so, it is because the eloquence of a statement continuously forces on Emerson a recognition that its source resides outside his possession in reason's power to persuade. This needn't entail ignoring entirely the empirical conditions and effects of language, but it does call for recognition of a nonempirical medium of eloquence and persuasiveness, a transcendental pragmatics of power that harbors a sense of disinterestedness divorced from theology and metaphysics and rooted in an historicist emergence of reason.

5. Emerson's development away from humanism, away from the essential link between speaker and statement, founds his identification of reason and fate, and his late description of eloquence as "the double force of reason and destiny" (*C* 7: 92). It suggests further why he diminishes the importance of the material conditions of the speaker and the audience in his lectures on eloquence, and emphasizes instead the power of the ideational structure of a statement. Over time he radicalized his understanding of the relations among truth, eloquence, and fate, finally locating all three, not in the speaker or listener but in the statement itself, the account made of things. Consider the following remark from the lecture on eloquence: "There is for every man a statement possible of that truth which he is most unwilling to receive,—a statement possible, so broad and so pungent that he cannot get away from it, but must either bend to it or die of it. Else there would be no such word as eloquence, which means this. The listener cannot hide from himself that something has been shown him and the whole world which he did not wish to see; and as he cannot dispose of it, it disposes of him" (*C* 7: 91–92). Eloquence is a "fatal force," operating irrespective of self-consciousness or artistic intention (*C* 7: 92). "The eloquent man is he who is no beautiful speaker, but who is inwardly drunk with a certain belief. It agitates and tears him, and perhaps almost bereaves him of the power of articulation. Then it rushes from him as in short, abrupt screams, in torrents of meaning. The possession the subject has of his mind is so entire that it ensures an order of expression which is the order of Nature itself, and so the order of greatest force, and inimitable by any art" (*C* 7: 92–93).

that nearly all readers have noted, did not affect his understanding of truth or reason in nature. Rather, it affected the overtly philosophical question of the *method* by which the individual can apprehend nature and reason. The development in Emerson's philosophy is reflected in the titles he gave to each phase: the method of Man, the method of nature, and the doctrine of fate. The shift between the first two, laid out in "The Method of Nature," pivots on the philosophical range Emerson attributes to his concept of Man and marks his turn away from conviction in the God within, that Stephen Whicher so effectively identified, the faith in a method of thought that returns the value of nature and the sceptre of reason to the will of Man.[6] "The Method of Nature" expresses his release of this last anchor grasped in nature, the active soul that founded his early humanism. And thus it marks the point at which Emerson first addressed an antihumanist conception of nature.

Recently much criticism on Emerson has demonstrated the scope of his early synthesis, whether emphasizing, as Sacvan Bercovitch does, its symbolic, representative nature, or identifying it in terms of compensatory psychological fables, intrinsically ironic acts of aggressive and creative reading, or its inevitable and defining return to the inappropriable otherness of nature.[7] In each case critics have sought to uncover the limits of the early synthesis and implicitly or explicitly its ideological status. Gains in our understanding of Emerson's rhetorical strategies, his psychological and social background, and the adequacy of the ideology of self-reliance to society in general have been substantial. And what emerges rather decisively from the body of recent criticism, both appreciative and critical, is the finitude of Emerson's humanist synthesis. But what is less often noted, and what I wish to stress, is that Emerson, at least after 1841, would not have disagreed with the principal claim that stands behind many of these studies. If he seized command of nature in 1836, then by 1841 he had given it up again, predicting later critiques of the individualist ideology of self-reliance by insisting, "There is no man," and later, "The individual is always mistaken."

6. Stephen Whicher, *Freedom and Fate* (Philadelphia: University of Pennsylvania Press, 1953); see esp. 20.
7. Sacvan Bercovitch, *The Puritan Origins of the American Self* (New Haven: Yale University Press, 1975), see 136; B. L. Packer describes Emerson's early synthesis as rhetorical mythmaking, identifying Emerson's primary fables as contraction, dislocation, ossification, and reflection (*Emerson's Fall: A New Interpretation of the Major Essays*, [New York: Continuum Publishing Co., 1982]); and Julie Ellison argues that the humanist synthesis consists in the ironic and creative gesture of a critical reader (*Emerson's Romantic Style*).

What I find most interesting then in recent readings of Emerson is the suggestion they hold that the humanist phase was a stage in a broader development in his thought, an evolution characterized by his sense that thought and action are primarily obedient, not authoritative. It has been convincingly shown that during the 1820s Emerson was uncommonly sensitive to the authority prior texts held over him.[8] Even in the 1830s he identified a moment of obedience in his humanist dialectic, although it was subsumed under the authority of individual thought. Certainly years of preparation stand behind the synthesis he developed to solder the "crack" in *Nature*, but it is important to bear in mind that he made the crucial revisions to "Spirit" and "Idealism" in the weeks between June and August of 1836.[9] His humanist phase lasted, then, a short five years out of a productive lifetime of writing that is conservatively estimated at thirty years. Unfortunately, continuing emphasis, positive and negative, given to this brief stage in his intellectual life has acted largely to preclude study of the development of his ideas. As important as it is to identify the limits of his early period—and certainly the fulsome affirmations given it in the past warrant criticism—in order to open up study of Emerson's later theory, it is necessary to treat the period more descriptively, giving full voice to the power of the humanist synthesis, neither to endorse nor to refute it, but rather to stage the tensions within it that motivate Emerson's later writings. For from 1841 to 1860 Emerson experimented with the possibilities available to thought and action after the grasp of humanist authority has revealed *itself* to be a form of fatal obedience.

Emerson's career began with his recognition of the fittedness of nature, reason, and Man, which led him to view nature as a text and the individual as a reader who, if he is not also a writer, finds his best ideas return to him with alienated majesty. If "modernity itself, is writing," then from the start it recognized its writing as contained within a re-

---

8. See Julie Ellison, *Emerson's Romantic Style*, esp. 36ff. In respect to Emerson's early sense of being submissive to earlier texts Ellison writes, "The inherited civilization is felt as a superego that assigns duties and evaluates performance and to whom we are 'answerable.' 'Consanguinity' defines an eternal present in which our fathers live on by virtue of our continued obedience to them" (46). Also see B. L. Packer's discussion of the relation between Emerson and Jones Very in *Emerson's Fall*, 186ff.

9. See Merton M. Sealts, "The Composition of *Nature*," in *Emerson's Nature: Origin, Growth, and Meaning*, ed. Merton M. Sealts and Alfred R. Ferguson (Carbondale: Southern Illinois University Press, 1979). Sealts writes, "The 'crack' he complained of was soon mended by unspecified revision of whatever stood in the manuscript between 'Discipline' and 'Prospects' so as to form one or both of the chapters now entitled 'Idealism' and 'Spirit'" (191).

flective gesture.¹⁰ Descartes read (proved) God in order to write (assert) the subject, and Emerson does something similar, although more radical, in *Nature*: he collapses the difference between reading and writing, maintained in Descartes by the ontological differentiation of God and the subject.¹¹ Indeed, Emerson's humanism can be powerfully cast as his discovery that the reader writes.¹² "The crucial freedom comes," Julie Ellison says, "when he changes his mind about criticism. For it is by the transvaluation of reading that Emerson makes possible the gratifications of the sublime. The (secondary) interpretation of (primary) inherited texts becomes a way of controlling, even of creating them."¹³ For the early Emerson, what is at stake is how well and

---

10. Francois Furet, quoted in *The Practice of Everyday Life*, by Michel de Certeau, trans. Steven Rendall (Berkeley and Los Angeles: University of California Press, 1984), 168.

11. That Emerson radically humanizes the Cartesian gesture is Cavell's point in "Being Odd, Getting Even," where he traces Emerson's advance on Descartes's proof of God and the cogito. Cavell's concluding remarks on Emerson's theory of reading suggest the point I am making here: "'Self-Reliance' as a whole presents a theory . . . of reading. . . . I have elsewhere called this the (apparent) paradox of reading; it might just as well be called the paradox of writing, since of writing meant with such ambitions we can say that only after it has done its work of creating a writer . . . can one know what it is to write" (289). I take this description to refer to the collapse in Emerson's early thought of the difference between reading and the work of writing that creates the author, and to affirm the modernity of the idea of self-reliance, not by suggesting that the individual is ontologically original but by asserting he is *adequate* to the transition by which reading is transformed into self-empowering writing. By adequacy I mean the mastery of the text achieved by obedient reading-become-writing (Cavell, 290), which suggests the (secondary) role of obedience in Emerson's early period.

12. Hughes's discussion of Emersonian correspondence makes related remarks, noting the role of language: "What matters is that language is both literal and figurative for Emerson. Not alternately, but at the same time. For the author it is literal, for the interpreting reader it is figurative" (*Emerson's Demanding Optimism*, 155). Language thus both determines a difference between the reader and the text and promises the identity of the reader and the text. In *Nature* Emerson resists the former effect of language, but, as Hughes notes, doing so depends on the prior condition of difference, with its implication of obedience: "Precisely this distinction between ME as reader or interpreter and ME as author is the one that *Nature*'s argument requires, with its emphasis on the spiritually responsive imagination, but that Emerson's purpose for *Nature* resists" (154). Emerson, of course, does not create the difference between the ME and the NOT-ME, he inherits it, and his writings take shape as responses to that inheritance. Hughes's remark sets in relief the response Emerson makes in *Nature*, which locates the poetic nature of language and privileges somewhat violently, the transformation it makes possible of the reader into a writer of nature.

13. *Emerson's Romantic Style*, 42. Packer makes a similar point in *Emerson's Fall*: "The assertion that a text reveals a meaning its author did not consciously intend (whether of unwitting folly or oracular wisdom) is the constitutive gesture of interpretation" (*Emerson's Fall*, 21). Both writers interpret Emerson's early phase in terms of a critical and ironic gesture that seizes power for the reader. Ellison is quick to see the corollary: if the reader always writes, then the writer always quotes, ironically. Emerson came to this conclusion more

how self-consciously the individual reads and writes nature. But to imagine we surpass modernity by attending to the reader is to underestimate it and to raise the question of what a politically and philosophically viable reader, somehow creative but not authorial, can be. The viability of the reader, and the subsequent authenticity of thought and action, must come, Emerson felt, from practice, a pure practice and not, specifically, from the reciprocity of theory and practice. Emerson came to see that the consequence of living within the dream of the fittedness of Man and nature is the reduction of relations to technocratic equations of power. But when one closely follows the philosophical valences of his language, not only the fittedness but also the fundamental *difference* between nature's reason and Man is revealed. His recognition of this difference cast the text of nature beyond the view of the reader/writer: the book of nature became the book of fate, illegible and dictatorially eloquent. Emerson conceived of it as an inscription written, not *in*, but *of* the sheer practice of life. He located the world's laws in the gestures that play across the face and the inflection of the voice, in the gait and rhythm of the body, in the irreducible dance of the individual's existence; he saw reason as a text from which we cannot withdraw and which can be read—and (re)written—only through obedience to its practice. Under the force of this vision he closed his lecture on nature's method at Waterville College in Maine and opened an inquiry into the wisdom of practice and the love of fate.

Emerson tracks the path of reason to the apprehension of fate by means of an appropriation and adaptation of the principal concepts of Western philosophy, and my procedure will be to follow the path he has traced. I start with a phenomenological account of his early period, beginning with the synthesis he forges in *Nature*. As I have suggested, Emerson turns from phenomenological humanism in the 1840s, but he does so in and through the terms of his early thought, and thus a precondition of understanding his antihumanism is an account adequate to the scope and eloquence of the early humanism. A phenomenological reading provides this, following the lead of Emerson's language and imagery. As Donald E. Pease points out in his remarks on "the transparent eyeball" image in *Nature*, the breadth and scope of Emerson's use of the metaphor of vision is great indeed.[14] Pease lists—and dismisses

---

slowly and, I would say, with, not irony, but the "terrible earnestness" he remarks in "Eloquence," the principle of strife with which he discerns the real from the illusory (*C* 7: 93).

14. Many readers of Emerson have noticed his use of the metaphor of vision, primary

as inadequate to account for the image—idealism, sublimity, death, cognition, protection, nature, the fathers, "I," and Divine Being. The description he settles on, "an image for the impossible act of sight seeing itself," aptly indicates, moreover, the philosophical roots and resonance of Emerson's idea.¹⁵ But in this connection it is worth noting that it repeats less the modern sense of reflection than the Aristotelian identification of the end of metaphysical discourse as the principle of thought thinking itself. "It is of Himself," Aristotle concludes in the *Metaphysics*, "that The Intellect is thinking . . . and so Thinking is the Thinking of Thinking."¹⁶ A phenomenological elucidation of Emerson's writings places them firmly in this broad context and indicates thereby Emerson's engagement and repetition of the fundamental principles inflected through Western philosophical discourse.

By emphasizing the phenomenological casting of Emerson's thought I hope to sharpen the lines of what is at stake in his early works, lines sometimes blurred by a lingering metaphysical dualism that is inappropriately applied to his thought. As suggested by the remarks above, a phenomenological approach situates Emerson's writings at the margin of modern philosophy and suggests why he generally ignores the perplexities of epistemological dualism. "When the soul is really present," as B. L. Packer notes, "Emerson insists, all *sense* of dualism ceases."¹⁷ Emerson's concerns rest instead with what he viewed as the more fundamental philosophical issue of describing and justifying a way of being in the world, a posture or attitude taken toward thought's

---

among them being Sherman Paul, *Emerson's Angle of Vision: Man and Nature in American Experience* (Cambridge, Mass.: Harvard University Press, 1952). Two other treatments have been most helpful: James M. Cox, "R. W. Emerson: The Circles of the Eye," in *Emerson: Prophesy, Metamorphosis, and Influence*, ed. David Levin (New York: Columbia University Press, 1975), 57–81, and Tony Tanner, "Emerson: The Unconquered Eye and the Enchanted Circle," in *The Reign of Wonder: Naivety and Reality in American Literature* (Cambridge: Cambridge University Press, 1965), 26–45.

15. Donald E. Pease, *Visionary Compacts: American Renaissance Writings in Cultural Context* (Madison: University of Wisconsin Press, 1987), 225.

16. Aristotle, *Metaphysics*, Lambda:9, trans. Hippocrates G. Apostle (Bloomington: Indiana University Press, 1966), 209. Pease's discussion of the problems and perplexities surrounding the image of the transparent eyeball compares in interesting ways with Aristotle's description of "The Intellect [God]" in the *Metaphysics*. Compare, for instance, Paul Ricoeur's discussion in *The Rule of Metaphor* of the poetic dimension of this founding principle of Western metaphysical thought, with Pease's description of the transparent eyeball as "the charged space something moves through to become something else, [which] refers to the very activity of making metaphor, the transition of one term into another (a movement, by the way, which also makes all quests for meaning and purposes possible)" (226).

17. *Emerson's Fall*, 145.

production of the diversity and difference in nature and society. Thus, in his early writings he sought a positive assertion of the humanist inheritance he identified for himself as the recognition of the founding capacity and scope of individual thought. A phenomenological interpretation shows the extent to which he relied on a vocabulary of vision to formulate this assertion, and in the course of doing so it draws out as well the complementary sense that nature is not objectively infinite, but rather consists of the manifestations that gather around the individual, and is in this regard a finite appearance. When Emerson writes that the individual is the creator in the finite, he does not imply that there is somewhere an infinite that disposes this creator—dwarfs him, as he says. Rather, he means that the only principle of creation, of evaluation, in nature is the finite principle of individual thought, acting where it finds itself and extending the individual's knowledge to the limits of his vision, to the horizon of his eye and world. Accordingly, Ellison notes, "When [Emerson] confronts God directly, he becomes the original of which God is the copy."[18]

My purpose, however, is to show not only that Emerson repeated the fundamental movement of Western philosophical thought but that his writings take their departure from the endpoint of that movement. They begin by giving voice then, through the imagery of sight, to the tradition's *completion*.[19]

Emerson views human being as thrown into the world, there to stand as the occasion, and in his early period the cause, of nature's appearance. This is evident in the motto to "Self-Reliance," which describes the human condition of being thus cast onto the rocks with hands and feet for power. I use a phenomenological approach to stress

---

18. *Emerson's Romantic Style*, 55.

19. In this respect especially my interpretation of Emerson bears comparison to the writings of Martin Heidegger. Like Heidegger after him, Emerson first found the origin of value in the effective historicity of the individual, thematizing the potential for self-appropriation through the metaphor of vision, and then later questioned and carried on a dialogue with this very potential, finally reaching an understanding of thought, will, and fate that compares directly with Nietzsche's philosophical writings and Heidegger's still uncharted later works. Recognizing this similarity provides, moreover, a useful perspective in the current debate over the significance and influence of Heidegger's political allegiances and investments in his theoretical work. Certainly Heidegger's historical situation should not be ignored, but I am encouraged by Emerson's different historical site and the obviously independent development of his thought to believe that Heidegger's theory can be preserved from many current political criticisms and certainly from such theoretically retrograde oppositions as that implied by Nicholas Rand's assertion that Heidegger's theories might be given "the license we grant poets," but cannot be treated "as though they were objectively valid truths" ("The Political Truth of Heidegger's 'Logos': Hiding in Translation," *PMLA* 105 [May 1990]: 446, 444).

the idea that is at the very center of Emerson's thought, the idea that the individual brings nature to presence, and, importantly, there is, therefore, no other nature but the one the individual gives rise to. Phenomenological vocabulary insistently reflects his assertion that nature occurs only there where consciousness is. If Emerson's transcendentalism is rooted in this conviction, then it is also true that the premise does not imply a subjectivist theory. Rather, it revises the question of self and otherness, indicating that otherness emerges in whatever way and with whatever value it does within the circle of the eye. Put otherwise, it indicates that our sense of otherness is always earned by the way we think, or, as it were, see.

For Emerson, the challenge to thought is to earn its reality and thus the individual's authenticity. I expect a phenomenological approach to clarify Emerson's early thought because it describes the *philosophical work*—which is to say, the work of thought—that characterizes Emerson's humanism. A phenomenological reading brings out the rigorously demanding way of living, or being, in society and the world that self-reliance stands for, a way of being responsible for yourself that takes its departure from the historicity of the individual. Emerson develops the idea of self-reliance out of a concern for the ordinary and deeply realistic everyday existence of the individual. Stanley Cavell's work on Emerson impresses me as close to the heart of Emerson's early conception of the individual, mainly because he credits the idea of self-reliance with being the thoughtful position of historical, finite individuals and with being the struggle for an earned reality. Emerson finds the issue of being human, of human being, in the immediate problem of the value we give to our world. His question is never, do we earn our reality? But rather, what reality do we earn? What nature do we raise to presence? Authenticity, he makes clear, as if it should need to be made clear, is not automatic. Rather, it is, as he said of thinking, the hardest thing of all to do.

Nature revolves around the principle of disclosure, or unconcealment, of the effective power of reason, and I take this principle to be the referent of the "Joyous Science" mentioned in the citation at the head of this introduction. When Emerson identifies himself as a professor of the Joyous Science, he indicates that the object of his study and profession is the science of nature's disclosure in visible effects of power, the science of the manifestation of reason's power. His theory and ethics come down to enabling the unobstructed presence of nature and regaining the innocence of nature's appearance by rejecting, ignoring, turning away from, the metaphysical apparatuses that accuse nature and formulate it in categorial orders that function to cheat and persecute (as he writes in "Compensation") its free disclosure. The Joyous Science refers to the pleasure of unconcealment and the science of power that attends it. It names a method of thought that finds value in the hierarchy of things as they are and as they show themselves to be, beyond the terms of any criterion of judgment that precedes active presencing. But if *Nature* introduces this "science," then it does so under the authority of a humanist prejudice. The early synthesis in *Nature* is characterized by Emerson's belief that *the individual* can will nature's disclosure.

In his early phase, the period from the publication of *Nature* to the delivery of "Man, the Reformer" (1841), Emerson draws to its conclusion the conception of Man as the end and purpose of nature. He develops and refines the meaning of his humanism in *Essays: First Series* (1841) and the addresses of the 1830s, but the theoretical foundation for the humanist synthesis is found in *Nature*, a work that is framed by twin images of the power of sight. The transparent eyeball figures the phenomenological resolution of nature through the human eye, and the coincidence of the axis of vision and the axis of things indicates the convergence of human sight and nature's appearance that is enabled by the emancipation of reason to a prospective posture, to the forward directedness of will implied by *matutina cognitio* (*CW* 1:10, 43). These images first of all indicate the phenomenological nature of Emerson's early method, and they complement the crucial central chapters of *Nature*, "Idealism" and "Spirit."

The primary importance of these two chapters resides in the transition Emerson makes from "Idealism" to "Spirit," for it is through this transition, and the *distinction* it indicates between the themes of the two chapters, that Emerson resolves the dualism in nature he could not otherwise reconcile. For Emerson, idealism was not an endpoint but "a temporary landing-place in a larger dialectic."[20] The thesis of "Idealism" had not, to his satisfaction, solved the problem of the "crack" in nature, and focusing attention on "Idealism" thus risks missing what Emerson gains in the "Spirit" chapter. It is therefore important to emphasize Emerson's critique of idealism, for through this critique he establishes the value of spirit, namely, the phenomenological centrality of will in nature.

It is well known that in "Spirit" Emerson argues that idealism is no more than a useful perspective, useful because by overthrowing the premise of materialism it renders nature pliant before human will. "Ide-

---

20. Packer, *Emerson's Fall*, 57. Endorsing Sealts's argument, Packer reasons that "Spirit" was the crucial late addition to *Nature* intended to solder its "crack."

alism" is not then the endpoint of nature's ascent to unity through the doctrine of uses; rather, it too is used. "The advantage of the ideal theory over the popular faith," he writes, "is this, that it presents the world in precisely that view which is most desirable to the mind" (*CW* 1:36). Emerson is frankly insistent about his *use* of idealism as a methodological tool, a useful hypothesis and no more. Idealism is valuable insofar as it has an affinity with and prepares for spirit. In itself, however, it fails the most crucial test of a unified system of thought: it fails to explain the origin and purpose of the universe, the whence and whereto of matter. Emerson quite explicitly denies any teleological value to idealism: "Three problems are put by nature to the mind: What is matter? Whence is it? and Whereto? *The first of these questions only*, the ideal theory answers" (*CW* 1:37, emphasis added). "Idealism" defuses the epistemological problem of dualism, rendering matter phenomenal, but it makes no progress on the teleology of nature. On the contrary, as Emerson uses it, idealism is critical, not affirmative. It establishes no principle; or in Emerson's more theologically colorful language, it "leaves God out of me . . . leaves me in the splendid labyrinth of my perceptions, to wander without end" (*CW* 1:37).

I labor this point in order to stress that one should look to "Spirit," not, as is often done, to "Idealism," to find the terms of Emerson's early thought. The two chapters carry entirely different philosophical emphases. Far from being repetitive of "Idealism," "Spirit" disposes idealism, and one recognizes its meaning only to the extent that one sees its greater eloquence. In "Spirit" Emerson extends the idealist hypothesis beyond the epistemological opposition of materialism and idealism, and thus beyond the terms of modern dualism in which idealism represents one method of responding to the problem of knowledge, and into the moral realm, where the idealist hypothesis acts as a propaedeutic for the assertion of Man's final causality in nature. If stress is placed on "Idealism" as the central chapter of *Nature*, then the work appears to revolve around the problem of knowledge and to be situated in a dualistic framework where Emerson's emancipatory claims appear either overstated or rhetorical and merely inspirational. Emerson's identification of spirit in response to a lack in idealism places his work instead, from its very beginnings, in a post-Kantian and nonepistemological context.

The chapter on spirit thus draws attention away from the problem that "Idealism" responds to—the problem of knowing the objective world, or, as Emerson puts it, of answering the question of *what* matter is—and it throws attention onto the moral questions of the origins and ends of nature. On its own, idealism resolves nothing and returns no principle in nature. Spirit, as Emerson explains it, consists in the moral response to these questions prepared for by idealism. To be more exact, spirit is the reflective gesture of thought that turns on the idealist hypothesis and asks what principle in nature it predicts. Idealism allows only one answer to this question: "When, following the invisible steps of thought, we come to inquire, Whence is matter? and Whereto? . . . We learn that the highest is present to the soul of man, that the dread universal essence, which is not wisdom, or love, or beauty, or power, but all in one, and each entirely, is that for which all things exist, and that by which they are; that spirit creates; . . . and we learn that man has access to the entire mind of the Creator, is himself the creator in the finite" (*CW* 1:38). It is worthwhile noting the similarity of Hegel's statement explaining the transition from Reason to Spirit in *The Phenomenology of Spirit*: "Reason is Spirit when its certainty of being all reality has been raised to truth, and *it is conscious of itself as its own world, and the world as itself*" (emphasis added).[21] Emerson's use of the term "spirit" here reveals itself as primarily philosophical, not theological, referring, like Hegel's, to thought's *recognition* of the centrality of consciousness in nature, or, as Emerson's standard trope would have it, the centrality of Man. Spirit is distinct from idealism precisely to the extent that the capacity to presence nature is implicit *but unrecognized* in the idealist perspective. And for this reason idealism, as Emerson describes it, is bound to both the dynamic of a dualistic interpretation of nature and a self-critical subversion of that dualism, a combination that leads to Emerson's statement that idealism leaves him in the labyrinth of his own perceptions. Following "Idealism" alone, one is indeed led to the conclusion that "[the idealist self's] identity is an illusion. . . . It watches without being able to distinguish itself from what it watches because it is itself an object of vision. It is itself apparent, not 'real.'"[22] Unequipped to recognize consciousness as the sole principle in nature, idealism remains a reactive hypothesis, blind to its moral, which is to say, its evaluative and pragmatic, consequences. The reflective recognition called for in "Spirit" shifts attention away from the epistemological problematic and directs it toward a

---

21. G.W.F. Hegel, *Phenomenology of Spirit*, trans. A. V. Miller (Oxford: Oxford University Press, 1977), 263.

22. Michael, *Emerson and Skepticism*, 64. Relating Emerson's argument to Hume's skepticism, Michael provides an excellent discussion of the self-destruction "Idealism" effects on its own premise of dualism, effectively showing that "Idealism" cannot adequately solder the "crack" in *Nature*.

moral conception of truth, which completes, as it were, the promise of idealist theories in general.

Critics have noted the similarity between Emerson's description and the Romantic sublime understood as an interpretive act, and the comparison cannot, I think, be discounted.[23] But what is at stake is the context in which one situates the interpretive act, or, precisely, whether or not Emerson can be shown to have recognized a (material) context in which all interpretations finally take place. Emerson's movement out of a dualistic world interpretation, his dismissal of the Kantian privileging of theoretical reason and its attendant privileging of epistemological discourse, represents a movement in thought that draws the sublime out of the narrowly aesthetic disposition given it in Kant's system and affirms the individual as the author of nature. *Nature* is written to demonstrate the eloquence of this movement, which is to say, its capacity to account for other interpretive schemes, specifically that of the opposition of a material and ideal world. Both appear to the perspective of self-reliance as interpretations. What is not conceived as an interpretation is the authorial power of the self, which recedes behind and beneath all its productions. This insight gave the idea of self-reliance its powerful hold over Emerson. It is a hold that cannot be loosened by the criticism that it too is merely an interpretation. So much the better, I imagine Emerson saying. Moreover, when this radical humanism does lose its hold over Emerson, it leaves him nowhere in nature to turn for grounding or context; and in his literalness, when he had nowhere to stand, he fell.

Spirit, then, refers to the phenomenological power of the individual, or thought's recognition that the individual is the occasion for the struggles of self and otherness that constitute nature.[24] Not a denial of

---

23. Cf. Ellison: "If it is a critic or reader who discovers his ability to create the meanings of the texts that threaten him, we have a truly 'hermeneutical' sublime, for the act of interpretation effects the crucial conversion" (*Emerson's Romantic Style*, 40–41).

24. Compare Pease's description of spirit as "afterthinking" (*Visionary Compacts*, 227ff.). Pease's aporistic account of spirit emphasizes the utter metaphoricity of nature and language's inability to grasp it, extending the logic implicit in *Nature* in a way that anticipates Emerson's own extension of his thought in his transitional writings. But Pease understates the theory of action sponsoring the early humanism, which anchors nature's metaphoricity and returns nature's law to the individual. As the transformative power by which the individual finds himself the author of nature's poetry and the receptor of its power, spirit is warranted by a theory of action, or as Emerson will put it later, by the perspective of life from the platform of action. A good deal is at stake in recognizing the universality Emerson initially attributes to this perspective: namely, the preservation of the philosophical cogency of the later writings. It is in this regard that I find limitations to Pease's insightful account. He

the world, Emerson's transcendentalism is a recognition of the active soul, that is, the soul "becoming" in and through the negotiations of difference that make up one's world. With this recognition comes an awareness of the "common root" from which the individual and nature proceed: the centrality of the human soul itself.

> And what is that root? Is not that the soul of his soul?—A thought too bold—a dream too wild. Yet when this spiritual light shall have revealed the law of more earthly natures,—when he has learned to worship the soul, and to see that the natural philosophy that now is, is only the first gropings of its gigantic hand, he shall look forward to an ever expanding knowledge as to a becoming creator. He shall see that nature is the opposite of the soul, answering to it part for part. One is seal, and one is print. Its beauty is the beauty of his own mind. Its laws are the laws of his own mind. Nature then becomes to him the measure of his attainments. (*CW* 1:55)

These lines should be appreciated not only for their exuberance but also for their radical content. They express the foundational thesis of Emerson's early theory. When he writes elsewhere, "The world is nothing, the man is all, in yourself is the law of nature; . . . in yourself slumbers the whole of Reason; it is for you to know all, it is for you to dare all," he does not describe a therapeutic fantasy posed within the limits of a dualistic universe (*CW* 1:69). Rather, the statement derives from the philosophical assertions in "Spirit," and it contains the imperative of Emerson's early thought: the command to dare to be accountable for the world, to recognize the source of nature's law in one's own actions, and thereby to realize the dignity that comes from an authentic relationship to the world. Emerson is far from denying the fact of limits in an individual's life, but his concern is never with how we can know and verify these limits, or even how we can predict their effects. Rather, he addresses the fact of limitation through moral terms, recognizing them as values. And his concern is invariably with how we relate

---

predicts the *form* of Emerson's later thought, brilliantly drawing it out of its embryonic expression in *Nature*, but because he does not fully articulate the cogency of spirit as Emerson put it forward, his account does not preserve the scope of spirit by which the *power* of the doctrine of fate is demarcated. Failing to reflect the emphases in Emerson's theory at the time he wrote *Nature*, Pease's reading cannot provide an account of the distinct theoretical premises of Emerson's thought at each of its stages, an account that is needed not only to identify the development and trajectory of his work but also to retrieve the eloquence of his final synthesis in "Fate."

to the conditions of our existence. Do we dwarf ourselves in nature, giving power over to the limits we perceive? Or do we recognize our power to appropriate and dispose all conditions under our interpretation of the world and thus to find a home in the world? "Spirit" is a thoughtful reflection on our power thus to own the world. Given this perspective, the problem of the intermittency of revelation would not have seemed fatal to Emerson. If he realized that human existence does not operate constantly at the level of authenticity, that he often finds himself a weed by the wall, still, the "Spirit" chapter describes more than the hope of authenticity written into the Orphic chants. It describes the philosophical work that earns the individual's authenticity and, conversely, the "lassitude" or ill will that accounts for its absence.[25]

On the foundation of "Spirit" Emerson writes his crucial early essays and lectures, his works up to "Man, the Reformer." In all the important early essays and addresses Emerson discusses and develops his belief that the whence and whereto of nature is Man, that Man is the sole principle in nature, and that on the foundation of Man it is possible to erect a new morality of self-reliance and compensation, the very morality he calls for in "The American Scholar" through his listing of the errors of historical Christianity. The emphasis on circularity in the method described in "Circles," and the corresponding emphasis on the inevitability of Man's standing, far from indicating a shift in Emerson's early project, as is sometimes thought, radically affirms the humanism of the early period.[26] Insofar as these essays and lectures share the appeal to Man's capacity to recover himself, insofar as they anticipate the decisive assertion in "Circles" that, place him where you will, Man stands, they reflect and repeat the discovery in "Spirit." I cannot then distinguish between the universality of the teleological assertion in *Nature* and some sense of a more modest or delimited claim in the later writings of the early period. Emerson's sense of the teleological

---

25. Packer, *Emerson's Fall*, 133.
26. Cavell reaches a different conclusion, asserting that *Nature* depends on a teleological method that Emerson immediately abandoned. He writes, "I am at present among those who find *Nature* . . . not yet to constitute the Emersonian philosophical voice" ("Finding as Founding: Taking Steps in Emerson's 'Experience,'" 79). Cavell's purpose is to distinguish the theoretical structure of *Nature* and "Experience," and certainly there is a crucial philosophical distinction between those two works. I will argue, though, that the distinction becomes apparent only insofar as one recognizes the shared foundation of *Nature* and such early essays as "Self-Reliance" and "Circles," a foundation manifest in the radical humanist teleology that sponsors each of them and that is indeed distinct from the theory behind "Experience."

and universal claims of Man is consistent from "Spirit" to "Man, the Reformer." Man is the creator in finite, and for that reason his authentic utterances speak the universal sense of nature. The claims of reason are of course practical for Emerson and to that extent are fitted to the finite context of practical action. The everydayness of reason's activity is figured in the conception of the individual as the creator in finite. In neither *Nature* nor "Self-Reliance" does Emerson suggest that Man is the principle of knowledge. Rather, Man's teleology is practical; indeed, the practical teleology of Man is the meaning of radical humanism and is the sole *fact* of Emerson's early period. So, without wanting to deny the emerging sophistication and refinement of Emerson's work between 1836 and 1841, I would insist this fact itself does not change.

It is here that I begin a reading of Emerson's works, on the base of his phenomenological conception of active reason and the practical humanity of spirit. By wedding the clarity of thought to exertions of will Emerson establishes the humanist nature of his theory. "The mind now thinks; now acts; and each fit reproduces the other," he writes, indicating that truth, the law of nature, is manifested and articulated through decisive acts of will and thus emerges within the horizon of the individual, the only space for Emerson's early synthesis within which relations can gain unity and order (*CW* 1:61). Truth in this sense is the living presence and centrality of human will manifest as the gathering disclosure of nature and as the clarity and eloquence of thought. Equally, the truth of "Spirit" consists in the eloquence of its thesis, the comprehensiveness of identifying consciousness as the evaluative center of nature. Indeed, *Nature* reflects that the power of philosophical modernism resides in the eloquence of this identification. The modern turn to the subject holds the potential to appropriate and dispose of all other principles. Emersonian spirit realizes this potential, disposing matter under mind, and God under Man, and affirming human will as the vehicle of highest reason, the signifying signified that affirms unity in its dispersions. In this way, Emerson both strains and remains faithful to the metaphysical tradition retained in philosophical modernism.

The strain in Emerson's synthesis will bear fruit in his writings after 1841, but in the early writings his fidelity to metaphysical thought is most emphatic. His insistence on the reciprocity of thought and will indicates that only by virtue of decisive willful acts can truth be affirmed. The structure and dynamic of metaphysical thought, that is, the premise of a transcending ground of value withheld from the interactions of power in nature, is thereby maintained. Whether Emerson refers to the ground as truth, the soul or Oversoul, Law, Omnipotent

Will, or Central Man, it remains essentially the same: the human principle that is withdrawn from and upholds the play of relations. Emerson's faith in such a principle appears throughout his early period, but nowhere more explicitly than at the end of "Compensation," the early essay that most describes the pure play of power, and thus the essay that most insistently demands an assertion of the withdrawal of the soul from that play. The soul is not a compensation, Emerson writes; it is not in the economy of compensatory power relations, the economy of the will's expression. Rather, it *is* that economy, its unity and its presence. The soul is the principle of the unconcealment of the economy of nature, the principle of decisive acts of will.

Emerson succeeds in the early essays in articulating the synthesis of thought and will as the foundation of the essential worth of Man. Locating value in the unconcealment of human power, he challenges the individual, not only to build his own world, which is inevitable in any case, but to take responsibility for that world by laying its relations bare. The imperative to self-reliance consists in no more than such an act of unconcealment or resolution that brings the universe into focus and thereby articulates the universal sense. Emerson speaks in the early essays to the moral and practical question of freedom, to how we engage and live in the world that is present to us. His essays put forward a manner of living in the world that consists in the imperative to disclose the relations of things as they are. Were one to read the meaning of the Joyous Science through the terms of this early synthesis, it would consist in a quite radical extension of Western humanism, effected largely through Emerson's anticipatory use of phenomenological method. The Joyous Science would refer to the work of human will by which the one Law, the soul, is unconcealed, and Emerson's professions would be those of authentic Man, of Man Thinking. Finally, however, it would describe still the well-established theoretical structure of metaphysical thought.

But, as I suggested, the value of a phenomenological interpretation of Emerson is not limited to its usefulness in explaining his early synthesis. Much more important than any possible clarification of the early work is the foundation it sets for understanding Emerson's middle and late periods of thought, the periods inaugurated in 1841 by the assertions in "The Method of Nature" and completed in the doctrine of fate. The language of phenomenology, because it captures Emerson's capacious sense of the power and adequacy of the individual, also sets in stark relief the implications of his turn away from human phenomenological centrality and its subversive consequences for the concepts of Man and nature's presence. Emerson overcomes his own phenomenological method, and one is therefore most likely to recognize the value of his later thought by following the clue that phenomenology provides, a clue that leads thought beyond the limits of phenomenology, self, and nature, and into the milieu of fate.

In 1841 Emerson places in question precisely the depth and authenticity of the individual's phenomenological centrality, the individual's power. His turn away from humanism consists in the recognition that the unity of active reason, the unified articulation of the world made possible by human reason construed as a phenomenological power, is superficial; which is to say, as Emerson often does from 1841 on, *Man* is superficial. The living presence of the individual, of Man Thinking, is undercut by this shift in thought. But Emerson's turn does not mark a mere reversal in his thought, least of all from Romantic idealism to materialism, or along the lines of such artificial oppositions as that between solipsism and a concern for social value. In view of its foundation in the dialectical sublation of oppositions, no simple reversal of the humanist synthesis is possible. Rather, the change in Emerson's writings reflects a philosophical movement of thought, the product of a self-exceeding development in the logic of humanist philosophy itself. And when this is recognized, it becomes possible to articulate an alternative interpretation of it that opens up an understanding of the later writings and suggests Emerson's embrace of obedience.

Toward this end, I will approach the passages in "The Method of Nature" and the essays and lectures that follow it, by reflecting on the reciprocity between thought and will that Emerson asserts in "The American Scholar" and by thinking of the shift in 1841 as a response to his new recognition of the failure of that reciprocity. When Emerson substitutes the method of nature for the method of Man, he indicates that Man's will is not adequate to nature, cannot resolve thought in a univocal expression, and thus that nature does not come to us through the terms of the individual's authentic speech. But rather than proceed then to reintroduce the dualism his early synthesis supersedes, he instead reconceives the relation of Man and nature, while still viewing the individual's constitution as the essential fact of human existence. That is to say, the turn to antihumanism reflects a change in Emerson's sense of our ability to own our legislative capacity in nature, not a rejection of that capacity. Conversely, the fact of the determinative power of the individual in nature is not principally what is at stake in Emerson's early work. Instead, as I said, the possibility of *recognizing* that fact and the consequences this would have for how one lives are

Emerson's main concerns. In his early period, he seems to have viewed these two matters as the same: that is, to be the central and legislative power in nature appeared to him as indistinct from at least the potential to recognize oneself as such. The practical imperative to visionary self-reliance followed logically. He came to see, however, that humanist self-recognition is a stage, not the end or telos, of thought's engagement of a radically human world. The distinction between these two positions is crucial to the argument I work out over the course of this book. Before going on then I want to draw out a few of its general implications.

Again, Emerson did not question the adequacy of an individual's constitution or organization—the plurality of conditions that he generally referred to as the soul—to nature. His early faith in Central Man stems from the recognition that there is only one fact in nature, and that is the individual's organization, his historicity. Rather than address this fact in a narrowly Kantian manner, however, Emerson viewed the fit of the soul and nature as exact and inevitable. I would press this, moreover, to suggest that Emerson conceived of the soul, the organization and constitution of the individual, not as the *condition* or *term* of experience at all. The dualism these words imply, if epistemologically necessary, misses Emerson's emphasis. His early faith is characterized not merely or even principally by his belief in the foundation of nature in the individual soul, but by the faith in human will to own its constitution, by the faith that Man exists, if not often, at least potentially and *essentially*, as the power of self-recognition. The soul is active presence for Emerson, and as such it *appropriates* conditions as the terms of freedom. For this reason Emerson says there are no circumstances and no past at our back. To be exact, then, individual will, in its act of self-reliant authenticity, is the *principle* of nature, adequate to all conditions of nature, a principle thus indistinguishable from the terms and conditions of its enactment, a principle that erases limitation by appropriating it as an aspect of its power. This may be a fable, and in his later period Emerson will say it is. But it is important to be clear what the fable is and is not. It is not the belief that nature is present only insofar as it is articulated by human will. The fable is rather that nature is only presence. And because it is a fable that, when he rejects it, Emerson sublimates into a higher "reason," it should be viewed as the condition for the possibility of his turn to the illusoriness of experience and later to the primordiality of fate. It is insufficient then to identify fate as conditions, historicity, or the individual's organization. Sensitivity to, and an explicit awareness of, such limits is reflected throughout Emerson's writings and is not definitive of his later period. Fate is rather those limits insofar as they are not seen, are invisible, and, most importantly, insofar as they *cannot*, even potentially, be brought to presence under the authority of the individual. It can't be overemphasized that the movement in Emerson's thought revolves around the issue of self-recognition or the failure of self-recognition, and the development in his theory occurs in respect to the method by which reason (later fate) is apprehended and manifested, either through a humanist or antihumanist philosophical method. Moreover, the critique of philosophical dualism of whatever stripe implicit in Emerson's early humanism shows that both his humanism and his antihumanism name the process of thought that precedes—conditions, if one wants to put it that way—all explanatory or interpretive approaches.

It can be readily concluded then that the turn in Emerson's thought does not justify the assumption of an ontological substance underwriting human being. The imagery of substance, of a ground that upholds, finds its final expression for Emerson in the humanist synthesis and loses force with the embrace of antihumanism. The superficiality of human being does not imply the depth of some other Being. Nature does not recede beneath human will, as that which sponsors and supports it. Rather, nature resides in a superficial dynamic, in a dynamic of the play of surface and depth that is itself textural. That is to say, nature becomes for Emerson the dynamic set in play by Man's superficiality, a power that does not then consist in the perpetual presencing of nature, but rather consists in the failure of that presencing activity, the passing of presence. One can follow Emerson's visual metaphors, particularly in the opening paragraph of "Experience," to describe this dynamic in terms of revelation and concealment, showing and withholding. Nature, he writes, does not like to be observed. But again, he dissociates the dynamic of nature's self-concealment from the assumption of a principle of depth that remains hidden behind all revelations and unconcealed by them.

The transitional lectures of 1841–42, including "The Method of Nature" and "Lectures on the Times," as well as "Experience," provide the opportunity to develop the theoretical nature of Emerson's antihumanist turn, and I will do so in Chapters 3 and 4. But for now I want to anticipate the consequences of this turn for Emerson's philosophical method and, specifically, its consequences for the meaning of the Joyous Science.

The turn to antihumanism both reaffirms the dynamic of revelation and concealment and, at the same time, subverts the ethos of phenomenological unconcealment. If the unconcealment of truth results in the superficiality of human will, then the activity of will nevertheless remains a process of disclosure. But what it now discloses is a world of surfaces, or purely exterior power. It will be through attention to this difference, which might be characterized by drawing a distinction between unconcealment and disclosure, where the former engages power under the principle of the universality, totality, and certitude of human will and the latter recognizes power in the disclosure of nature as the unprincipled interplay of forces, that I will bring the meaning of the Joyous Science to clarity.

Emerson wrote his journal entry on the Joyous Science in July of 1841, apparently as he was composing "The Method of Nature," and thus in the midst of the period when he turned from humanism to antihumanism. This suggests that the Joyous Science, if it in a sense looks backward to the early works, actually articulates and comes to fulfillment in and through the shift to antihumanism. And indeed, Emerson's ethics of disclosure could not properly be realized as long as he worked within the terms of humanism. As he came to see, the humanist withdrawal of the soul from the fluctuations of nature, the withdrawal essential to any metaphysics, is contrary to the meaning of the Joyous Science and in fact suppresses its meaning. To be sure, Man Thinking is the principle of nature's appearance, but it is a partial principle that depends on the retreat of the soul from showing forth. Under a humanist interpretation, then, the disclosure of nature remains subordinate to and obscured by the enclosure of Central Man, and to that extent the Joyous Science—the science and law of the appearance of nature as the play of power—remains incompletely represented. The Joyous Science, realized as *nature's* method of disclosure, could appear only at the moment Emerson gave up the withdrawal, the epoche of the soul, by which the disclosure of nature is figured within the decisiveness of Man. If the sense of the Joyous Science can be made to accord with the ethos of unconcealment central to his early phase and thereby be shown to be one interpretation of that ethos, it finally does not describe individualistic unconcealment. Rather, it describes the manifestation of nature's sheer relativity, which is to say, an appearance that enacts the power of nature not by enclosing it in epochal presence, but rather by presenting the slippage from presence that characterizes power relations.

After 1841, Emerson views this withdrawal as nature's function, not Man's. He concedes that the individual cannot keep pace with, or own, the fluctuations in nature, and he works out the Joyous Science in distinction from the faith that Man's decisiveness can articulate nature's power in a univocal statement. The consequences for his later ethics are considerable. As long as ethical demands are based on the principle of *adequate* revelation and the assumption that nothing in nature necessarily eludes presence, the phenomenological imperative to self-reliance results. But at the point Emerson recognizes all utterances as inadequate to nature's disclosure, he sees the aggression of self-reliance as necessarily giving rise to so much "talk," as opposed to authentic speech. The self-recovery available to the individual is revealed as belated and repetitive. Emerson might have embraced an ironic posture in reaction to this discovery, but the existence of the doctrine of fate is evidence that he did not and also demonstrates, retrospectively as it were, the literalness of his earlier humanism. Most importantly, it formulates the conduct Emerson felt was possible for human beings within the play of the method of nature: in the absence of the capacity to appropriate nature, right human conduct consists in obedience, which is in turn manifest by the sheer practice of life.

Certainly, Emerson did not immediately recognize affirmative consequences of his turn from humanism. "Experience" testifies to the devastating effect of his apprehension of the superficiality of Man, a thought that strips Man of his power and dignity, of his depth and certitude in nature. If the early essays had forged a noble resolution to the aspirations of the humanist tradition, then the transitional lectures and essays bespeak the collapse of that resolution as much as they do the initiation of a different practice of life. Sorting out the tone of the transitional writings is undoubtedly a complicated matter. Indeed, most of Emerson's mature arguments are made in "Experience." The movement from "Experience" to "Fate" does not consist in the discovery of a new argument, but rather in a change in attitude, registered in a new tone taken toward the position set out in "Experience." By labeling the lectures and essays of the middle period transitional, I mean to indicate that they reveal an Emerson who is uncertain and tentative, unable to locate an affirmative possibility within the terms of the antihumanist critique. The transitional works emphasize the diminution and situation of the power of human will in the world. Emerson's call for patience at the end of "Experience," a gesture of passivity and inaction typical of 1844 but inconceivable to the boundless humanist confidence of a few years before, attests that he initially experienced the science of power as a diminution—to the point of effective failure—of human action, of conduct.

The question raised for the late period of Emerson's work is, therefore, what are the consequences for human action, for how we live our lives, of the failure of Man to own his existence? In "Fate" Emerson develops his response. His return to the question of conduct is not surprising; he has, in fact, never left it. It is quite reasonable to view the body of Emerson's writings as an extended inquiry into the issue of human worth, of how we are to act humanly and with dignity. He struggled to track the possibility of living a dignified life through the largely uncharted territory beyond, first traditional values, then finally even the presumed unity and substantiality of the individual. His inquiry unsettles and dissolves not only traditional conceptions of human worth but even his own early and radical humanist formulations. And it leads Emerson to descriptions of society based on a doctrine that ignores the metaphysics of unconcealment in favor of an apprehension of the use of power. Here Emerson's pragmatic intuition comes to completion beyond the scope of phenomenological method. Man remains the vehicle of nature's appearance and power, but beyond the humanist synthesis that locates this phenomenological medium at the center and origin of nature. In short, the phenomenological causality of Man is situated after 1841. The ethical and political effect is to turn emphasis away from the responsibility of Man and toward the dispersal of power, such that power is not finally always seen as performing the labor that returns the authenticity of the individual. On the contrary, the individual is now viewed as itself disposed in the play of relations, in the play of disclosures that have no depth, no inside. The Joyous Science is the science of such sheer and exterior power, naming the joy of immersion in power as against the fear implicit in the act of withdrawal. Emerson's mature pragmatic ethics have their root in this joy.

Under the doctrine of fate, Emerson traces out the possibilities for a practice that refuses the critical distancing typical of his early phase and equally refuses the paralysis and passivity of his transitional works in the 1840s. His intellectual honesty and literalness, the "terrible earnestness" he speaks of in "Eloquence," required that he present fatal conduct in all of its modes, and that included prominently describing it in terms of power relations (*C* 7:93). But it would entirely miss Emerson's point to leave the impression that his later ethics consisted in a release of the individual to a callous irresponsibility and society to a politics of self-interest, rendering both devoid of the claim of reason. Attention to Emerson's philosophical development convinces me he did not abandon reason, but rather revised his understanding of reason and the method by which it is apprehended, coming to find it in the everyday practice of life by which the past is drawn into the future and identifying obedience to that practice as the means of apprehending the coherence of nature. In so doing he endorsed a philosophical life of wonder and obedience, rather than assertion and command. Emerson figures this practice in the image of listening posed against the constitutive force of speech and sight. In the figure of the auditor averse to the ironic gesture of authority, Emerson finds the model of a thoughtful posture that can receive and lay out the account of things and in so doing engage the power of reason manifest in the eloquence of the ordinary.

Part I

STANDING

The philosophy of the erect position: God made man upright.

A man is a method; a progressive arrangement; a selecting principle gathering his like to him wherever he goes.

There is no time to roses. There is simply the rose. It is perfect in every moment of its existence. Before a leaf bud has burst, its whole life acts; in the full blown flower, there is no more; in the leafless root, there is no less. Its nature is satisfied & it satisfies nature, in all moments alike. There is no time to the Rose. But man is always postponing or remembering. Man does not live in the great Present but with reverted eye wails for the past or wasting his riches, stands a tiptoe to foresee the future. So shall Man one day live with living nature, happy and strong in the deep present. There is no time to just men. The profuse roses blow.

The only speech will at last be Action.

There can be no greatness without abandonment.

—Emerson, *The Journals and Miscellaneous Notebooks*

The synthesis Emerson develops in *Nature* indicates both his allegiance to philosophical discourse and the place of his theory in the field of philosophical thought. His sense of having discovered a fundamental truth in active reason is evident in the early journal entries, which reflect a growing understanding of modern philosophy. In 1826 Emerson saw in reason only the mechanistic rationalism of the eighteenth century, still to his mind dominant in Unitarian thought, and wrote, "Bare reason, cold as cucumber, was all that was tolerated in aforetime, till men grew disgusted at the skeleton."[1] But by 1831 he had revised his assessment to find in reason itself the terms for overcoming alienation: "Suicidal is this distrust of reason; this fear to think . . . [t]o reflect is to receive truth immediately from God without any medium."[2] Emerson's excitement over his discovery was at times unbounded, but from a more distant perspective it is possible to see that his new conception of reason is consistent with the philosophical developments of the early nineteenth century.

Emerson is positioned at the point in modern philosophy when the a priori structures governing judgment, structures initiated by Descartes and brought to systematic expression by Kant, were coming apart. The rationalist tradition was in the midst of its transformation from a reflective to a self-reflexive methodology. His two descriptions of reason show this transformation occurring in his thinking as well, and it is easy to understand what he found attractive in the self-reflexive method. Its eloquence and power rests in the assertion that logic is self-motivated. Hegel's dialectic is the premier description of the progressive principle in reason, and, whether directly influential or not, it is certainly re-

---

1. *Selections from Ralph Waldo Emerson*, ed. Stephen Whicher (Boston: Houghton Mifflin Co., 1957), 8.
2. Ralph Waldo Emerson, *The Journals and Miscellaneous Notebooks*, ed. William Gilman et al. (Cambridge, Mass.: Harvard University Press, 1970), 3:279. Hereafter cited as *JMN*. Cf. *CW* 1:xxiii.

peated in Emerson's remark in *Nature* that there must be "somewhat progressive" in the theory of nature (*CW* 1:36). For Hegel, any determination of a concept yields that concept's other and the consequent desire to bring otherness to actuality in a new concept. Hegelian method thus consists in the dialectic of desire and reflection, which finds an internal contradiction in logic and compels reason to reach behind reflective forms of judgment, as in the same manner Hegel had faulted Kant for failing to go behind the veil of appearances. Considered in a more general way, Hegel's dialectic expresses a broad philosophical movement toward a recognition of the reciprocity of thought and action, which gives reason a practical rather than contemplative, an historical rather than synchronic, foundation.

The precedent of German dialectical thought, of the discourse of reason understood as a progressive, active principle, provides Emerson with an account of nature and experience that not only fits within the terms of reason but for which reason is the medium of value; which is to say, it provides him with a single and unified discourse of value. The recognition of reason's adequacy to nature, as the 1831 journal citation makes clear, first presented itself to Emerson as a discovery of the centrality of individual thought and the complicity of thought and nature. He construed reason as historically emergent in the actions of the individual and, as the next two chapters will show, developed this idea in a more insistently individualistic manner than was typical of his time. Emerson was inundated in the onto-theological tradition; when the universality of reason, which he had doubted in the 1820s, did appear to him, it brought the full content of that tradition within the scope of the individual. He thus draws to its logical endpoint the theological and philosophical faith that Man is nature's end, and concludes that nature properly thought about derives from the effects of the individual's constitution and that the individual should know himself or herself for the informing principle of nature.

Emerson's simultaneous discovery and identification of reason and the "God within" indicates the philosophical dimension of his thought. The strictly philosophical evolution of his work begins here. At the same time, then, it begins amid a philosophical context that has abandoned a narrow lexicon or taxonomy of reason and replaced it with an understanding of reason as the amorphous and fluid activity of spirit. If Emerson's theory fits into the broad contours of Kantian thought, repeating the idealist premise that all experience is dictated by the organization of the individual mind, then the emphatically moral cast Emerson gives to his discovery unsettles idealist structures of thought, opens experience to the full play of the mind's constitution, and places responsibility on the individual to own the sense of nature. Emerson's philosophical novitiate takes place, moreover, at a time when to be reasonable was appearing to many philosophers to mean recognizing that language in all its particularity and diversity is the vehicle of reason. He therefore understood the primary challenge to human existence as residing in the moral issue of the success or failure of the individual to articulate his vision and in the consequences that success or failure has for the quality of his life.

To the extent Emerson recognizes and emphasizes the unleashing of reason to the poetic use of language, it becomes figures, metaphors, images, and narratives rather than concepts that carry the arguments in his writings. Because this can have the effect of obscuring their philosophical content, of suggesting that Emerson was not primarily concerned with philosophical ideas, which, it has long been held, enter his writings only peripherally and largely inadequately, I will focus my effort on drawing out the philosophical content of his metaphors and making clear their explanatory scope. It is important to do so, moreover, not only to establish the centrality of his philosophical concerns but also because in *Nature* and the essays and lectures of the early period Emerson formulated the poetic/philosophical vocabulary he would use throughout his lifetime. His later writings draw heavily on the value he earns for his central terms, both carrying that value along and adapting it to formulate his new explanations of "the always interesting topics of Man and Nature" (*CW* 1:122).

1

Vision and Thought

Emerson sets down the practical imperative of his early thought in the opening paragraph of "Self-Reliance" when he writes, "To believe your own thought, to believe that what is true for you in your private heart, is true for all men,—that is genius. Speak your latent conviction and it shall be the universal sense" (*CW* 2:27). These sentences describe a hyperbolic conception of freedom, freedom conceived as the immediate expression of personal conviction unconstrained by regulations or rules. But Emerson does not merely embrace the premise of pure expressivity, he weds it to a comprehensive theory of value that he says affirms, shall affirm, "the universal sense." Here I find what is characteristic about Emerson's early thought, as well as the central premise of the idea of self-reliance: the claim that radical freedom shall issue in universal value.

The humanist faith underwriting Emerson's early essays is nowhere more apparent than in these opening lines of "Self-Reliance," and the claim they make indicates the extension of humanist thought that he developed in his early essays and lectures. The nature of self-reliance, as of the revolution in thought and action that Emerson conceived under that name, can best be appreciated by comparing it to Kant's ethics. As David Marr writes, "Emerson's early doctrine of self-reliance bears close resemblance [to Kant's ethics], especially in so far as both Emerson and Kant regarded mere social conformity as a form of self-inflicted punishment."¹ And indeed, the comparison could be justified simply by virtue of the surprising similarity between Emerson's language and the formulation of the Categorical Imperative. Emerson's claim that individual freedom will have universal effect closely resembles Kant's famous assertion that pure freedom can be the basis of universal law. When placed side by side, the statements show their similarity: Kant's imperative commands the individual to "act only on the maxim through which you can at the same time will it should become a universal law."² Emerson's phrasing seems intended to extend Kant's formula: "Speak your latent conviction and it shall be the universal sense." What the two statements share is a pietistic faith in the power of individual will to bring about essential value. Kant's initial intuition, like Emerson's, speaks to the uncanny possibility that human will has the power to create value. Kant in fact concedes this sense when he writes in reference to the Categorical Imperative, "The thing is strange enough, and has no parallel in the remainder of practical knowledge. For the a priori thought of the possibility of giving universal law, which is thus merely problematic, is unconditionally commanded as a law without borrowing anything from experience or from any external will."³ The distance between Kant's rational imperative to moral action and Emerson's call to self-reliance is significantly shortened in consideration of this statement.⁴ It is, nonetheless, well known that for Kant the faculty of freedom ultimately conforms to natural law and accordingly is informed by the structure of cognitive judgment. Kant moderates the power he gives to the will by asserting that the transformation of pure freedom to universal law occurs through the mediation of theoretical reason—freedom legislates universal laws by appeal to the ra-

---

1. David Marr, *American Worlds since Emerson* (Amherst: University of Massachussetts Press, 1988), 63.
2. Immanuel Kant, *The Groundwork of the Metaphysic of Morals*, ed. H. J. Paton (London: Mayflower Press, Hutchinson University Library, 1947), 88.
3. Immanuel Kant, *Critique of Practical Reason*, ed. Lewis White Beck (Chicago: University of Chicago Press, 1949), 142.
4. Stanley Cavell indirectly remarks this similarity when commenting on a passage in "The American Scholar," which also founds universal truth on apprehension and articulation of one's deepest convictions. "The contrast to the superficially private," Cavell writes, "which the *most* private can reach, Emerson characterizes sometimes as necessary, sometimes as universal, thus exactly according to the characteristics Kant assigns to the a priori" ("Aversive Thinking: Emersonian Representations in Heidegger and Nietzsche," *New Literary History* 22,1 [Winter 1991]: 141). And later, commenting on the same lines I have cited from "Self-Reliance" and passages from "The American Scholar," Cavell concludes, "As for Kant, for Emerson this vision is an inception of the moral life" ("Aversive Thinking," 143).

tional forms of classical logic. If defining acts of human freedom overlook all particular practical maxims, they do not for Kant overlook theoretical reason itself or its manifestation in reason's public use.[5] On the contrary, freedom works through what Kant takes to be the inviolable structure of logic and only thereby returns the universal law of the world. The practical imperative in Kant's thought is finally then the command to be logical, for only thereby, under Kant's premises, can it be efficacious.

Nonetheless, Kant, at least in the above lines, comes close to expressing, and certainly his intuition implies, the humanist thought that Emerson sets out in the opening lines of "Self-Reliance." The advantage of juxtaposing the passage from "Self-Reliance" and the Categorical Imperative is that it sets in relief the innovative nature of Emerson's practical call. It indicates that Emerson's early ideology, unlike Kant's ethics, *does* extend the humanist intuition to infinite proportion, that Emerson refuses to retreat from the hyperbole of radical freedom to any definitive *theoretical* structure. His imperative thus relies on the skeptical release of the will from antecedent conditions, on the abandonment of such conditions, including especially the conditions of rational cognition. Emerson's relegation of theoretical reason to a secondary role characterizes his early thought and differentiates it from Kant's system.[6] It founds the moral utopianism of his early period. If Emerson's early unwillingness to concede any historical conditions is well known, emphasizing his difference from Kant shows that self-reliance consists of a will that equally knows no formal conditions, and suggests why when he asks in his 1837 journal, "Who shall define to me an Individual?" he is more directly and forcefully confronted with the contradiction contained, and repressed, in rational constructions of individuality, and why he goes on to characterize the individual as coming "armed and impassioned, to parricide thus murderously inclined, ever to traverse and kill the Divine Life" (*JMN* 5:336–37). Self-reliance inhabits this contradiction, taking the destruction of a priori principles of action and value as the condition for individuality and for the return of the "Divine Life" to human being.

---

5. Ellison, citing the following passage from Emerson's journals, notes his more solitary conception of freedom: "A trust in yourself is the height not of pride but of piety, an unwillingness to learn of any but God himself" (*JMN*, 3:279). She concludes, "[Emerson] avoids heresy by making God the creator of the self-reliant soul, but insists on an exclusive relationship to the deity that allows him to reject public opinion. Refusing to respect any authority but God makes him God's equal" (*Emerson's Romantic Style*, 53, 54).

6. For a different conclusion, see Marr, *American Worlds since Emerson*, 63ff.

But if Emerson repudiates Kant's rationalism, he continues the larger humanist project, implicit in Kant's practical philosophy, of locating human foundations of universal value. It is important that he continues it free of the limitation theoretical reason places on practical reason. Bringing practical reason out from under the dominance of theoretical reason, he pushes to the foreground the foundation of humanist ideology, the faith that individual freedom is the sole transcendental condition of value, that the human voice creates the world, or, to be more exact, articulates the value of the world. Only in this respect does Emersonian "transcendentalism" succeed in transforming the private to the public, the particular to the universal. And accordingly, the account of self-reliance requires a distinct means of thematizing, or figuring the "sense" of, the universal sense. For this Emerson relied on figures of vision. In metaphors of vision he found a medium of value adequate to the soul's becoming, a medium traditionally attached to the capacity of speech and thereby illustrative of the power of eloquence. Vision captured the sense of sovereignty that Emerson attached to self-reliant articulations.

By tracing self-reliance to a phenomenological capacity, it becomes possible to situate Emerson's practical imperative in the command to see clearly, to render the world transparent through our actions and to speak its transparency. The imperative to speak one's latent conviction is revealed thereby to be vision's imperative, the command to act authentically in the world by seeing things as they are. This explanation provides a way of understanding Emerson's early belief that radical human freedom enables the universal sense and that value emerges wholly as the immediate manifest effects of action.

THE IMPERATIVE TO SEE THINGS AS THEY ARE

One of the more engaging of Emerson's descriptions of self-reliance is found a short way into the essay, where he writes, "The nonchalance of boys who are sure of a dinner, and would disdain as much as a lord to do or say aught to conciliate one, is the healthy attitude of human nature" (*CW* 2:29). Emerson raises through this description the image of an attitude of indifference that accords with an unconditioned will. He goes on to fill out the idea: "A boy is in the parlour what the pit is in the playhouse; independent, irresponsible, looking out from his corner on such people and facts as pass by, he tries and sentences them on their merits, in the swift summary way of boys, as good, bad, interesting, silly, eloquent, troublesome. He cumbers himself never about consequences, about interests: he gives an independent, genuine verdict" (*CW* 2:29). As a description of self-reliance, this statement is dominated by the sense of a will emancipated from crippling responsibility and released to the disinterest that characterizes the boy's attitude before he is "clapped into jail by his consciousness" (*CW* 2:29). It undoubtedly reflects the unconditioned spontaneity most often associated with self-reliance. However, the statement is equally interesting for the capacity of judgment that it connects to the boy's attitude. Indifference is set out as a posture of immediate judgment, and, moreover, the posture from which *genuine* judgment derives. If the boy's attitude is one of irresponsibility, then the effect of his attitude is evaluation of the most authentic kind.

The description is important here because it reveals the relationship between a conditionless will and genuine or right judgment that I have suggested is at the center of Emerson's early theory. Emerson intends that the self-reliant attitude be opposed to rational purposiveness, to the kind of teleological endeavor that consists of the imposition of a priori categories on thought, and he makes this clear when, a few sentences later, he characterizes the boy's attitude as the posture of "neutrality," indicating an attitude that simply ignores antecedent criteria of judgment. The boy's neutrality, his innocence, stands for an indifference to all prior criteria and thereby results in genuine evaluations. But in no sense does self-reliant neutrality indicate a broad indifference to value. Judgments that issue from neutrality are then not inconsequential or frivolous, and I question readings that identify the whimsy of self-reliance with ineffectiveness or with a merely critical effect. It is not at all accurate to understand the boy's attitude as incapacitating or only playful. On the contrary, it grounds judgments that "must always be formidable" (*CW* 2:29). Emerson says he writes whim on the lintels of his doorpost to protect his genius, not to disarm it, and to protect it principally by naming, under the label "whim," an attitude of thought and action that, by dismissing theoretical and normative conventions, opens the space for authentic evaluations.

The boy's innocent attitude thus conjoins emancipated will and the capacity for genuine judgment and turns attention to the problem of how emancipated will, predicated as it is on the dismissal of all criteria of value, can be understood to be the basis of evaluations of the most veritable kind. The solution is found, of course, in the link that exists between the boy's healthy attitude and the method of skeptical, phenomenological judgment that Emerson elaborates over the course of his writings.[7] The manner of the boy's judgment accords with the description of skepticism briefly described above and formulated most acutely in "Montaigne, or the Skeptic." Neutrality carries the meaning of the suspension of judgment that Emerson identifies in "Montaigne" as the principle of skepticism. The boy is neither a critic nor a believer; his back is turned on the conditions of criticism and belief, but at least in his early phase, the point is to indicate that this skeptical gesture initiates the process of authentic judgment. Emerson's remarks show that judgments of the most formidable kind occur because conditionless will is irrevocably linked to sight and enables true sight of the world. "The child sees better than the man," Tony Tanner writes; and indeed, the boy is marked, as the skeptic will be later, by the unprecedented capacity to "look out" from a corner of the world and to judge without blame or prejudice, standing as an innocent observer in the midst of the world.[8] Although the statement comes from "Montaigne," Emerson could as well have written of the self-reliant individual that "everything that is excellent in man . . . he will see and judge" (*C* 4:161). And like the skeptic, the boy can say, "I neither affirm nor deny. I stand here to try the case. I am here to consider, *skopein*, to consider how it is" (*C* 4:156). There are certainly important differences between the skeptic and the self-reliant boy, most of them determined by the shift from humanism to antihumanism that intervenes between the writing of the two essays. Nonetheless, it is profitable to note the continuity between them. It reveals the emphasis Emerson places on the phenomenological act and the connection he draws between it and a skeptical attitude. In the earlier essay, this act affirms value; genuine evaluations of the world result from *skopein*, from the activity of looking absent informing categories of sight, from a willed attitude of perceptual innocence.

The relation of self-reliant will and phenomenological clarity is evident, moreover, in the preeminent figure of self-reliance, as of the en-

---

7. Cavell emphasizes this point in his discussion of "Self-Reliance" in "Being Odd, Getting Even." He develops his reading by posing the Emersonian idea of the self against Descartes's skeptical cogito, and by showing that the skeptical subject, which is the enduring problem/solution of critical philosophy, is performative. By drawing a connection between a formal cogito and Emerson's idea of individuality, Cavell demonstrates that Emerson's skeptical approach is rooted in self-performance, and that in Emerson's use of it the fundamental axiom of modern epistemology, as well as the set of problems it initiates, thereby gives way to issues of action.

8. "Emerson: The Unconquered Eye and the Enchanted Circle," in *Critical Essays on Ralph Waldo Emerson*, ed. Robert Burkholder and Joel Myerson (Boston: G. K. Hall & Co., 1983), 314.

tirety of Emerson's early philosophy of the erect position. I have in mind the figure of the upright position that Emerson evokes midway through the essay, complaining, "Man is timid and apologetic; he is no longer upright; he dares not say 'I think,' 'I am,' but quotes some saint or sage" (*CW* 2:38). The upright position, Man standing, refers to a willingness to act in the world, principally a willingness to act by speaking one's latent conviction and thereby affirming one's fundamental identity. Upright innocence stands opposed to a contemplative posture, marking rather the suspension and unsettling of presuppositions that results from what he calls daring action. Elsewhere Emerson makes clear, however, that uprightness signifies more than daring action; it signifies action specifically *in the service* of seeing clearly.

He took the figure of uprightness from Milton's description in *Paradise Lost*, where it refers to the attitude of Man at his creation. But more importantly, he calls it up in this essay from his own earlier writings, which show that he thought of the self-reliant attitude in terms of a way of seeing. "I ought to have no shame," Emerson wrote in his 1835 journal, "in publishing the records of one who aimed only at the upright position more anxious that the thing should be truly seen than careful what thing it was" (*JMN* 5:43). Uprightness thus converges in Emerson's figural argument with the boy's attitude and means the capacity to see without shame, to observe innocent of prior conditions. Indeed, *to do*, in Emerson, primarily means to see, to make visible, and correlatively, to speak is to lay out the appearance of nature as the context in which self and otherness are mutually disposed. Uprightness is then a means or an attitude that illuminates the interrelations that make up the immediate context of one's world. The figure does not represent a solipsistic posture in any traditional sense. Emerson is far from denying otherness: natural or human. Rather, his discussion is directed toward elucidating the manner by which the self and otherness are made apparent, toward revealing through authentic action the effective proximity of the self and other in the world. Instead of appealing to conditions or principles that by prescribing action effectively obscure it, he describes the method of sight that enables nature's unmediated manifestion. The boy's formidable verdicts stem from trusting his own view of things and thus presenting things as they are. It makes sense then that Emerson would identify the "Trustee," the "aboriginal Self on which a universal reliance may be grounded," not principally as Instinct or Spontaneity, but as a phenomenological capacity, the "involuntary perception" to which "a perfect faith is due" (*CW* 2:37). The final trustee of the individual, and of his world, is the effective, inevitable, and unmediated disclosure of nature brought about by being in the world in a state of unconditioned will, of "unaffected, unbiased, unbribable, unaffrighted innocence" (*CW* 2:29).

In summary, the complementarity between self-reliance and Emerson's sense of skeptical judgment settles self-reliance in the context of a phenomenological method that relies on acts of unconditioned will to illuminate the relations in one's world. My intention is to stress that this in turn suggests the reciprocity of thought and action, sight and will, that underwrites Emerson's early method. There is no more forceful illustration of this phenomenological sponsorship of identity than the essay "Circles." By turning to "Circles," and then later to a discussion of "Compensation," it is possible to solidify this point and suggest the eloquence of Emersonian humanism. But as the power and scope of his humanist synthesis are displayed, it will also be possible to suggest the points at which it will be eclipsed later in his writings.

"Circles" begins, of course, with Emerson's well-known claim that the eye is the first circle, and implicitly then with the claim that the circle of the eye sets the limits for the manifestation of nature. In a sense, no more need be said about the essay: all of nature is thus pulled within the horizon of Man, and the universality of the self is justified. This is saying enough, however, only if one keeps in mind that the power of vision is a double-edged sword. If the eye gathers nature for the individual, and for the individual's potential universality, then the horizon of the eye can as well become fixed and freeze the fluctuations of natural appearance, imposing a single limit on nature and thereby establishing a static structure of value according to which natural presence is determined and repeated in continuous re-presentations. Precisely such sedimentation and repetition of a particular order acts to create normative and theoretical values, retrospective constructs, that interpret and thus dominate our lived experience. It halts the coincidence of vision and the onwardness of nature and creates an artificial divide between self and nature, diminishing the individual to a merely functional self-identity, to the dwarfed condition spoken of by the Orphic poet in *Nature* (*CW* 1:42). Emerson's attack on conventions in "Circles" is directed at such evaluative structures that survive in enduring or fixed horizons of the eye. In a litany of phrases and sentences he makes clear that his central value is the manifestation of pure onwardness: "There are no fixtures to men," "no past at my back," "Life is a series of surprises," "The continual effort to raise himself above himself, to walk a pitch above his last height, betrays itself in a man's relations," and most characteristically, "We can never go so far back as to preclude a still higher vision" (*CW* 2:182, 188, 189, 182, 183). He writes, "There is no outside, no enclosing wall, no circumference to us" (*CW* 2:181). As is well known, Emerson's purpose is to show that thought is progressive, that it progresses by virtue of its reciprocal dependence on the emancipatory activity of the will, that every progressive act opens a new horizon, transforms the past into a new value and overrules repetition by appropriating all of nature and the past to its articulation of the present. If all appearances emerge within the eye's horizon, then the prolific activity of forward-directed will, *matutina cognitio*, assures that there can be no limit to the circles we draw around nature, to what we can see (and finally to how we can find ourselves). Thus Emerson writes, "Our life is an apprenticeship to the truth that around every circle another can be drawn; that there is no end in nature, but every end is a beginning" (*CW* 2:179).

The foundation of Emerson's early humanism is set in relief in this essay and shown to consist in nothing less than the appropriation of God's perspective. In response to his skepticism about what an individual can be, he offers the individual as the compass that surrounds and manifests nature. Emerson's purpose is to teach God in Man, to teach Man to inhabit the perspective of the "flying Perfect" (*CW* 2:179). Emersonian transcendentalism does not put forward a version of humanist ideology upon which we can critically reflect; rather, it consists in the formula of humanism itself.⁹ When he writes, "Our globe seen by God, is a transparent law," he indicates what the nature of our humanized apotheosis would be: it will occur as our ascent to, or inhabitation of, the attitude that wills the transparency of nature. If the world's transparency now flees before us as quickly as the "flying Perfect," then

---

9. The resilience of Emerson's conception can be made evident by considering Jeffrey Steele's remarks in his study of the reader's response to Emersonian transcendentalism. Steele asserts the need to distance oneself from Emerson's rhetoric: "In order for our identification or absorption in the voice of a text to appear within the field of critical reflection, a reciprocal act of distancing is necessary. At the same time that we try on and speak through the Transcendentalist mask, achieving a liberating sense of freedom, we must maintain the awareness that we are acting" (*The Representation of the Self in the American Renaissance*, 10). But the identification of the "flying Perfect," or the Oversoul, as the act of reflective withdrawal or distancing by which vision is sustained indicates that Emerson's humanist faith is not founded in the unconscious, as Steele suggests, but in the power of reason to recover the individual's historicity for thought. The eloquence and appropriative power of self-reliance thus becomes apparent with our recognition of its prediction and inclusion of just the distancing gesture Steele says will contain it. The critical and ironic act that Steele intends to delimit the scope of the text, here the concept of self-reliance or active will, in this case enacts it and thus reinstantiates its "infinitude."

this is the very fact that commands the phenomenological destruction of all contemporary horizons of presence, and the attitude that is directed toward the future. The teaching implicit in "Circles" is a justification of the emergent self, for it identifies the permanence of Man as that which stands at the center and defines the circumference of the system of onward natural appearances. Emerson anticipates this fact in *Nature* when he writes that Man "is placed in the centre of beings, and a ray of relation passes from every other being to him" (*CW* 1:19). He expresses the self-recovering exuberance of the individual most poignantly, however, in "Circles," writing that the authentic individual "cannot have his flank turned, cannot be outgeneralled, but put him where you will, he stands" (*CW* 2:183). Richard Poirier captures the humanism of Emerson's early thought, as well as its resilience, in contemporary terms when he writes, "Emerson may sometimes sound deconstructionist . . . [b]ut he insists . . . this very same temporariness [of the circular philosophy] is instigated and perpetuated by the human will."[10] The phenomenological destruction of the eye's horizon creates "a new generalization" by virtue of Man's will, and without fail its first effect is the recreation, the ecstasy, of the individual (*CW* 2:183).

The method described by "Circles" thus reveals much more than a method of sight. The argument emphasizes that the value of self-reliance, as the central agency in Emerson's early theory and the imperative of human existence, resides in the complicity of vision and will that it names. It consists of the conflation of emancipated will and the process of sight figured in "Self-Reliance" as the boy's innocent observation. The attitude of uprightness enacts the method of "Circles," effecting the coincidence of vision and nature both within an horizon of the eye and as the condition for overcoming any horizon. The exertions of unconditioned will upon which it relies, by overcoming prior appearances—destroying them through the phenomenological act of turning attention away from them ("Let us rise into another idea: [the preceding idea] will disappear," Emerson writes)—produces a clearing of the space in the eye's circle, within which a new manifestation of nature appears (*CW* 2:179). Emerson conceives no end to this process; it is not as if eventually the true horizon of the eye, and thus of nature and the individual, will be found. Rather, the *true* horizon is found each time a previous horizon is overcome; the true horizon is the emergent horizon—the flying perfect—that discloses the individual as the clear-

---

10. Richard Poirier, *The Renewal of Literature: Emersonian Reflections* (New York: Random House, 1987), 16.

ing that enables the appearance of nature's onwardness. The activity of overcoming one circle, moving to another, to a new epochal unity within which the world is transparent, is the fundamental value of self-reliance. Self-reliance is rightly thought of then as the agency of a phenomenological destruction and presencing, the agency of overlooking or seeing beyond one's current horizon to a new manifestation of nature. The identity of the individual is raised through the articulation of a new circle. To see beyond is to see truly, and in this sense self-reliance, being in the upright posture, is to dare to think.

"Circles" describes a phenomenological method for which there is no permanence of value; it affirms a method of the ongoing fluctuation of nature for which "the universe is fluid and volatile [and] permanence is but a word of degrees" (*CW* 2:179). It develops the reciprocity of the eye and the will that is anticipated by the figural logic of "Self-Reliance," and it indicates the mutual dependence, the coimplication of thought and will, that Emerson writes of in "The American Scholar" (*CW* 1:61).

But insofar as the dynamic of nature's appearance is consolidated within the limits of the willful eye, to the extent Emerson insists "on the radical identity of 'I' and 'eye,'" it needs to be said that it is in principle incorrect to describe nature as the flux of appearance and disappearance.[11] Moments of authenticity consist, rather, of a dynamic of phenomenological destruction and presence, for nature never eludes the ecstatic presence of the individual, and it never passes then from appearance. Nature never disappears any more than Man does. It remains utterly transparent within the circular, epochal unity of presence enabled by the individual.[12] In this respect Emerson's language in "Circles" generally, and his remarks about permanence in nature especially, is misleading, suggesting a blindness in his conception or an overstatement in his language. If deep unto deep discloses a vast affirmative, then that affirmative names the permanent principle in Emerson's early

11. Joel Porte, *Representative Man: Ralph Waldo Emerson in His Times* (New York: Oxford University Press, 1979), ix.

12. Michael's discussion of "Emerson's cipher of the world" offers an alternative interpretation that emphasizes the dependence of self-possession on "the grasp of the other" (*Emerson and Skepticism*, 136, 138). I cannot reconcile Michael's conclusion that self-definition is achieved when the individual is disposed by another's explanation with Emerson's disparaging description of the moment of being so disposed: "Then already is our first speaker not man." Moreover, Emerson goes on to suggest a response that emphasizes the individual origins of self-presence: "His only redress is forthwith to draw a circle outside of his antagonist. And so men do *by themselves*" (*CW* 2:181, emphasis added).

method, consisting in the affirmation of Man. The content of nature's presence may defy the fixity of retrospective categories, but the fact of natural presence itself is not placed in question. And it will not be questioned as long as Emerson affirms the one principle the early thought maintains, the principle Poirier rightly identifies as the permanence of active will, the depth of human being in nature. If it is not then wrong, it is misleading to describe "Circles" as "a sustained vision of a world in flux," even if in some sense it describes a universe that works "in terms of an endless metamorphic process that has neither beginning nor end."[13] It is misleading because Emerson withdraws from the flux precisely the reflective distance necessary to sustain the vision and bound it by the individual. It may be difficult to read "Circles" without sharing in the pleasures of perpetual self-recovery, but it is well to bear in mind that the identification of active will at the foundation of the method of "Circles," when viewed retrospectively from "The Method of Nature," marks not its infinitude but the limits of the method and marks it precisely by delimiting the efficacy of human will, what Emerson calls in the later lecture the platform of action.

It is well to bear this in mind particularly when considering the role of language in Emerson's early method, for the limitations that will later be recognized for vision apply as well to speech. It is clear from the opening lines of "Self-Reliance" that Emerson formulates his practical imperative in terms of speech. Speech, for Emerson, carries out the function of *logos* prior to its sedimentation as a fixed account of nature; which is to say, Emerson, consistent with a tradition in Western thought that begins with the Greeks, views authentic speech as utterances that operate reciprocally with thought's intuition to lay out the living account of *phusis*, or nature. The central role this gives to speech is evident in many places in Emerson's writings. He writes, for instance, "The organ of language [is] the subtlest, strongest, and longest-lived of man's creations, and only fitly used as the weapon of thought and justice"; or elsewhere, "Always the seer is a sayer. Somehow his dream is told. Somehow he publishes it with solemn joy" (*CW* 1:110, 84). Speech, then, as Emerson describes it in the early period, is the principal, perhaps the only, weapon of thought and justice, where these terms nearly synonymously represent the proportionate and rounded articulation of the object.

---

13. Michael T. Gilmore, "Emerson and the Persistence of the Commodity," in *Emerson: Prospect and Retrospect*, ed. Joel Porte (Cambridge, Mass.: Harvard University Press, 1982), 72; Porte, *Representative Man*, x.

Speech, moreover, is a central part of the dynamic of phenomenological destruction and affirmation implicit in the idea of self-reliance. It effects the unity of nature by overthrowing conventional articulations and decisively asserting new formulations of nature, broadly through the poetic act of creating metaphors. Indeed, the power of speech is rendered in terms of the creative power of poetry, as a human capacity to give just account of emergent nature—of the Rose.[14] As such, it is wed to the phenomenological destruction of value that initiates self-reliance and is an expression of the value of nature inherent in the clearing it establishes. If "Self-Reliance" affirms the individual as the very possibility of nature's presence, then speech realizes that potential. Emerson describes an individual who bespeaks his or her engagement of nature, an individual coincident with the proliferation of nature, writing, "I run eagerly into this resounding tumult. I grasp the hands of those next to me, and take my place in the ring to suffer and to work, taught by an instinct that so shall the dumb abyss be vocal with speech. I pierce its order; I dissipate its fear; I dispose of it within the circuit of my expanding life" (*CW* 1:59).

Emerson views authentic speech, then, as unbound by the customs embedded in social linguistic structures, as expression that derives from abandonment of customs and conventions. "The way of life is wonderful," he writes in "Circles," "it is by abandonment" (*CW* 2:190). And he goes on in "Spiritual Laws" to invoke the figure of oratory to indicate the reliance of true utterances on the gesture of abandonment that grounds speech in thought's illumination. Noting that our public speaking "has not abandonment," he asserts, "Somewhere not only every orator but every man should let out all the length of all the reins; should find or make a frank and hardy expression of what force and meaning is in him" (*CW* 2:83). At stake in this call is the implication of choice, and authentic identity, in the speech act. Decisiveness itself consists in speaking one's belief and thereby articulating the order of one's world. To speak with abandon, with attention to one's own latent convictions irrespective of prior accounts, clarifies the emergent relations of the epochal unity of the eye and expresses the organization of nature's appearance, expresses thought, whence reciprocally it derives. The return of dispersive acts of will to the humanist synthesis of individual identity is thus mandated by the identity of will and speech under the concept of decision or choice. Insofar as decision consists of severing, or cutting off, one's vision, the unity of the individual

---

14. Cf. Gertrude Reif Hughes, *Emerson's Demanding Optimism*, 73ff.

emerges through the act of speech. Decision here, of course, implies no rational deliberation and presupposes no a priori identity but instead refers to the utterance necessarily entailed by seeing truly. Decision involves a fundamental and necessary trust in one's own thought. To decide—and thereby to identify oneself—means both to believe your private heart, your latent convictions, and to speak their appearance as the emergence of nature. Speech renders the eye's horizon, and in so doing frames and articulates the contemporaneous disposition of the self in the world, and the decision *implicit already* in a self-reliant posture in the world—in uprightness—thus becomes explicit, and the world's relations become transparent for it. Self-reliance can be described as the phenomenological resolution effected by decisive speech. Authentic speech is convicted by what is seen truly and held accountable to its expression. Perhaps it is more accurate to say it is the conviction of the self-reliant individual welling up in the form of language. In either case, however, speech expresses the identity of the individual in and through the ecstatic unity of nature's transparence.

In this respect speech is the fundamental practical act of Emerson's early thought. But it should be added that although speech is the medium of nature's appearance, it cannot be divorced from, nor can it properly be understood as, a power or faculty that precedes nature's appearance. Rather, as noted above, speech is settled in the phenomenological dynamic of destruction and affirmation and takes shape as a consequence of that dynamic. Inasmuch as authentic speech derives from the involuntary perception to which, Emerson tells us, we owe the greatest fidelity, the boy and the skeptic alike first *see* and then judge by speaking what is seen rightly.

That such perception depends on the spontaneity or instinct of abandonment from prior conditions of thought provides the terms for affirming the mutual dependence of unconditioned will and thought that sponsors the early phenomenological humanism. But it also gives the appearance of the precedence of will. And, to be sure, Emerson's early writings do privilege the capacity of the will to overcome and then, through utterance, to circumscribe and manifest nature. But the method described in "Circles" and implicit in the early work shows that in a more general sense, will and speech serve the process of nature's appearing: *phusis*. Thus if Emerson's central concern in the early writings and addresses is to teach an emancipated will, and if his confidence rests in the faith that such will can own the world and render it transparent for thought, then, from a retrospective view again, the emphasis in "Circles" on the precedence of nature's appearing predicts Emerson's later dissociation of speech and natural presencing. Indeed, Emerson will come increasingly to identify thought, not with the clarification and resolution of nature possible under the authority of a decisive will, but with the indeterminate and, he will say, illusory flux of nature extrinsic to the will's performance. His faith here in the appropriative power of speech, its adequacy to the fluctuations of nature, thus mirrors his blindness, mentioned above, to the permanence of the soul's withdrawal in the circular method. And just as the soul's withdrawal can be accounted for only by the preemptive valorization of the will, so his confidence in authentic speech depends on substituting for nature's temporality the linearity of the will's actions, which privilege the "now" and the present. In both cases Emerson describes the form and content of emancipated will as interactive with but not as a part of nature, and in consequence the situatedness of the will, of authentic speech and of the decisiveness of the soul within a temporality framed on the oscillations of nature's appearing and disappearing, is unacknowledged.

Emerson's later thought is founded on the recognition of the primordiality of this oscillatory movement, as I will show in Part II. What is crucial to note now is that awareness of this oscillation is guarded from its redetermination within a dialectic of presence and absence and thus from its reappropriation by the humanist dynamic of the will, only by preserving the power of the humanist synthesis as it is overcome, a preservation and disposal that is in turn accomplished by externalizing the function of the will itself, or put otherwise, by fully articulating its power. My purpose is not served then by diminishing the scope of the humanist dialectic. Any hasty diminution of the will's not insubstantial power to gather its history in a contemporary articulation of the self and the world can only lead to reductive and retrograde self-interpretations, not to mention misleading interpretations of Emerson's work. Accordingly, to further draw out the measure of his humanism and its reliance on the preemptive priority of will, I discuss in the following section the ethics of the doctrine of compensation as an outgrowth of his affirmation of the will.

VALUE BEYOND THE SPIRIT OF REVENGE

In the opening paragraph of "Circles" Emerson writes: "One moral we have already deduced in considering the circular or compensatory character of every human action" (*CW* 2:179). His reference is to "Compensation," and the remark indicates the close connection he sees between the phenomenological method of thought described in "Circles" and the theory of value that he develops in "Compensation." Each circle, each limit of the eye, is the compensation of an act, each phenomenological resolution of the individual in and through the utterance of the clearing within the eye is its own reward. The method of "Circles" shows the intimacy Emerson contemplated between the imperative to self-reliance and the doctrine of compensation. The doctrine is straightforward: the value of an act, as of the just individual, is given immediately as the relational structure of presence that the act manifests.[15]

Emerson develops the meaning of compensation in direct relation to the dynamic of emancipated will and natural appearance and describes it as an effective, pragmatic theory of value. The "philosophy of the erect position," with its imperative to abandonment, could support no other theory of value, for no authentic criteria of value can exist prior to the active elucidation of the horizon of the eye. Value—compensation—is found only in the articulation, the manifestation of the clearing within the eye enabled by abandonment, that is to say, in the visible effects of authentic action. The discussion in "Compensation" therefore describes value in terms of disposition within a system of interrelationships, and Emerson's heavy use of economic imagery in the essay accordingly reflects the dispositional nature of value. However, the doctrine of compensation does not for that reason oppose the claim to universality implicit in self-reliant acts. Insofar as speech articulates the clearing within the eye, it lays out the economy of self and nature, the economy of presence. Emerson's deep conviction in the constitutive power of self-reliant actions entails that the context in which an individual act is disposed, and thus according to which it gains value, is itself the effect of phenomenological resolution. That is to say, authentic speech disposes the self according to its own dictation of the economic order within the clearing of the eye. On the basis of this conception of evaluation, Emerson often repeats that the Last Judgment occurs every day: the circle detached by speech provides the terms of its own immediate and self-evident justification. The imperative to self-reliance and the doctrine of compensation thus converge in the act of authentic

---

15. See Sherman Paul, *Emerson's Angle of Vision*, 98ff. Paul's discussion of the doctrine of compensation remains one of the best, implying the affinity between phenomenological and pragmatic method, presence and its effective articulation of relations in nature.

speech. The doctrine of compensation complements the ecstasy of Man; it explains the value of the Rose that exists without reference, the theory of value that derives from the presence, the justness of the Rose that is without time because time collapses into it.

Emerson's first concern in "Compensation" is to carry out the refutation of retrospective theories of value that is implied by the imperative to self-reliance. His argument, albeit figural in nature, is sweeping in breadth, and can be measured against the suggestive scope of Christian doctrine, both as a religious faith and an anthropological structure. Emerson develops the doctrine of compensation in opposition to the structure of Christian reward, posing it as a repudiation of the premise of Christian eschatology, which is for him the principal instance in Western culture of all theories of value that rely on a priori or antecedent evaluative foundations.

"Compensation" begins with a description of a fire-and-brimstone preacher, a man "esteemed for his orthodoxy," laying out the doctrine of the Last Judgment. "He assumed," Emerson writes, "that judgment is not executed in this world; that the wicked are successful; that the good are miserable; and then urged from reason and Scripture a compensation to be made to both parties in the next life" (*CW* 2:55). An "ordinary" representation of the Christian myth, the description is made interesting by Emerson's gloss of the teaching implicit in the preacher's sermon: "The legitimate inference the disciple would draw was,—'We are to have *such* a good time as the sinners have now;'—or, to push it to its extreme import,—'You sin now; we shall sin by and by; we would sin now, if we could, not being successful, we expect our revenge tomorrow'" (*CW* 2:56).

When Emerson says that the preacher's sermon describes the divinely sponsored replacement of the sinner by the good individual, emphasizing that the good expect to have "*such*" a time as the sinners have had in this world, that they expect, that is, the very compensations the sinner gets in this world, the rewards of this world, he unmasks the supposed metaphysical truths of Christianity as human values and sets the discussion of metaphysical thought on the ground of the acquisition of power. In fact, the preacher, at least in Emerson's portrait of him, is quite frank, acknowledging that the promise of Christianity is no more or less than eventual revenge. Emerson's concern, beyond the striking rhetorical effect of reducing Christianity to motives of revenge, is to make clear that the preacher's doctrine defines the essential value of the afterlife as the displaced satisfactions of this world, the postponed gratification of all-too-human desires. However, his objection to the preacher's sermon, and his reason for stating his surprise that "no offence appeared to be taken by the congregation at this doctrine," is hardly its humanist foundation (*CW* 2:57). He has no intention in "Compensation" of renovating metaphysical doctrine under a new description, which would presumably invigorate the afterlife, giving it credibility. On the contrary, he draws Christianity under the umbrella of humanist thought in order to set in relief the *human* value and effect of Christian doctrine, to question its worth when that worth is not hidden behind the veil of metaphysical faith.

Standing beneath and sponsoring Emerson's gloss of the preacher's sermon, then, is a revaluation of the Christian myth that treats it under the assumptions of his radical humanism. He begins his discussion of fundamental compensation, of the sources of value we find in ourselves and in the world around us, by bringing the paradigm of Western metaphysics and eschatology down to its human foundation, posing it there in relation to human action and in terms of its human worth and thereby implicitly questioning both the motives of those who hold to Christian doctrine and the effective value of the doctrine. His purpose is to indicate that the structure of evaluation intrinsic to Christianity is itself faulty and to replace it with the doctrine of compensation.

It is not enough, however, merely to note that Christian doctrine has its roots in human desires; the doctrine of compensation can be explained, and more importantly gains its force as an alternative theory of evaluation, only insofar as one understands the failure of human potential that Emerson identifies with the embrace of Christian doctrine. It implies a failure, not just of the metaphysical belief but of the believer as well. Emerson's argument is not only against the illusion of metaphysics but against what that illusion entails for the way we live our lives, and it is this result—the human disposition entailed by Christian metaphysics—that explains the value Emerson attaches to the doctrine of compensation. Of course, Emerson does not provide an "argument" against Christianity. To understand his position I find it necessary to reconstruct the argument implied by the narratives and figures he provides. In this case that means the narrative of the preacher's sermon and, specifically, its most important aspect, the figure of revenge. For, again, it is revenge that names the value of Christianity, not only as a metaphysical faith but, more importantly, as a disposition of human beings in the world.

In order to develop the figural meaning of revenge, I will exploit the fact that Emerson's use of the figure, especially in connection with Christian doctrine, anticipates more recent discussions. Indeed, his representation of Christian metaphysics as a mode of revenge indicates his place perhaps at the head of the rich literature that has grown up around the figure of revenge, most notably its central use in the writings of Friedrich Nietzsche, who, given his extensive reading of and admiration for Emerson, may well have derived the figure from him.[16] Nietzsche, in any case, shows in explicit terms the significance it holds, not only as a criticism of metaphysics but as a figure of an alternative, human way of being in the world.

In *Thus Spoke Zarathustra* Nietzsche writes the following of revenge, "This, indeed this alone, is what revenge is: the will's ill will against time and its 'it was'"[17] Heidegger, in his discussion of this statement, points out that the final phrase in the sentence, "time and its 'it was,'" should not be taken to refer to two distinct things; rather, time's "it was" is the basic attribute of time, which, Heidegger writes, "identifies the foundation of time in its entire and intrinsic time essence."[18] The "it was," then, does not refer to the past alone but rather to the fact of time's passing. When Nietzsche writes, "'It was'—that is the name of the will's gnashing of teeth and most secret melancholy," he speaks of the will's aversion to the very fact of the passing of time, and of its inability to control time's movement.[19] To suffer transience is, for the will, to be powerless in the face of time's becoming. What Nietzsche's statement indicates is that revenge consists structurally of the will's inversion on the continuum of time, its turning back on time's passing and taking a regressive attitude in an attempt to bring time's transience under its dominion. Revenge is properly termed "ill will" to the extent that it describes the will's assumption of a posture contrary to its natural direction coincident with time's linear passing. Nietzsche's description indicates, moreover, that revenge is fundamentally reactive, reacting in the broadest sense to the fact, the power, of time's passing: ill will is predicated on a sense of impotence. "Revenge is driven by the feeling of being vanquished and injured," Heidegger

---

16. For a discussion of Emerson's anticipation of Nietzsche's critique of the metaphysical tradition as a system of thought governed by the spirit of revenge, as well as a treatment of the differences between Emerson and Nietzsche on this topic, see my "'Compensation': Exteriority beyond the Spirit of Revenge," *ESQ* 33,2 (1987): 110–19; see also Mark Edmundson, "Emerson and the Work of Melancholia," *Raritan* 6 (Spring 1987): 120–36.

17. Friedrich Nietzsche, *Thus Spoke Zarathustra*, in *The Portable Nietzsche*, ed. Walter Kaufmann (New York: Viking Press, 1954), 252.

18. Martin Heidegger, "Who Is Nietzsche's Zarathustra," in *The New Nietzsche*, ed. David B. Allison (New York: Delta Publishing Co., 1977), 73.

19. Nietzsche, *Thus Spoke Zarathustra*, 251.

writes; which is to say, it is driven by reaction to a prior force.[20] Here then is the significance of Nietzsche's description; it indicates that revenge describes a manner of the individual's disposition in the flow of time that is reactive and fundamentally impotent.

Given Emerson's repudiation of retrospection—presciently enough he calls it "the disease . . . in the will"—and his affirmation of emancipated will, one could expect his use of the figure of revenge in the narrative at the beginning of "Compensation" to correspond to Nietzsche's meaning (*CW* 2:62). It does so first of all in regard to the reactive nature of revenge. As I pointed out above, Emerson asserts that Christian doctrine promises "*such*" values as the sinners have on earth, and he thus indicates that it limits willful activity to a reactive posture. Christian will is defined by its reaction to the power of sinners on earth; the doctrine of the Last Judgment defines an afterlife in reaction to the values of this world. The reduction of the Christian myth to the value of revenge thus reveals, on the one side, the humanist and willful foundation of the supposedly metaphysical doctrine and, on the other side, the merely derivative evaluations possible for Christian will. The preacher's sermon hardly teaches the denunciation of human desire, exertions of will; rather, it perverts those exertions, turning them backward in a retrospective posture that looks to prior actions in order to define value and consolidate power.

It is clear, moreover, that Emerson understands the disease in the will in terms of temporality, but his descriptions emphasize the phenomenological nature of time's passing, which is to say, the fact that time inheres in the will's manifestation of nature's onwardness in the progressive appearances of nature. The attitude of a healthy will is self-reliance, which, as I showed in the previous section, is a posture that enables the unobstructed appearance of the whole of nature through the coincidence of the axis of vision and the axis of the thing. Nietzsche's remarks give clarity to the fact that the phenomenological activity of self-reliant will and the coincidence of the axis of vision and the axis of the thing describe the appearance of nature *as* time's passing. The "wholeness" of nature made present by a self-reliant attitude is manifest process, the appearance of temporality itself, or the appearance of active will. The meaning of the doctrine of compensation is rooted in this interactive appearance. The alternative attitude, the ill will that in this essay as elsewhere Emerson describes as sensualism, turns reactively away from the whole unfolding appearance of nature

---

20. Heidegger, "Who Is Nietzsche's Zarathustra," 71.

and, rather than recognize it, obscures it behind obstructive evaluations derived from the partial representation on which it fixes attention. Under the condition of a diseased will we turn away from the onwardness of nature to fix the world under a single interpretation: "Whilst thus the world will be whole, and refuses to be disparted, we seek to act partially, to sunder, to appropriate" (*CW* 2:61).

Such action is, of course, not done for its own sake. It is carried out in an effort to control the power of nature by subsuming it for selfish ends. "The ingenuity of man has always been dedicated to the solution of one problem," Emerson writes, "—how to detach the sensual sweet, the sensual strong, the sensual bright, &c. from the moral sweet, the moral deep, the moral fair; that is, again, to contrive to cut clean off this upper surface so thin as to leave it bottomless; to get a one end, without an other end" (*CW* 2:61). Emerson's criticism is directed at a disposition in the world that of essence fixes nature under a static representation. The depth it cuts off is the depth of a healthy will, which is to say, a healthy attention to the flow of nature in and through an active will. Sensualism refers to the selfish desire to sever and accumulate, fixing the world in a single, partial portrait and concealing the whole of nature's unfolding appearances behind it. It consists of the desire to hoard nature under the static terms of one's self- and world-definition. In the terms of Nietzsche's statement above, sensualism is the desire to deny the passing of time and gain the selfish satisfaction of creating a picture of unchanging eternity. Sensualism, on this reading of it, should not be opposed to otherworldliness and metaphysics. For Emerson, it is opposite to the meaning of humanist spirit and to spiritualism, and thus opposite to the willed coincidence of vision and nature. And in opposition to a spiritual reception of the world, sensualism founds, precisely, otherworldly interpretations of Being.

Emerson's refutation of the preacher's doctrine thus focuses on the concealment of natural onwardness it entails: "The fallacy lay in the immense concession that the bad are successful; that justice is not done now. The blindness of the preacher consisted in deferring to the base estimate of the market of what constitutes a manly success, instead of confronting and convicting the world from the truth; announcing the Presence of the Soul; the omnipotence of the Will: and so establishing the standard of good and ill, of success and falsehood" (*CW* 2:56). Christian will represents a method of thought that failing to disclose the world in its authenticity, defers the value of actions to a displaced criterion: "the base estimate of the market." It disposes of individual action in a sensualist evaluative structure that conceals the act behind a partial criterion. Not the Rose, but a diminutive representation of the Rose—what the Rose is taken to refer to—is manifest. The Rose is obscured. The preacher's doctrine teaches the imposition of a mediate criterion of value on acts of will with the consequence of concealing their true value. It presupposes that justice is not done now and concedes success to skulking and postponing. The preacher's congregation ought to have taken offense at his doctrine, Emerson believes, because it is a doctrine of deceit.

Emerson's larger purpose in his early essays is to show that when "the intellect is at once infected" by the disease in the will, sensualism gains control over thought, and vengeful desires determine the interpretive criteria that measures nature (*CW* 2:62). Human ingenuity is thereby put to the service of establishing an interpretation of the world that apportions its value, distinguishing nature quantitatively, rather than recognizing the qualitative whole of natural presence. "The radical tragedy of nature," Emerson concludes, "[is] the distinction of More and Less" (*CW* 2:71). When distinctions are established that divide natural presence, the presence of nature is cast along a line that measures it as discrete parts, enumerates it, but is incapable of presenting its completeness. Justice is displaced to the end of time, and indeed comes to name revenge on time.

If Emerson's conception of compensation depends on recognizing the full presence of nature, nature's completeness, within the horizon of the eye, it is, as one would expect, defined and articulated by the will. Such recognition is impossible for an eye conditioned by ill will, for revenge turns on the epochal presence of nature raised by our actions and judges it to be partial, whereas Emersonian justice recognizes the completion of nature, the purpose of the world, in every rounded economy of effects manifested by an act. I take this to be Emerson's meaning in statements such as the following, where he affirms the full presence of nature in a particular thing: "So do we put our life into every act. The true doctrine of omnipresence is, that God re-appears with all his parts in every moss and cobweb. The value of the universe contrives to throw itself into every point" (*CW* 2:60). The distinction of more and less creates specious terms for implicating value that eludes the universe brought to presence by our will. Emerson writes that God reappears in every part of nature precisely in order to deny the partiality of nature, to indicate that the presence of nature is complete in every circle of the eye drawn by the will. When, on the other hand, a mere aspect, condition, or circumstance of nature's presence is isolated, fixed, and thus made to stand for nature's effect and value, it loses its innocence as a part of the unfolding whole of nature's appearance and becomes doubly responsible: responsible both for a false evaluation of the world and for the concealment of nature. As Emerson's remark cited above indicates, the greatest part of man's ingenuity has been aimed at accomplishing this revenge, and it is in this respect one can understand his claim that "the history of persecution," the history of sensualist revenge on nature, "is a history of endeavors to cheat nature" (*CW* 2:69).

For Emerson, the preacher's sermon rehearses the long-standing institutionalization of the persecution and obstruction of *phusis*. And it is not difficult to understand why the Christian myth characterizes so well for Emerson, and Nietzsche, the revaluation implicit in all metaphysical thought. It demonstrates in explicit and historical terms the attempt of theological, social, and cultural wills to power to suppress time's passing, to suppress the sheer power and presence of the will's becoming. Indeed, Christianity can appear to be the master narrative in the West of value systems that oppress and wreak revenge on contemporary and immediate manifestations of nature in the name of a displaced, sensual satisfaction. The richness of the figure explains why Nietzsche would write, "For *that man be delivered from revenge*, that is for me the bridge to the highest hope, and a rainbow after long storms."[21] Nietzsche usurps the language of ideality in order to describe an embrace of the power of will in the world. To overcome the spirit of revenge would be to think becoming in a way that does not feel repugnance toward time's passing and therefore does not insist on eternal values—does not force a single aspect of nature to bear responsibility for the whole. It would be to return to the will its innocence and its health, to bring the will into harmony with the unfolding of nature in time, with the condition of transition, enabling the will to speak its essential truth as the wholeness of the world, to speak its latent conviction as the universal sense.

The doctrine of compensation should be read then out of Emerson's call to presence the *wholeness* of nature through the actions of authentic will beyond the spirit of revenge. Emerson's argument is forthright: presence becoming, think temporality, see time. Put otherwise: compensation inheres in the presence of self-reliant will's onwardness, not only in the world but, for Emerson, as the world. For Emerson's description of the preacher's error implies, as well, the identity that I have insisted he asserts between will and natural presence. The state-

---

21. Nietzsche, *Thus Spoke Zarathustra*, 211.

ment implicitly equates the "Presence of the Soul" and the "omnipotence of the Will." The presence of the soul is nothing but the disclosure of the will as the appearance of time's passing. If the fallacy of Christian metaphysics, as generally of the structure of thought it represents, is its reactive, obscuring nature, then it will be corrected—the concept of the Last Judgment will be overcome (or redefined) and justice will be done now—by recognizing that compensatory value is nothing but the unconcealment of the will in the world, its effects in the world. In place of the preacher's representation of a dead and unreachable compensation "urged from reason and Scripture," Emerson sets the value of the "aboriginal abyss of real being," which is not a metaphysical substrate or a fixed origin of existence, but the onward, relational power, the "vast affirmative" of human will (*CW* 2:55, 70). The one secure thing in all of Emerson's early writings, as noted above, is the enabling depth of human will emancipated from the constraints deriving from the disease of retrospection and thus released to the manifestation of its own innocent becoming. The basis of value in the doctrine of compensation is the living, moral sense of an act, and the moral sense consists of the complete disclosure of the economy of effects intrinsic to the act. Nature and compensation are present in the circle of the eye, and the determination of the more or the less of that circle is irrelevant to its value. Nothing remains hidden; everything shows its disposition in the articulation of the essential thing, the Rose. The Rose is not situated in time because the Rose is temporality itself. Not a figure of eternity, the Rose is the active appearing of nature, the manifestation of transition, the disclosure of process. For Emerson the essential thing, the Rose, is then the temporality of omnipotent will.

The two modes of compensation that Emerson goes on to identify in the essay reflect two ways of looking at the effect of emancipated will, two perspectives that can be taken on healthy will. These two perspectives are implied in my discussion so far under the description of the wholeness of the appearance of the will as nature's onwardness and the description of the interrelations set in place by will. Compensation, in the early phase of Emerson's writings at least, referred to both. And broadly, it is this distinction that Emerson has in mind when he describes the two modes of compensation:

> Every act rewards itself, or, in other words, integrates itself, in a twofold manner; first, in the thing, or, in real nature; and second, in the circumstances, or, in apparent nature. Men call the circumstance the retribution. The causal retribution is in the thing, and is

seen by the soul. The retribution in the circumstance, is seen by the understanding; it is inseparable from the thing, but is often spread over a long time, and so does not become distinct until after many years. (*CW* 2:60)

The distinction Emerson draws between "the thing" and "circumstance," and the fact that he aligns causality with the thing, is the most important part of this description. We normally think of causality in terms of the circumstantial effects of an act. An act is said to cause this or that effect, and its value—compensation—consists of the effect. However, the potential for a sensual understanding of compensation derives precisely from this way of thinking, from the understanding's point of view. Insofar as we detach one effect or set of effects, discretely available over the apparent material, linear appearance of time, from the full array of effects—from the thing itself—we engage only its sensual value. Reduction to sensual value is an essential threat as long as the appearance of nature is governed by the temporality of the will. In the above lines Emerson withdraws the meaning of causality from the potentially sensual interpretation of the understanding and returns it to the real nature of the thing: "The causal retribution is in the thing." The principal question this raises is what the thing is, and it isn't hard to predict the answer: it is the will. Showing why, however, suggests more about the seductive eloquence of the philosophy of will.

There is a strong temptation to answer this question by appeal to an analogy to the perspective of the understanding, and thus to describe the thing as the manifestation now of the full effects of an act, the collapse of the linear unfolding of circumstances over time into the radical temporality of the presence of the thing *now*. Emerson, too, is tempted to engage in such analogy. Indeed, most of his descriptions of compensation rely on a perspective that sees effects displayed discretely over the material appearance of time. He writes, for instance, "In Nature, nothing can be given, all things are sold," and thereby appeals to an understanding of value for which an act is rewarded by the purchase it makes on an effect in nature (*CW* 2:63). Analogy to the perspective of the understanding is evident, as well, when Emerson turns to the teaching of fables in order to clarify the meaning of compensation: "Prometheus knows one secret that Jove must bargain for; Minerva, another," he tells us, suggesting that the "in-working of the All" consists of the interaction of effective powers (*CW* 2:62). In both cases Emerson describes the nature of the essential thing by analogy to the appearance of interrelated effects of action, implying that the thing, the primary compensation, consists of the immediate manifestation of all of these effects in a single, simultaneous presence: that the whole is the sum of its parts. The clarity of such descriptions, which accord very well with the image of the circumference of the eye enclosing the interaction of the relations that gather around an act, drawing them back from their linear unfolding into a ball of simultaneous effects, is undoubtedly useful as an analogy. However, the weakness of depicting the principal meaning of compensation by analogy to the understanding's perspective is that it blunts the effect of Emerson's revaluation of the thing by allowing the thing to remain understood according to circumstantial, pragmatic effects. If the understanding's perspective is, obviously, not erroneous, it is a secondary perspective that can provide only a secondary description. Emerson sets the thing in opposition to circumstances, and we should attempt to know it in its own terms.

An act is compensated primarily, then, by integrating itself in the thing; compensation is integration in the thing. The thing does not precede the act. Emerson's emphasis is rather on the act's integration. The act integrates with nature—it enables the coincidence of vision and nature—in one of two ways: with the thing or with the circumstance. The natural appearance enabled by the act can be construed, therefore, either as the thing or as circumstances. If it is construed as the thing, the thing is the causality of the act. That is to say, the thing is causality with respect to the value of the act, not the effects of a cause. The thing is the act's value *as* its cause. We understand the thing, and thus compensation, distinct from circumstantial attributions, by divorcing the meaning of causality from the sensual interpretation that links a single cause with a single effect: the causality of circumstances. The thing does not fit within a chain of causal relations; the thing is itself the cause, the act. The act integrates itself with the thing by effecting the thing as itself, or as its manifest value. I could say the act manifests itself as the thing, which would mean that it manifests itself as the gathering of the act's integration—the interaction of which it consists, the gathering of nature. If putting it this way seems to imply that the thing is the manifestation of the act's effects and thereby seems to return to an analogical account of the thing, it at least stresses the wholeness of the thing, as against the partialness of effects. The thing is the whole manifestation of the act, its intrinsic causality, its full phenomenological presence, its horizon.

Emerson's discussion of polarity supports this explanation of compensation insofar as it indicates the illusoriness of circumstances and reveals the balanced nature of the world's economy, thereby throwing its value back on the whole. It repudiates the belief that action can gain us a singular success, by showing that every success is bound to its other half, a failure, as every failure is bound to a success. Determinations of more and less refute themselves: "Every sweet hath its sour; every evil its good" (*CW* 2:58). Emerson's purpose is to show that sensual criteria of value, insofar as they depend on inappropriate, partial representations, are faulty. They are the great tragedy of life to the extent we believe in them. The law of polarity thus indicates the ultimate indifference of circumstances. I should say, it indicates the innocence of circumstances, for Emerson does not deny circumstantial limits as a way of viewing compensation. Rather, he denies that circumstances should be isolated in order to fix meaning. An act can be rightly viewed as unfolding according to circumstances. But its primary value consists, in these terms, of the innocence and harmony of its economy of effects taken as a whole. Circumstances alone convict one of nothing, but rather return the individual's conviction to the sense of the whole economy of the act. Thus, Emerson concludes the discussion of polarity by asserting that "the true life and satisfactions of man seem to elude the utmost rigors or felicities of condition, and to establish themselves with great indifferency under all varieties of circumstance" (*CW* 2:59). And he adds, "These appearances indicate the fact that the universe is represented in every one of its particles" (*CW* 2:59). He can hold this position only if he assumes the transparency of circumstances and their service to the will that predicts them.

Emerson's attraction to the idea of polarity, and his use of it, reflects the centrality of will in his thought. Exertions of will define a fundamental dualism in the world, or, put otherwise, they produce things that consist of a body of relations, an economy of effects. The effects of will are interrelated in the world, yet their very complexity is the will's compensation. In "The American Scholar" Emerson describes action as a resource of nature's dualistic appearance: "The final value of action . . . is, that it is a resource. That great principle of Undulation in nature, that shows itself in the inspiring and expiring of breath; in desire and satiety; in the ebb and flow of the sea, in day and night, in heat and cold, and as yet more deeply ingrained in every atom and every fluid, is known to us under the name of Polarity." But he adds that the laws of polarity "are the law of nature because they are the law of spirit" (*CW* 1:61). The argument behind the discussion of polarity repudiates evaluations of life that employ sensual criteria in order to distinguish more and less valuable actions and thus affirms that the causality of a thing is always cast back to the activity of will: that when truly seen in its balanced wholeness, the thing is self-aware will, or an attitude based on the awareness of will's causality, rendered in and through its actions.

Finally, the value of the thing inheres in the essential implication—drawn from the will's effects or simply the fact of its efficacy—of its causality. This implication, present to the understanding as the necessity of a cause prior to every effect, gives itself to reason, to the "invisible steps of thought" Emerson refers to in the "Spirit" chapter of *Nature*, as the possibility of self-recognition, self-accountability, and self-responsibility. The value of the thing is therefore available only to reason, and the principal compensation for an act inheres in the quality and direction of the human being who articulates his world. The first and most important sense of compensation can be understood best as a way of viewing our reality, a perspective we take, as essentially the attitude of healthy will that reveals ourselves to ourselves as the single thing that is nature. For Emerson the attitude of the individual, the manner in which he or she addresses the world, preempts the dominance of circumstances and determines their value. The first order of compensation thus derives from the way the individual integrates in nature, how he or she views the world and dictates circumstances.

That the description of compensation contains an equivocation was clear even to Emerson. His purpose is to describe compensation as an ongoing process that occurs at every moment of the individual's life. His humanist synthesis depends on viewing presence as the very activity of life, on viewing the soul as the process of living. Yet it seemed clear to Emerson in his early period, and was in any case necessary for his humanism, that the process was self-manifest. The identity and integrity of the individual depends on the soul's withdrawal from the compensatory process of life. "There is a deeper fact in the soul than compensation," Emerson concludes, "to wit, its own nature. The soul is not a compensation, but a life" (*CW* 2:70). As the process of full self-articulation, the soul is in fact both a life and a compensation, and Emerson's early humanism is founded on the conviction that this doubleness in the soul is an essential ingredient of being human. His description of the soul presses and unsettles sedimented structures of the metaphysical tradition in the West but finally falls within its most essential paradigm. The soul both *is* the pure temporality of nature and is the principle of withdrawal from that temporality that makes it manifest to itself and manifest as the central cause in nature.

Emerson will soon enough restrict and diminish this faith in the centrality of will in the world. The task for readers of his early essays and lectures, as I see it, is not to critique his position—and especially not with a reactionary argument against metaphysics—or to anticipate Emerson's own critique of it, but to recognize the force of thought that led Emerson in the 1830s and early 1840s to embrace it. My remarks have been intended to show that force of thought to be the omnivorous power of the will to articulate its situation and in so doing to claim its adequacy as source of its situation, transforming limits into the terms of identity. The failure to do so is at base the preacher's fallacy. His fallacy consists of the metaphysical gesture by which he grants substance to circumstantial limits and judges the world by them. Emerson's acute understanding of the formal workings of the will (and ill will) leads him to dismiss the preacher's doctrine and with it to dismiss the notion of fixed limits. And he is left, then, with the manifesting power of healthy will as the sole principle in nature. Nothing remains but the capacity of will to show nature; there is no other principle, and unless the law of causality is to be forfeited (as it will be), all the world must be traced to omnipotent will.

The eloquence of Emerson's early thought surely stems from his insight into the logic of the will, for from within the hegemony of the will's temporality, we are set on a path toward identifying the centrality of healthy will in nature, the imperative to self-reliance, and the determination that value, compensation, can be nothing but the manifestation of will, the circle of the eye ever drawn about onward action. Whether viewed by reason or by understanding—that is, as the simultaneity of self-recognition or through circumstantial limits—retribution is the world we build. To suggest, on the contrary, that the world manifested by will is partial, or even illusory, that it is anything but our being in the world, would depend on the assumption of and backward glance to another world elsewhere, and thus it would depend on the preacher's fallacy. If one can retrospectively recognize Emerson's blindness to the contingency of the will's instructuration of nature, then it is also clear that the recognition of its contingency must be earned and that it *can* be earned only by embracing, articulating, and exhausting the logic of the will. It seems crucial, then, to recognize what Emerson does accomplish in his early period. He succeeds in his early writings in defending the authentic presence of the self and the world from the stultifying metaphysics represented by the preacher's doctrine. He struggles with the implications of having abandoned the extrinsic grounds of human and natural legitimacy contained in and represented by the preacher. The value of his early thought consists in its release of human being from bondage to the disease in the will that vengefully divides it from nature.

EMERSON'S TRANSCENDENTALISM

I began this chapter by suggesting that Emerson shared Kant's intuition of the basis of moral value in freedom but substantially altered the conception of transcendence attached to it, maintaining the immediate transformation of private will into universal value for the individual. The phenomenological terms of my discussion draw out the difference in Emerson's notion of transcendence and indicate he understood transcendence as a convergence of morality and thought more radical than Kant imagined. Unrestricted by the Kantian distinction of theoretical and practical reason, Emersonian transcendentalism inheres in what is presented by the clearing of the eye, the space opened up within the horizon of the eye. His, then, is a humanist and phenomenological transcendence, not a rationalist one. It is height, the upright posture, understood as the activity of rising above normative conventions—which for Emerson means all principled determinations of thought—and seeing truly. To see truly is to establish a phenomenological opening in which the self and the world appear and, moreover, in which they appear immediately as manifest compensation. Transcendence, the upright posture, and height are all comprehensible as nothing but this phenomenological opening.

Emerson altered the meaning of transcendence then mainly by indicating that it is a matter of action, not contemplation, by inverting the traditional priority of theory over practice and rendering universality finite. "The preamble of thought, the transition through which it passes from the unconscious to the conscious," Emerson tells the listeners of "The American Scholar," "is action. Only so much do I know, as I have lived" (*CW* 2:59). And he later adds, "Thinking is the function. Living is the functionary" (*CW* 1:61). The imperative in Emerson's thought is to act rather than to deliberate, and, specifically, to act in such a way as to establish the eye's opening, to clear the area of the eye's horizon. "Self-Reliance" compels us to action that destroys the mediate forms of thought that obscure and diminish the individual. Action accordingly precedes and enables thought. The fundamental imperative standing behind "Self-Reliance" is not Kant's imperative on freedom to legislate rationally, an imperative that presupposes thought's priority over action, but the Emersonian command to act freely and give rise to thought as the presence of oneself in the world, to ignore the external language of grounds and principles and to "speak rather of that which relies, because it works and is" (*CW* 2:40). The imperative is to the innocence of action that is taken *in order to* think, to see, clearly.

The centrality of speech, as noted above, indicates the mutual dependence of will and thought. Speech manifests the soul, lays out its compensatory relations and thus its justice. Whatever limitations Emerson would later find in language's access to Being, in the early period authentic speech is the organ of the *universal sense*, the enactment of transcendence and height, and, as I will show in the next chapter, the agency by which we nurture and husband nature's finite presence. It derives from the abandonment of extraneous teleological structures, realizing universality in no fixed final cause, following no pregiven path, and having no definite goal. Writing recently of the convergence of thought and morality found in Emerson's early writings, and explicitly comparing it to Heideggerian theory, Stanley Cavell gives a clear indication of the still compelling power of this synthesis: "The morality is neither teleological (basing itself on a conception of the good to be maximized in society) nor deontological (basing itself on an independent conception of the right), and the thinking is some as yet unknown distance from what we might think of as reasoning."[22] Emerson, of course, did think of it as reasoning, and I've suggested why he did, but Cavell's remark rightly reflects the adventurousness of Emerson's take on reason's claim to utter the *logos* of nature. Emerson conceived of speech contemporaneous with the act of will, speech that, in his favorite description, voiced the transition of thought. The only authentic value for Emerson is the disclosure of the world effected by emancipated will. Critics who read self-reliance strictly in terms of the imperative to abandonment are in an important sense then not mistaken. Genuine verdicts do reflect the utterance of an unconditioned will. From the perspective of rationalist conventions of thought they are evaluations made without aim, random shots in the dark. The boy's attitude produces judgments—achieves self and natural determination—without purpose or goal, as scattered assertions whose only intent is "the shooting of the gulf . . . the darting of an aim," and whose only end is illuminating the unknown transition, "advancing on Chaos and the Dark" (*CW* 2:40, 28). However, Emersonian transcendence, as developed in the early writings, thereby identifies individuality, not the dis-

---

22. Cavell, "Aversive Thinking," 143.

persal and fragmentation of the will, and it does so because assertion reveals a phenomenological clearing and because speaking articulates the boundary of sight—because emancipated will entails the justice of compensation. Emerson's phenomenological method returns individuality in the practice of uprightness, the nonchalance of the boy's attitude of abandonment that *as such* passes genuine verdicts. The judgments of innocent sight resolve the truth of the world under the justice of the individual and thus invariably return Man as the universal sense.

When Emerson asks, "Who shall define to me an Individual?" his answer reflects the dynamic of will and thought that allows speech to gather the power of *phusis* under the compensatory mark of Man. At such moments the individual recognizes itself as the ecstatic utterance of nature's appearance. "The soul knows no persons," he writes, but adds, "It invites every man to expand to the full circle of the universe, and will have no preferences but those of spontaneous love" (*CW* 1:82). Out of his skepticism Emerson initially found a deeper faith in love, in the possibility of practical transcendence and individuality through the uncanny decision that heeds the "awful invitation . . . to blend with [the dawn's] aurora" (*JMN* 5:337). His call on the individual to trust himself means to accept nature as it is given, to find himself as the particular vision of nature his actions give rise to. Emerson's principal concern in the early essays is to describe the meaning and manner of this sort of relation to nature and the individuality it entails, and his writings of the period effectively respond to the rationalistic and dualistic criticism of the apparent subjectivity of self-reliance. The criticism fails because his idea of the individual exceeds the terms of rationalism. He replaces a subjective domination or construction of nature with an imperative to attend to and acknowledge the foundation of the relations of self and other in the effects of one's actions and thus to recognize not the opposition but the nearness of self and other. Self-reliant speech may have little to do with being responsible to society in the narrow sense of rational reckoning, as Emerson's critics often said. But Emerson struggled in his early essays and addresses to demonstrate that it has everything to do with being responsible to human being in the broad sense, in the sense of recognizing the quality of our being in the world and by extension the quality of the societies we form.

2

Culture and Ownership

In the preceding chapter I describe Emerson's thought in terms of an essentially moral project, built on the interdependence of theoretical and practical ways of being in the world, which knocks down the long-standing opposition between *theoria* and *praxis*. He viewed his work from its very earliest stages as a call on his readers to change the way they live. Thus, it was with a practical change in mind that Emerson stood before the students of the Harvard Divinity School in 1838 and said, "It is my duty to say to you, that the need was never greater of new revelation than now" (*CW* 1:84). The "Divinity School Address" has long been remembered for its attack on the contemporary state of religious faith, as it should be. In the address, Emerson isolates what he views as the errors of traditional Christianity. But in so doing he returns the question of faith to the power and conduct of the self-reliant individual. "The question returns," he writes, "What shall we do?" His answer rejects all principles of action and value extraneous to the self-trusting individual, asserting that "all attempts to project and establish a Cultus with new rites and forms, seem to me in vain. Faith makes us, and not we it, and faith makes its own forms" (*CW* 1:92).

Emerson recognizes the very heart of the matter, the ethic, of his early synthesis, in the attitude of self-reliance, and he uses the addresses and lectures of the 1830s in particular to develop and to teach this ethic. In "The American Scholar," for instance, he writes of the duties "such as become Man Thinking. . . . They may all be comprised in self-trust" (*CW* 1:62). From self-reliance stems the command to authentic speech, and thus the self-reliant individual is to see clearly in order to "tell his brother what he thinks" (*CW* 1:63). "But speak the truth," Emerson writes, "and all nature and all spirits help you with unexpected furtherance" (*CW* 1:78). An active, emancipated will is at the origin of authentic speech: "It is the raw material out of which the intellect moulds her splendid products. A strange process too, this, by which experience is converted into thought, as mulberry leaf is converted into satin. The manufacture goes forward at all hours" (*CW* 1:59). The conversion of experience to thought goes forward by virtue of authentic individual activity, by virtue of the single fact and principle in nature, "the one thing in the world of value . . . the active soul,—the soul, free, sovereign, active." "This every man is entitled to," Emerson goes on to write, effectively summarizing his humanist faith, "this every man contains within him, although in almost all men, obstructed, and as yet unborn. The soul active sees absolute truth; and utters truth, or creates" (*CW* 1:56).

Emerson's early transcendentalism had always carried a practical and pragmatic value, and that he increasingly emphasizes the practical value of his thought in the lectures and addresses of the later 1830s and early 1840s represents no particular shift in his thinking and certainly reflects no opposition in his mind between transcendentalism and practical power. It more likely indicates his frustration at not adequately communicating the practical content and foundation of his thought. When a fundamental shift in his position does occur, it will not be founded on, nor will it be possible to articulate it through, the terms of the opposition between transcendentalism and practical power. That opposition never has a place in Emerson's theory. There is, instead, a continuous thematic development in his ideas from the transcendental works to the earliest of the supposedly more practical lectures that came later. Nowhere is Emerson's effort to demonstrate the practical power of his early humanist thought more evident, or to my mind more successful, than in "Man, the Reformer," where he achieves a powerful expression of the significance of the radical humanism he espouses in "Self-Reliance" and a clear statement of its everyday value. "Man, the Reformer" is, moreover, the last of Emerson's humanist works and the lecture that marks the endpoint of that period in his thought. It describes the value for society and the individual of the critique implicit in the idea of self-reliance. In it Emerson shows that the assertion that the world comes to effective appearance—to value—through authentic individual action initiates a fundamental and far-reaching revolution both for the individual and for society. Indeed, his description of the revolutionary content implicit in his early thought could hardly be more comprehensive than it is in the well-known opening section of the lecture. Dismissing all previous reform movements as in comparison limited in breadth, he writes:

> In the history of the world the doctrine of Reform had never such scope as at the present hour. Lutherans, Hernhutters, Jesuits, Monks, Quakers, Knox, Wesley, Swedenborg, Bentham, in their accusations of society, all respected something,—church or state, literature or history, domestic usages, the market town, the dinner table, coined money. But now all these and all things else hear the trumpet and must rush to judgment,—Christianity, the laws, commerce, schools, the farm, the laboratory; and not a kingdom, town, statute, rite, calling, man, or woman, but is threatened by the new spirit. (*CW* 1:146)

The threat of the new spirit is the threat of self-reliance. Attacks on the ahistoricity of Emerson's early thought misunderstand or ignore the critical element of social engagement written into the idea of self-reliance, and it is still crucial to answer this perhaps most enduring misconstrual of Emerson's thought. The insistence and dismissive vigor with which it is often put forward is well represented by Quentin Anderson's remark that "our finally effective performance is put off to the coming of some New Jerusalem. . . . What is offered as a consummatory experience . . . can have no issue in action; its very character as an experience claims so much of the world for the self that it leaves us nothing to act on."[1] An unbiased reading of Emerson's works simply can't support this assertion. Founded on the reciprocity of thought and action, self-reliance is rooted in precisely action; it refers to a manner of living in the world that takes its point of departure from the abandonment of social institutions and categories of thought, that is to say, a manner of being in the world that proceeds from an all-inclusive phenomenological destruction of value, and earns the value of the world through contemporary action and evaluation.

By focusing on "Man, the Reformer," I wish to address the question and the problem of the moral revolution that Emerson conceived under the name of self-reliance, a revolution he believed would have

---

1. Quentin Anderson, *The Imperial Self: An Essay on American Literary and Cultural History* (New York: Alfred A. Knopf, 1971), 45.

broad political and social consequences. He envisioned a revolution that would be fought in the arena of the individual's life, where politics and society are not abstractions but lived realities. He imagined it would be fought over the attitudes and dispositions of the individual. In this chapter I will show that to the question What is the nature of the revolution implicit in the idea of self-reliance? the best answer looks to the practical consequences of inhabiting the attitude of healthy will.

THE DOMESTICATION OF CULTURE

Emerson provides the general terms for describing the revolution of self-reliance in "The American Scholar," when he writes, "This revolution is to be wrought by the gradual domestication of the idea of Culture" (*CW* 1:65). His reference to culture is twofold, calling for both a national culture and a self-culture. The richness of the statement rests in more than just the implicit equation he here, as typically elsewhere, draws between national and private culture, however. Quite apart from the issue of developing a national culture that turns from European models, the statement also implicates the fundamental meaning of self-reliance for the individual. Emerson had devoted a lecture series in 1837–38 to the topic of culture.[2] This is not surprising given that culture was a common enough nineteenth century and Unitarian topic, but it is nonetheless important because by 1841 his treatment of culture had extended the concept beyond the parameters of fixed contexts, either theological or political.[3] More importantly, his specific concern had come to be with the *domestication* of culture, suggesting a sense of culture as intrinsic rather than extrinsic to the individual. My discussion begins with this suggestion, for the idea of self-reliance evolved in conjunction with his developing understanding of culture and the process that domesticates it; and the value of reform, the poli-

---

2. For an in-depth discussion of the lecture series "Human Culture," see David Robinson, *Apostle of Culture: Emerson as Preacher and Lecturer* (Philadelphia: University of Pennsylvania Press, 1982). Robinson emphasizes the relation between Emerson's idea of culture and the principle of his early synthesis, the active soul: "The element of the 'progressive' . . . is at the basis of this definition of culture. . . . There is no better definition of the active soul . . . than this description of the progressive moral nature of man" (115). He shows, moreover, the extent to which in "Man, the Reformer" Emerson consolidates the themes and topics developed in the lecture series.

3. See Robinson, *Apostle of Culture*, 9ff.

tics it entails, and more widely the "revolution" he predicted in his early thought thus depend largely on uncovering what he meant by culture's domestication.

The domestication of culture for the individual means, first of all, the return of the idea of culture to the individual from its alienation in institutions and thus the return of responsibility for evaluations in general to the individual from its displacement in extraneous principles or criteria. The statement initially suggests an understanding of culture in terms of individual growth, as a means of building the individual: "The main enterprise of the world for splendor, for extent, is the upbuilding of a man" (*CW* 1:65). To this extent the revolution of self-reliance consists in the reform or the rebuilding of the individual subsequent to assuming a self-reliant posture in the world. The individual's "upbuilding" does not result, however, from the appropriation of a cultural past, and culture does not consist, not principally at least, in a body of material deemed usable for the project of building up the individual and society. Emerson consistently poses his thought against precisely such alienated and alienating traditions, and I would stress that his conception of culture cannot then be understood in terms of the appropriation of an essentially alien cultural past. The idea of culture must instead be radicalized along the lines of his phenomenological method. Self-culture, and the idea of self-reliance it is founded on, is not merely a transformative capacity or much less a rationally purposive activity. Rather, inasmuch as Emerson takes self-reliance to be the only authentic attitude of the individual, he cannot construe culture as a separable body of beliefs or conditions, a history. For the self-reliant posture, history's value is invariably contemporaneous, and culture is manifest in history's contemporaneity, or say its momentariness. Appropriation of a usable past would presuppose a prior, inauthentic alienation of the past and, as it were, a kind of untrusting detour to self-trust, a failure fully to recognize ourselves as the phenomenological cause of nature. If the revolution of self-reliance consists in the domestication of the idea of culture, then, given the phenomenological power of the self-reliant attitude and the destruction implicit in it, culture cannot be understood in the terms implied by the adaptation of a usable past or the sure development of a rational future. Culture, too, would contain at its center, as both an initiating and an ongoing gesture, a destructive moment inconsistent with the construction of the self out of a cultural past, or any conception of the self purely as a sociocultural construct, and indeed inconsistent with the very notion of enduring cultural forms. Thus, if the "upbuilding of man" is to accord with the imperative to self-reliance, the individual must be built up subsequent to the abandonment of constructed values. The principle of Emerson's early thought accordingly places a demand on us to reconsider the meaning of culture and to recognize in it the momentary illumination found in an emergent, phenomenological process. When Emerson writes in "Human Culture" of the individual's "own Culture,—the unfolding of his nature," and says that this is the "chief end of man," he suggests that culture is the present work of the soul, not the terms, past or progressively built up as the future, of one's nature.[4] And accordingly, culture consists not in the production of one's constitution but in the manifest process of unfolding one's nature or, better, in the attitude that attends to that process, and by attending cultivates it.

It is in this respect that I say Emerson's idea of culture has a phenomenological foundation, being a matter of attitude and attention, a way of relating to manifest effects in nature. He sets aside the idea that culture is the rational arrangement of human nature, an education or edification that proceeds by way of prescription and informing, and embraces culture as the contemporaneous activity of bringing nature to appearance. Culture thus names the fundamental ethos of Emerson's early period, as indeed, although in different ways, of all of his writings. It names the process by which we earn our reality; a process of enabling nature's presence by bringing it from behind concealments.

Certainly Emerson describes culture as instruction and education, but it is "the educating of the eye" (*EL* 2:216). He has in mind the education we gain by engaging nature. "The only motive," he writes, "is the ambition to discover *by exercising* his latent power" (*EL* 2:215). The upbuilding of the individual refers to the expansion of our immediate scope of vision that results from gathering within our personal economy wider articulations of nature. It assumes no value separate from the individual's gaze and consequently does not pose levels or ranks of culture, or a separate ideal to be attained. When Emerson speaks of the domestication of culture, he has in mind the individual's recognition that in an authentic state, culture consists in the duty of the individual "to *coax and woo* the strong Instinct to bestir itself and work its miracle, [which] is the end of all wise endeavor" (my emphasis).[5] The "miracle" worked renders nature new under the organization of the individual, the perspective of the individual, to put it

---

4. *The Early Lectures of Ralph Waldo Emerson*, ed. Stephen Whicher et al. (Cambridge, Mass.: Harvard University Press, 1959), 2:215. Hereafter cited as *EL*.
5. Cited in Whicher, *Freedom and Fate*, 84.

another way. Emerson undoubtedly valued conversation, lectures, history, and art as stimuli and provocations to the individual, and it has often been noted that his lecture style suggests he identified his role in such terms, provoking his listeners to self-reliance. But culture does not consist in these external provocations or much less in their objects; it is rather the immediate work of thought and will. And the revolutionary content of self-reliance begins with the recognition of it as such. The domestication of the idea of culture draws value back from conditions that situate the individual. It refers to the work of recognizing one's centrality in nature and bearing responsibility for the order of things. As the citation above indicates, this includes (but is far from limited to) taking responsibility for the political and social relations of one's world.

Emerson's statements then have philosophical significance when in "Man, the Reformer" he develops the idea of culture under the general figure of the farmer, writing, "A man should have a farm or a mechanical craft for his culture," and adding, "In general, one may say, that the husbandman's is the oldest, and most universal profession" (*CW* 1:150, 152). The reference to the figure of the farmer hardly implies a rustic doctrine of rural withdrawal, the forerunner of 1960s back-to-nature movements. It is a figure for a practical philosophy, a way of being in the world and of relating to society and the world, and although Emerson's argument is embedded in figures and narratives, his treatment nonetheless accords in striking ways with Hegel's and Marx's discussions of the value of labor. The idea of cultural husbanding does not simply imply building or willing. It refers to a certain kind of building, the sort of building—willing—that nurtures the world, that is near to it and brings it to presence within the compass of the eye. "Manual labor," Emerson writes, "is the study of the external world" (*CW* 1:150). Husbandry integrates with the world—as the first compensation of actions is their integration with the thing—and cultivates both self and the world through labor that reforms nature. Labor neither masters already-operative forms nor collapses the distance between the laborer and nature. As Emerson conceives of it, labor studies nature with a kind of affection that seeks to draw it out of concealment by merging with it and becoming its condition, by speaking it. The articulation of nature is not lost then to the whims of the speaker but is earned by the fatality of his instinctual actions, by the self-reliance that works and is and, in its working, resolves nature. The revolution of self-reliance derives for Emerson from attention to our labor, attention to the nature that gathers around us quite apart from our subjective desires but as a consequence of our constitution, of the labor incessantly carried forward in virtue of the interaction of our constitution and nature. The function of culture, Emerson makes clear in his 1837–38 lecture series, is to afford us recognition of this interaction. "It will be seen at once that in the philosophic view of Human Culture, we look at all things in a new point of view from the popular one, viz. we consider mainly not the things but their effect on the beholder. And this habit of respecting things for their relation to the soul—for their intrinsic and universal effects, it is a part of Culture to form" (*EL* 2:222). The remark draws culture and labor together and predicts Emerson's later assertion "that every man ought to stand in primary relations with the work of the world, ought to do it himself, and not to suffer the accident of his having a purse in his pocket, or his having been bred to some dishonorable and injurious craft, to sever him from those duties" (*CW* 1:152). "The philosophic view of Human Culture" amounts to a dismissal of a priori value and an embrace of what would come to be called the pragmatic maxim: value resides in the effect of a thing, or in general the effects of nature. By aligning this pragmatic tendency with culture, Emerson indicates his confidence in active reason or the power of will to draw out the effects of nature. The doctrine of the farm is thus raised in value to a figure of a "future orientation . . . tinged with the finite," a figure of the power of the individual to cultivate nature's emerging effects.[6]

Emerson develops the complicity of culture and labor through his criticism of trade and his fictional description of John Smith's workers in "Man, the Reformer." The description serves both to distinguish between authentic and inauthentic labor and to give practical statement and body to his call for self-reliance, indicating that the revolution it predicts is not abstract but is found in the manner of our work in the world. "Is it possible," he asks,

> that I who get indefinite quantities of sugar, hominy, cotton, buckets, crockery ware, and letter paper, by simply signing my name once in three months to a check in favor of John Smith and Co. traders, get the fair share of exercise to my faculties by that act? . . . It is Smith himself, and his carriers, and dealers, and manufacturers, it is the sailor, and the hide-drogher, the butcher, the negro, the hunter, and the planter, who have intercepted the sugar of the

---

6. Robinson, *Apostle of Culture*, 153.

sugar, and the cotton of the cotton. They have got the education, I only the commodity. (*CW* 1:150)

The distinction sets the laborer, the slave, as the agent that has an immediate relation to the world, who obtains the "sugar of the sugar, and the cotton of the cotton." Figurally, Emerson indicates the capacity of manual labor to subvert formal hierarchies of value, to step out into the space in which nature's order is articulated and to dictate nature's contemporary value. The education that the workers receive is the influx of instruction that results from recognizing themselves in the effects of their labor. Work enables this instruction in two senses: work both departs from the secondary relation to nature that mediates its value through preestablished norms of thought and action, and is, secondly, the medium through which a new order in nature is articulated.

Emerson's emphasis on labor contrasts with and refutes his still-current reputation for spiritual abstraction and mystical flights to worlds elsewhere. Rooted in individual toil, phenomenological husbandry depicts a concrete manner of engaging one's world as it is, which is to say, engaging the only reality the individual can know, the reality in which he finds himself, into which he is cast and recast. By self-reliance Emerson means specific actions taken by concrete individuals in specific contexts. His refusal to rank the particular contexts in which individuals find themselves, and his alternative ranking of how one acts where they are, suggests the everyday realism of his theory, as well as his rejection of the reductiveness of normative descriptions, which can lead to only representative and typical self-identifications. He directs attention instead to determinations of the self and world that result from real engagement of the world through action.

The emphasis placed on manual labor shows, then, that Emerson understands reality to reside in the actions the individual takes and by which he forges the world's laws and husbands the emergence of nature's value. Manual labor signifies a manipular process, the manipulation of the world that gives it value, brings it to presence, shows it to the eye. Typically, he couches his argument in figural language, but it's clearly the absence of such an immediate manipular relation to the world that he laments in his description of buying products from John Smith and Co. "[It] were all very well," he says, "if I were necessarily absent, being detained by work of my own . . . *then should I be sure of my hands and feet*" (*CW* 1:150, emphasis added). Elsewhere he adds that each should take "bravely his part, *with his own hands*, in the manual labor of the world" (*CW* 1:149, emphasis added). The emphasis on the figural value of hands and feet refers to the husbanding of the world by manipulation through labor.[7] That he explicitly extends the idea of labor to embrace all "spiritual faculties"—"We must have a basis for our higher accomplishments, our delicate entertainments of poetry and philosophy, in the work of our hands"—reflects again his rejection of the opposition between *theoria* and *praxis*, setting thought on the basis of action (*CW* 1:150). Moreover, the statement shows that Emerson's conception of labor includes the activity, the performance, of all people, to the extent that their actions establish an immediate relation to the world, insofar as through their labor they "begin the world anew, as he does who puts the spade into the ground for food" (*CW* 1:147). Emerson had no need to limit his conception of authentic labor to a single class of people or actions. His use of labor, like the doctrine of the farm, refuses the distinction between the literal and the figural, and depicts, therefore, attitudes of the individual that he holds important for human existence, but not social or political roles that are *de facto* privileged. He does not fix class distinctions to establish the terms of participation in authentic labor. "I do not wish to overstate this doctrine of labor," he writes, "or insist that every man should be a farmer, any more than that every man should be a lexicographer" (*CW* 1:152). Rather, his purpose is general: to endorse the figural value of manual labor, the activity of a healthy will in distinction from the retrospection and ill will of a contemplative posture, as the foundation of authentic human being. His purpose is wider and less polemical than to privilege a class or a type of labor, much less a class or type of laborer; it is to pose the politics of phenomenological husbandry, the assertion that the fundamental political act is that by which we bring nature to authentic presence, against traditional conceptions of political action in which the value of an act is mediated by institutional structures and representative values.

The doctrine of the farm is Emerson's figural way of indicating that the site of reform is a way of being in the world, and of emphasizing that conduct is the field on which we declare our worth. "Human labor," he writes in "Compensation," "through all its forms, from the sharpening of a stake to the construction of a city or an epic, is one immense illustration of the perfect compensation of the universe" (*CW*

---

7. For a related discussion of the figural value of hands and the complicity Emerson asserts between thought and manipular labor, as well as a discussion of the similarity between Emerson's and Heidegger's representations of thought through figures of the hand, see Cavell, "Aversive Thinking," 136ff.

2:67). Similarly, in "Man, the Reformer" he adds, in a vast appropriation of God's perspective for the laborer, "labor is God's education . . . he only is a sincere learner, he only can become a master, who learns the secrets of labor, and who by real cunning exhorts from nature its sceptre" (*CW*, 1:152). Emerson's point is clear and consistent with the premises of "Self-Reliance" and "Compensation": the work we do, our actions in the world, brings to presence the world we live in, our value and the value of nature; and our duty, the task of thought, is to own nature through a withdrawal that resolves the effects of work without divorcing them from us, that renders us identifiable as the very unfolding of our nature. The doctrine of the farm, and the conception of culture it carries, describes the principle of work at the core of self-reliance as a cunning activity that simultaneously gives and withholds the distinction between worker and work, a cunning that releases the individual to the incessant self-overcoming of "Circles" and yet insists that wherever he is placed Man stands. The cunning inheres, as I have said, in the turn of speech that spontaneously exhorts nature, stands near to it as its visible work, drawing its power from it by encouraging its onwardness. Identity resides in reason's cunning voice: the voice of the husbandman, ever newly discovered in his work, who refuses hypostatization and earns a reality that eludes reification.

To explain the value he attaches to labor is, however, only Emerson's first intention in the description of John Smith and Co. Beyond that his purpose is to indicate the failure of the way of being in the world that finds its representative expression in the relations of trade and commerce, of the capitalist economic system emerging around him. Emerson's criticism of trade is, of course, well known and typical of transcendentalist writings. But if he poses commerce against the farmer, it is not always noticed that he does so in a deeply metaphorical way that serves principally to develop his phenomenological thesis.

Emerson found in the institutions of commerce a phenomenological falseness that cheats the individual of his integrity and reality of its presence. His recognition of this falseness, evident in the comments above, is reinforced by his description of the character of John Smith's workers: "They have some sort of self-sufficiency," he writes, "they can contrive without my aid to bring the day and the year round, but I depend on them, and have not earned by use a right to my arms and feet" (*CW* 1:150). The criticism is not directed merely at aspects or attributes of the system of commerce; it does not call for adjustments that would correct the "blacker traits" of the system of trade but leave the system intact and apparently justified (*CW* 1:148). Instead, Emerson denounces the essence of commercial exchange, and denounces it on the grounds that it is an inauthentic manner of being in the world: "The general system of our trade . . . is a system of selfishness; is not dictated by the high sentiments of human nature; is not measured by the exact law of reciprocity; much less by the sentiments of love and heroism; but is a system of *distrust*, of *concealment*" (*CW* 1:148, emphasis added).

What I want to emphasize in Emerson's criticism is the coupling of distrust and concealment, because it indicates the phenomenological stakes of his critique. His early thought centers on the potential for phenomenological authenticity and his criticism of trade is principally aimed at the self-concealment and thus self-dwarfing it causes. The repression of authentic individuality carried out by trade (but not only by trade, Emerson adds, but by "all the lucrative professions and practices of man") consists then of the phenomenological incapacitation of the individual: it "requires of the practitioner a certain shutting of the eyes" (*CW* 1:148). The criticism gains scope in consequence of the phenomenological allusion, and this is important to its revision of the arena of political action. Emerson's attack on the system of trade dismisses the marketplace as the site of social and political action, but dismisses it both literally and figuratively, indicating, not that it is a harsh system—a jagged world of reality that we might be forgiven for wanting to escape—but that it is a false system; which is to say, it is no system at all and reflects an illusory world. As I suggested above, Emerson reverses commonsense prejudices about realism; it is the marketplace that is an abstraction, an idealization, a formal construction. Indeed, the market figures a pernicious formalism that Emerson uses as a trope for the displacement of power from the self to a metaphysical principle. His description thus speaks not only literally to specific actions but, more importantly, figuratively to essential human attitudes, and indicates the individual is (self-) displaced from the site of his individuality to the extent he does not know himself according to his labor in the world. The distrust implicit in the system of trade is distrust in oneself—the absence of self-reliance. The "concealment" is the concealment of the individual who rather than disclose himself through the performance of labor hides behind the labor of others, or simply behind a refusal to own his labor.

Commerce is Emerson's most compelling example of a mode of evaluation that obscures the intrinsic value of the individual. Predicated on the mediation of the marketplace—the base estimate of the marketplace, Emerson wrote in criticism of the preacher in "Compensation"—it defines a system that cannot reveal the value of a thing. The marketplace assumes a formal measure of value, which replaces the immediate effect of action in the specific or local context in which a thing acts. Commerce is dependent on criteria of value that are extraneous and logically prior to the labor that produces a thing: the value and instruction that comes from the "sugar of the sugar" has little to do with its value on the market in Boston. If as a commodity, as an object for the market, a thing cannot show its compensatory value—cannot, that is, truly be a *thing*—then Emerson insists here that the product of labor is not a commodity. The effects of labor are rendered commodities only by the system of trade itself. Emerson viewed the authentic product of labor as the unconcealment of the individual. The individual emerges for Emerson from the relation that exists between labor and product before it is mediated by market forces, the relation by which the product of labor is self-disclosing compensation, not the displacement of the individual behind the value of the commodity. By criticizing the system of trade he intends then to show that the individual disposed in the world as in a marketplace is cheated of the self-growth and self-expansion that results from an immediate relation to nature, is cheated of the possibility of recognizing himself in the world through the actions he carries out. Thus hidden by the *apparent* self-reliant ethic of the laws of the market is the absence of an authentic relation between labor and what it produces: the failure of the individual is concealed by the apparent success of commerce. Emerson encourages the reader to recognize that "the market" cannot be found anywhere, because it has no existence, is itself an earned reality but a degenerate one, and that insofar as we locate our politics within its precincts, they are formalized. Conversely, he encourages the reader to seek an alternative site of labor and political action.

What interests me now is the clue a phenomenological reading provides for discovering the site of politics that he substitutes for the market, for here I think one gains a concrete sense of the reform Emerson has in mind. His critique of trade through the terms of distrust and concealment indicates both the duty of the political individual and the location of authentic politics that he substitutes for the model of the merchant in the marketplace. To be self-reliant implies, not the deployment of oneself and one's energies in and through the institutions of trade or any structural marketplace of value. Rather, it involves reversing the attitude that seeks value in a priori structures or extraneous criteria of value, and through one's actions becoming integrated with the unfolding process of nature.

The recognition that the market has figural, not literal, value for Emerson goes far toward explaining his ambivalent attitudes toward trade. He does not claim that self-reliance is impossible in the world of commerce: self-reliance is an attitude that can inform any labor. But equally, the market figures forth an attitude, or a way of evaluating our world, even the world of commerce, that is fundamentally opposed to self-reliance. Emerson distinguishes these two attitudes in "Man, the Reformer" through his characterization of "the first and second owner of property"—the "owner" as against the "watcher"—and by indicating that the foundation of reform inheres in the phenomenological power of the former (*CW* 1:150). His use of the imagery of sight and manipular action that informs his early essays is evident here as well. It is the first owner who carries out his duty to cultivate nature's economy of presence, to bear responsibility for it, to own it by bringing it within the compass of his eye, and to acknowledge himself thereby. The first owner of property engages and uses it, is integrated with it. He nurtures his property against its natural enemies. He "gets only as fast as he wants for his own ends"; thus, his property "does not embarrass him, or take away his sleep with *looking after*" (*CW* 1:151, emphasis added). His relation to it is not retrospective, that of a backward glance, but the onward vision of self-reliant will. It is a healthy relation "of masterly good humor, and sense of power, and fertility of resource . . . of those strong and learned hands, those peircing and learned eyes, that supple body, and that mighty and prevailing heart" (*CW* 1:151). The owner is integrated with nature as the milieu of his work. In contrast, the son who inherits his wealth has "his hands full—not to use these things,— but to look after them. . . . He is converted from the owner into a watchman or a watch-dog," into a speculator rather than a worker (*CW* 1:151).

The first owner, finding himself through his labor, figures the authentic human attitude—the life and spirit of self-reliance—that recognizes the return of self-identity as the product of labor. It is this life that is present, whether synchronically for thought or diachronically for history, as the instantiation of a compensatory system of value. The life of the soul is a power to create an epochal unity within which nature appears, the power of the farmer to husband nature's presence, the power of labor that *owns* the economy of presence. The dynamic of labor and production, action and effect, returns the focus of the economy of value it produces to the unity of the individual and thus grounds humanist claims for self-identity. To view that economy as a marketplace, as a formal field of relations cut off from human causality, abstracts its lived reality and fails to note that the interplay of compensatory values is set in action and encompassed by the individual. Emerson's early writings seek primarily to indicate the possibility open to the individual to find himself as the gathering and unity of the economy of presence instituted through labor. For this reason he claims that inasmuch as we are "sure of [our] hands and feet," inasmuch, that is, as we recognize ourselves in our labor, compensation will return the sense of individuality as the clarity of the relations of the self in the world.

The figure of the first owner describes the practical condition of "height" that Emerson identifies with virtue in "Self-Reliance," and its difference from the abstract mastery of the heir—who, detached from the immediacy of labor, inhabits the structurally metaphysical posture of the watcher, the master who watches after his wealth and thus is ultimately slave to the ends that define his wealth—expresses the imperative of the early thought. The second owner is unrelated to the world, has no access to nature, is "guarded by walls and curtains, stoves and down beds, coaches, and men-servants and women-servants from the earth and the sky" (*CW* 1:151). Inasmuch as the son has no manipular relation to nature, performs no authentic labor, he is reduced to "a puny, protected person . . . the menial and runner of his riches," and is concealed from himself as well (*CW* 1:151). Against this morally impoverished condition Emerson poses the decisiveness of the initial owner's labor. Nearness to nature derives from the work of hands and feet—it is principally hands and feet that connect us to the earth and sky. Labor establishes nature's scope, severs nature at its limits, and in thus casting nature cultivates its presence and earns its love. Emerson's Edenic description of naked innocence is a phenomenological rendering of what it would be like to live in a world for which we have borne responsibility. The owner is one "whom nature loved and feared, whom snow and rain, water and land, beast and fish seemed all to know and to serve" (*CW* 1:151). For Emerson nature is always reformed: "What is man born for, but to be a Reformer, a Re-maker of what man has made; a renouncer of lies; a restorer of truth and good" (*CW* 1:156). The conditions, the terms of nature into which the individual is thrown, are given value at the fingertips of the owner, where they come into focus as the content of his work. At stake, however, is how we remake them.

In "Man, the Reformer" Emerson extends his argument against a degenerate way of being and knowing ourselves. Do we conceal ourselves behind the market, denying our central relation to it and hoarding a false identity, dwarfed by the relations we set in play? Or do we acknowledge ourselves in the expenditure of our actions, the labor of our cultivation, enown ourselves as what we nurture to presence by externalizing, spending, our labor? Emerson eventually comes to view this expenditure as unrecoverable, but for the early Emerson only one answer to these questions is possible. Self-reliance resides in the self-recovery of the free activity of labor. By describing authenticity in this way, Emerson indicates the new site of politics and reform he identifies in this lecture and more widely in his early period. No longer the public arena of alienated human spirit, political activity for Emerson occurs in and through the territory defined by one's action, the field of one's phenomenological ownership. The revolution and reform that he predicts under the name of self-reliance is found in "the gradual domestication of the idea of culture" inasmuch as that phrase entails being in the world as its *owner*, as the agency that cultivates nature. It implies a revolution that will consist of a change in the way we exist in the world, from the irresponsibility that posits principles of value beyond the self to the upright posture that takes responsibility for the world and does so not least of all by recognizing the limit of the world to be defined by the scope of individual labor, by knowing that "no kernel of nourishing corn can come to him but through his toil bestowed on that plot of ground which is given to him to till" (*CW* 2:28).

At root, the ethics and politics of self-reliance depend on staying at home within the limits of one's power, and certainly for this reason, too, Emerson integrated the sense of domestication into his theory of culture. For the word "domesticate" revolves, of course, around the root *domus*, or house. To domesticate is to dwell in as a house, or to make a part of one's household, to bring into the fold of one's home, to naturalize. This represents a distinct development within Emerson's humanism from the doctrine of use in *Nature* to the more sophisticated themes of the doctrine of the farm. Not to use but to become at home with power, to take up dwelling with it, to see *it*—culture, the capacity to cultivate nature—as the site of authenticity and political duty, is the imperative of the doctrine of the farm. Emerson believed the revolution self-reliance predicts would emerge as the gradual ability to be at home, to set up household with our phenomenological power, to dwell *with* that power as we dwell *in* the world it manifests. And equally, political action would come to consist in the process of clarifying and properly uttering the meaning of the world in which we dwell. The very activity of cultivating nature, which again consists in the two movements of recognizing our centrality and bearing responsibility for nature, is the meaning of politics and results in what Emerson takes political action to be: the interrogative attitude in the individual that demands of institutions that they answer to the citizen's sense of right and wrong. The early writings enlarge politics beyond the sphere of institutional value to include the plurality of social relations carried by the description of making or building. Even this description, however, may not state the matter clearly enough, for to be at home with the *idea* of culture is not really to domesticate it. There remains some distance between such dwelling and the idea of culture—between the site of politics and the activity of labor—as long as it is concealed behind an idea. The profound practicality of self-reliance, a practicality that will eventually explode the humanist foundation Emerson appeals to in his early phase, does not give itself up to an idea or, in a sense, to language. Even Emerson, it seems, first spoke of it in a poor, external way. The logic of self-reliance will turn out to be more extensive than the *idea* of domesticating culture; it will lead to the practice of dwelling *as* cultivation. One's dwelling in the world—one's home and labor and worship—is to be his or her politics. Self-reliance teaches a way of being in the world for which the privacy of one's home is the political sphere, the private is the public, and political duty is to the solitude of dwelling with oneself. Although only partially understood in 1841, for Emerson the proper way to be in the world, the proper manner of living, makes of the act of building a domicile.

TRANSCENDENTAL POLITICS

When at the end of "Man, the Reformer" Emerson predicts "there will dawn ere long on our politics, on our modes of living . . . the sentiment of love," he makes clear his belief that the site of reform, defined by the nurturing and husbanding acts of the self-reliant individual, is the essential relation of love (*CW* 1:158). The "politics of love" mean for Emerson no mere sentimentality; he is far from suggesting that we reform society by encouraging brotherly love. Rather, the meaning of the politics of love should be read out of Emerson's general phenomenological approach. What he stresses in "Man, the Reformer" is his belief that individual authenticity can be a powerful political force. He thus defines the motive of authentic politics. In a certain respect, moreover, Emerson will maintain this belief even after he turns from his humanist faith. Certainly, the notion of individual authenticity will no longer have validity for him, but the basic idea that the individual acts in a specified situation with political or public effect, causing change and new value, and that the individual is the only means for realizing such effect, will endure. What will not endure is the universality and centrality of the phenomenological power of the individual rooted in self-recognition, and thus the very foundation of politics in love will be set aside. Still, it is worthwhile to note that the roots of the activity described in "Power" and "Wealth" can be found in the reformer described in this lecture and in the self-reliant individual in general. In both cases the description of the efficacy of human being derives from Emerson's insight that the individual, human will activates, energizes, and thus brings to effective presence and power the forces in a situation or context and that the individual has the capacity thus freely to overlook and manipulate forces that Emerson will eventually conclude are fatal.

In "Man, the Reformer," he urges the humanist version of this insight, asserting that political reform is settled in the activity of the authentic individual, that the site of the political—of reform and revolution—is the husbandman's relation with nature. The "prosecution of love" names a phenomenological disposition in the world, an attitude we take on the world, and a means by which we convict it and ourselves. Emerson poses his understanding of politics against the assumption that the political arena is defined by an abstract marketplace notion of the public, for the abstraction of politics from the field of individual perception establishes its institutional nature, as well as its alienated status. Traditional politics, defined by public institutions, material and immaterial, represents for Emerson another instance of the alienated world in which Man dwarfs himself. Fundamental reform can occur, therefore, only insofar as politics itself is redefined. In the absence of a redefinition of politics, reform will amount to no more than an incidental shifting of power from one group to another. Emerson's stakes are higher. He wishes to relocate political action, taking it out of the realm of alienated institutions, domesticating it, and in consequence destroying all institutions of political authority. The political reform Emerson has in mind depends, however, less on the abolition than the *revaluation* of political institutions. He is far from being a political nihilist in this lecture. His purpose is not negative. The phenomenological destruction he calls for wipes away the *alienated value* of political institutions. Political institutions are rather to gain their value within the scope of the eye; the individual is to own those institutions and only thus to take political action and determine political value. In short, politics is to be brought to the bar of individual conscience. In this respect, Emerson's purpose in "Man, the Reformer" is to show that it is the duty of all people to judge for themselves. He views politics as he views the world, in terms of the dynamic of destruction and regeneration that is settled in human action and that verifies human worth. The institutions of society are no different for him than the institutions of thought. They too are to be brought to judgment through each act of the individual. Fundamental political duty is thus "the duty that every man should assume his own vows, should call the institutions of society to account" (*CW* 1:153). Emerson's ideas about reform at bottom amount to the humanist and pragmatic call to "revise the whole of our social structure, the state, the school, religion, marriage, trade, science, [to] explore their foundations in our own nature" (*CW* 1:156). We can hardly but understand this call in tangible terms. The duty of the individual is to recognize political action in the work he or she does in the world, and the site of politics is the context made present by that work. Implicitly Emerson rejects the idea that institutions can be reformed through a single act of revolution. Reform inheres, instead, in the attitude of the individual that maintains a *constant* challenge to institutional authority, that demands that an institution show its worth each time it is used, an attitude that locates the individual at the periphery of the scope of institutional authority, looking on it as a possible, not actual, power and thus effectively reinventing the institution with each use of it. Emerson assumes that institutions are at the disposal of the individual and gain their value through the actions of the individual. This belief is embodied in the individual who accepts the authority of society's institutions only insofar as he or she gives them authority, who thus scrutinizes the world to locate the right course of action and only then instrumentalizes political institutions in order to carry out his or her verdict.

For such individuals the site of politics is local, limited to the scope of their effective actions. Figuratively, to be sure, but nonetheless for reasons that stem from Emerson's basic beliefs, he consistently advised his readers to attend to the issues of their own community before going far and wide in search of political causes. If he does not limit the nature of work to physical acts, he does argue against the merely formal assumption of a political posture, absent any immediate integration with the political scene. As a practical matter, then, Emerson's political theory requires that we make judgments and pursue political action only within the scope of our effectiveness and immediate knowledge. He renounces the universal applicability of political, social, or cultural values. Rendering politics responsible to individual conscience, Emerson deflates abstract concepts at least insofar as the criteria for judging them are assumed to reside outside the context of presence manifested by individual action. Fundamental political values, such as equality, liberty, and justice, cannot, for Emerson, be judged outside the terms established by individual action. It is precisely this fact that throws political judgment back on conscience and renders it synonymous with moral judgment. Justice emerges in and through the context of action that inheres in a situation. Emerson's thought places extraordinary weight on the individual's capacity to judge rightly, and we can give credence to this capacity, it seems to me, only if we recognize it as the endpoint of Emerson's humanist theory, as the ability to unconceal the laws of the situation fully, to render it absolutely exterior. Broad justice inheres in the balance, the harmony, of a situation when wholly unconcealed, not in any of its parts. Justice, it can be said, consists precisely of being conscientious. The basic duty of the individual is to nurture to presence every aspect of a situation, to bring before the eye all of its parts, in order thereby to reveal the justice of the situation.

Justice then is an immanent quality and has little to do with the judgments that society may bring to bear on it, a fact emphatically made by Emerson in "Self-Reliance," when, to the challenge that unknown to him his beliefs may do the devil's work, he responded by asserting, "If I am the Devil's child, I will live then from the Devil" (*CW* 2:30). Emerson found justice in the clarification and accountability of one's situation and not by comparison to others. He believed that life establishes its own terms of value, which derive from authentic action itself: "There are creative manners, there are creative actions, and creative words; manners, actions, and words, that is, indicative of no custom or authority, but springing spontaneous from the mind's own sense of good and fair" (*CW* 2:57). This is no less true of political action, and it is still valuable to point out that just political action can be decided only within the terms of the individual's world, and it is before the scrutiny of the individual that justice emerges and shows itself.

Emerson's early thought reaches its completion in the idea of the politics of love. His faith here as elsewhere in the early writings is humanist: "The power, which is at once spring and regulator in all efforts of reform, is faith in Man, the conviction that there is an infinite worthiness in him which will appear at the call of worth" (*CW* 1:156). Our worthiness consists of husbanding the world out of an interrogative attitude, questioning its institutions and values, demanding that the world give account of itself in every aspect and finally that we thereby give account of ourselves, that we know ourselves and the world in and through our actions. Emerson would have us own the institutions of society rather than the reverse, a relation that, of course, depends on the dissolution of everything stable in them. His attitudes are traditional and revolutionary. He would have us be true to our world, see it clearly, and see the operation of institutions in it clearly. Real reform, real political revolution, he believed, returns to authentic human being and will occur when every individual is true to the world he manifests, sees it for what it is, holds its contents responsible to his vision, and, moreover, holds himself responsible to his world-defining actions.

Part II

FALLING

No one has surmounted
The Destiny yet
Not one has accounted
To Conscience his debt.

This world is a palace whose walls are lined with mirrors.

You shall have joy, or you shall have power, said God, you shall not have both.

Genius is very well but it is enveloped and undermined by Wonder. The last fact is still Astonishment, mute, bottomless, boundless, endless Wonder.

Nature is a silent Man.

—Emerson, *The Journals and Miscellaneous Notebooks*

The thought Emerson had in the summer of 1841 and that he groped to express in his lecture of that summer, "The Method of Nature," must have seemed to him unprecedented. He had taken himself to be operating at the advanced edge of reason, the point at which reason is tool, medium, and content of an ongoing revolution, where it is brought to effective identity with the use of language and thus democratized as the eloquence of the everyday actions of the individual. His vision had been of the identity of the philosopher and the poet, the return of philosophy to its home in the poetic use of language. His essays and lectures had put the vision of a humanized philosophy into action, embodying the essence of reason as he saw it in fluid metaphors, whose philosophical value re-formed in each new context of the individual's life. Most readers have recognized "Circles" as his strongest statement of that vision. With its enduring but infinitely malleable figures of the eye, the horizon, and Man, it expresses Emerson's deep faith in the essence of humanist thought: the resiliency and integrity of the individual and the primacy of a philosophical view of life. So if we have grown accustomed to the issue of "the end of philosophy" and "the ends of man," it is still possible to retrieve Emerson's astonishment at the idea that forced itself on him in the summer of 1841 and to understand how unprecedented must have seemed the thought he uttered: "There is no man; there hath never been" (*CW* 1:122).[1]

Nonetheless, he recognized the consequences of the thought. Philosophy becomes for him the profanity of seeking a cause or anchor where

---

1. The phrase "the ends of man" is taken from the title of Jacques Derrida's essay in *Margins of Philosophy*, trans. Alan Bass (Chicago: University of Chicago Press, 1982), 109–36. It is pertinent that Derrida concludes his essay by noting that a critique of "the signified" and "a break with the thinking of Being" will take "the form of a critique of phenomenology" (134). Emerson's transitional period, consisting of a turn from and a delimitation of the phenomenological centrality of Man Thinking, thematized explicitly as the failed referentiality of language and including in "Experience" a delimitation of the discourse of Being, bears substantial resemblance to the critique Derrida predicts.

none can be found, and poetry recedes from the grasp of everyman. If one recalls that in his early essays the cause of causes was the poetic capacity to recover the unity and proportion of the individual from the contrariety of experience, then it isn't surprising to find that truth is displaced to utterances that occur on no day on the calendar.

Readers have long recognized the early years of the 1840s as a period of crisis in Emerson's works. The philosophical interpretation of Emerson I have put forward in the preceding chapters enables a particular kind of clarity in the understanding of that crisis, for a philosophical reading presupposes the continuity of reason, the sublative *Aufhebung* that "Circles" identifies with the progress of Man and that "The Method of Nature," through a geologic transfiguration of the circular image, transfers to nature. Emerson's crisis stems from this transference and the challenge it poses to humanist conceptions of reason, and it consists in his struggle nonetheless to maintain the viability of reason. And the clarity a philosophical interpretation allows depends on the reader also remaining faithful in the face of this challenge to the continuity of reason. Indeed, maintaining a philosophical approach at all depends on fidelity to reason. It is not gratuitous, then, that at this point in an interpretation of Emerson, and parallel to his crisis, the reader too should meet a crisis in the faith in reason. Emerson's readers' crises are poignantly expressed in the critical perplexity created by this lecture in particular and this period in general, as well, specifically, as the critical violence perpetrated on the lecture. Readers' doubt in reason, which ironically often takes shape as an unwillingness to entertain apparently counterrational thoughts, is not gratuitous, because it is at this point in Emerson's writings that a faithfulness to the historicity of reason embedded in his thought warrants in the reader not a sharing of the *commanding* posture of Central Man but rather an *obedience* to the self-overcoming of Man. Beginning with "The Method of Nature," fidelity to reason demands in the reader a turn from the appropriative command given by a critic's distance from his subject and puts in its place the self-effacement that obeys the dictates of reason rather than the claims of Man. *In the name of reason* the reader is called upon to give up the humanist presumptions that modernism defines as the substance of reason and reading.

Somewhat paradoxically, then, my intention to sustain a philosophical interpretation of Emerson's writings depends on faithfully following the lead of Emerson's language to the ends of philosophy and Man. The "*relève (Aufhebung)* of humanism," Jacques Derrida has noted, is a "trembling . . . from the *outside*" that finds its principal strategy in a reversal of the master tropes of humanism, turning them against themselves.[2] A philosophical approach to Emerson's transitional writings, because it relies on the discourse of reason, consists similarly in maintaining and carrying along the philosophical content of his principal figures, even as they are used to refute and overcome themselves. Indeed, this maintenance and carrying along is the condition of humanism's "trembling," and in Derrida no less than in Emerson, it is the surviving essence of reason and philosophy. The clarity it makes possible is of the scope (the reason) of what is overcome in the shift from the method of Man to the method of nature.

That the overcoming of humanism requires self-effacing obedience to reason nonetheless raises the most decisive challenge to the value of a philosophical interpretation, as, indeed, to the value of philosophy itself. The integrity of philosophical discourse and the claims of reason have traditionally relied on the universal foundation they give to our experience of the world. Aristotle initiates First philosophy by distinguishing the science of Being qua being from the various regional sciences, and the early Heidegger continues the tradition by raising the question and the difference of Being and beings. "The end of philosophy" would then mark the end of a universal discourse of Being. Interwoven with the issue of sustaining a philosophical reading of Emerson—and moreover against his own banishment of philosophy from the method of nature—is the very fate of this discourse. The self-overcoming of philosophy has presented itself historically as the collapse of the universal discourse of Being into regionalism, and the subsequent ascendancy of political discourse. To identify "the end of philosophy" has held the promise (however we value it) of raising political discourse to subsumptive prominence, a promise fulfilled in the ideological critiques that dominate contemporary discussions of value across disciplines. In this context it might seem at best naive, and at worst feudal, to identify "the end of philosophy" as the initiating gesture of a doctrine of obedience, and it might seem so whether this reveals the trajectory of Emerson's thought or not.

But this appearance reflects a reactionary presumption of philosophical universality, whereas the viability of a philosophical reading depends precisely on accomplishing philosophy's dissociation from the claims made for it as a universal science, without forfeiting reason. Indeed, a philosophical interpretation must fall back on reason and emphasize that "the end of philosophy" signifies principally the end of

---

2. Derrida, "The Ends of Man," 134, 135.

Man, which is to say, the end of the dream of *apprehending* a universal discourse of value or, rather, the unveiling of such discourse as fundamentally political and, as such, regional. It does *not* signify the end of what philosophy has called reason or *logos* and what Emerson calls first nature and later fate. Nor, in the same vein, does Emerson question the centrality and determinacy of the organization or historicity of the individual. Rather, "the end of philosophy" poses for him the question of reason made unavailable to individual apprehension and expression—the question of the inadequacy of self-reliant speech to the individual's constitution. Precisely this question is raised by Emerson's turn from the method of Man to the method of nature. But as I take Derrida to suggest, only reason can watch its own withdrawal from Man, and therefore a philosophical interpretation alone can trace the contours of this question as it emerges in Emerson's writings. Beyond this expository value, a philosophical approach to Emerson's transitional writings maintains an interpretive focus on the movement of reason at precisely the moment in its progress—its withdrawal from presence—when it has proven itself most likely to divert attention away from itself. Emerson's shift to the method of nature and his insistent, if not obsessive, attention to the elusiveness of nature demonstrate, moreover, that *his* focus remained on the turns of reason. By following him one thus marks the path of reason beyond a recoverable dialectic and uncovers, not the end of philosophy, but its call for an attitude of obedience to the irresolution of reason's turns.

3

The Falling Away of Man

The turn from humanism to antihumanism in Emerson's thought, which his reconsideration of the relation between Man and nature effects, is located chronologically at the time between the delivery of "Man, the Reformer" and "The Method of Nature." Inasmuch as the former provides Emerson's most effective statement of the political value of his early thought and the latter contains the first groping critique of his early thought and the seeds of the definitive work to follow, it is surprising that neither of these lectures has received a great deal of attention. Clearly, 1841 was an important year for Emerson. Nonetheless, "The Method of Nature" has been dismissed as a weak and uncertain lecture, a lecture that confused its listeners, that remains ineffective in written form, and that must surely represent fundamental confusions in its author. Against this characterization one can place the following remarks from the lecture, which reveal a powerful realignment of the images, figures, and themes that had come to mean most to Emerson:

> The festival of the intellect, and the return to its source, cast a strong light on the always interesting topics of Man and Nature. We are forcibly reminded of the old want. There is no man; there hath never been. The Intellect still asks that a man may be born. The flame of life flickers feebly in human breasts. We demand of men a richness and universality we do not find. Great men do not content

us. It is their solitude, not their force, that makes them conspicuous. There is somewhat indigent and tedious about them. . . . How tardily men arrive at any thought! how tardily they pass to it from another! The crystal sphere of thought is as concentrical as the geological structure of the globe. As all our soils and rocks lie in strata, concentric strata, so do all men's thinkings run laterally, never vertically. Here comes by a great inquisitor with auger and plumb-line, and will bore an Artesian well through all our conventions and theories, and pierce to the core of things. But as soon as he probes one crust, behold gimlet, plumb-line, and philosopher, all take a lateral direction, in spite of all resistance, as if some strong wind took everything off its feet, and if you come month after month to see what progress our reformer has made,—not an inch has he pierced,—you still find him with new words in the old place, floating about in new parts of the same old vein or crust. The new book says, "I will give you the key to nature," and we expect to go like a thunderbolt to the centre. But the thunder is a surface phenomenon, makes a skin deep cut, and so does the sage. The wedge turns out to be a rocket. Thus a man lasts but a very little while, for his monomania becomes insupportably tedious in a few months.

In the absence of man we turn to nature, which stands next. (*CW* 1:122–23, emphasis added)

Up to this paragraph in the address Emerson had seemed more or less to follow the themes of the early essays, and especially of "Man, the Reformer." In these lines, however, he introduces a problem that has been absent since *Nature*, and by so doing indicates a renewed sense of the inadequacy of the humanist synthesis he developed in the earlier works. His assertion that we are "forcibly reminded of the old want" that there is no man, speaks both to the philosophical/theological problem of individuation most evident in the Platonic tradition and to Emerson's *own* early recognition of the problem of the individual. His reference is to the desire implicit in the ancient and modern humanist project, the desire to locate value and knowledge in the individual. The old want is the desire that nature should be *for* man, that human beings should be the end of nature, its redemptive resolution. Emerson had thought to solve the problem through the ascent to spirit, reason's recognition of itself as the cause of the world's appearance. In these lines he announces that the humanist synthesis is faulty, that the old desire is not satisfied and has never been satisfied. The journal entry that stands behind this passage shows, as R. A. Yoder notes, the growing influence of Heraclitus on Emerson's thought.[1] But the entry indicates, as well, that Emerson now poses Heraclitus against the prominent figures of the "Trismegisti," the group of Neoplatonic thinkers that he identified as spokesmen for the powers of reason. In the journal he identifies the sages, whose thunder is a superficial phenomenon, as "Confucius, Menu, Zoroaster, Socrates," and, having critiqued them, concludes, "Ever & forever Heraclitus is justified who called the world an eternal inchoation" (*JMN* 7:457). The dismissive reference to the Trismegisti marks, then, Emerson's turning from the power of active reason aligned with humanism and his embrace of Heraclitus as a figure of an alternative wisdom, which is the wisdom of the method of nature rather than the method of Man. It is important to keep this opposition in mind when reading "Experience" as well, because the essay is grounded in a Heraclitean conception of nature and *logos*, and Emerson recalls the figures of the Trismegisti *only* in the "Reality" section and only in order to set their superficiality against the justice of Heraclitus's vision. As a consequence he provides a jarring depiction of the philosophical ideas of reality and Being as surface phenomena.

At stake in his turn is, of course, the status of nature as preeminent in its ontological secondariness, the seeming paradox of saying nature *stands* in its secondariness. Emerson does not assert the primacy of material nature and puts forward, therefore, no empiricism here. The nature he turns to remains the expression of spirit. But the falling away of Man indicates the signified has gained methodological priority over the signifier. Emerson's use of a geological figure suggests that he has in mind by nature the layers of expression of which memory consists, and if so, then he turns from an understanding of expressivity as the immediate manifestation of nature—the method of Man, where nature consists in the contemporary act of *remembering*—to an understanding of nature as the interlayering of memory that invariably precedes any expression. In Emerson's language, this structure of memory is our constitution. We might follow one strain of twentieth-century thought in call-

---

1. R. A. Yoder, *Emerson and the Orphic Poet in America* (Berkeley and Los Angeles: University of California Press, 1978), 40. Yoder's discussions of Emerson's poetry, especially the later poetry, derive from his analysis of Emerson's methodological shift in 1841, to which he often alludes. He gives excellent expression to the full range of Emerson's antihumanist method, the method of nature, when he concludes "there is no hint of anything behind or below this 'perpetual inchoation' to make transcendence even conceivable—nature contains all" (41). See also David Porter on Emerson's substitution of Becoming for Being in connection with Nietzsche's reading of him (*Emerson and Literary Change* [Cambridge, Mass.: Harvard University Press, 1978], esp. 201).

ing it the unconscious, as some critics have, or another by emphasizing its linguistic structure. Indeed, Emerson will figure nature as language, as Cavell notes, and materially considered, memory certainly manifests itself in the languages of nations and cultures.[2] It seems important to me, however, to recognize that for Emerson, either of these ways of speaking would represent no more than tropes through which we figure the elusiveness and recession of nature from referentiality. Memory, insofar as it is distinguished from the act of remembering and thus is characterized as a system of relations, an irresolute texture that carries the potential for resolution but equally renders any decisive utterance fragmentary and superficial, better captures Emerson's sense of the method of nature's secondariness and equally carries the sense of phenomenological temporality implicit in the revision of nature. As memory, nature is time's "it was," to borrow a phrase from Nietzsche. It is the incessant withdrawal from presence, nature's passing, the passing of presence. It is memory, but memory that, when it gives itself, does so only in articulations inadequate to its complexity. By embracing the method of nature, Emerson concedes that as an act of remembering, active reason is invariably belated, and that perception is rooted in what is secondary, illusory, dreamlike, and, when acted upon, superficial. The turn indicated in the passage cited above therefore leads me to reconsider, and to dismiss, the tradition in Emerson criticism that grounds Emerson's thought in the centrality and depth of human power, the mastery of nature, and the philosophy of self-culture.

Emerson's shift in thought could not be more explicit. The reformer and the sage, both privileged figures in his theory up to this time, are here brought under definitive criticism: neither understands nature; neither is integrated with nature; both are surface phenomena caught in a stratum of thought without knowing it and destined to repeat the same thought. But if the passage is explicit, many critics have been reluctant to credit the full scope of the shift in thought it indicates and have insistently read the relation of Man and nature humanistically. Whicher, for instance, early on addressed the lecture but aligned it thematically with "Circles," asserting, it now appears inaccurately, that the essay and lecture were written contemporaneously. Sherman Paul follows Whicher's lead, stating, "The method of mind, Emerson believed could also be seen in the method of nature."[3] Neither writer

---

2. See, in particular, Cavell, "Genteel Responses to Kant? In Emerson's 'Fate' and in Coleridge's *Biographia Literaria,*" *Raritan* 3 (Fall 1983): 47ff.
3. *Emerson's Angle of Vision*, 108.

gives the emphasis or priority I believe Emerson intended to the fundamental figural difference between the assertion in "Circles" that Man invariably stands, place him where you will, and the opposed assertion in "The Method of Nature" that Man is absent and nature stands. By subsuming the theme of the lecture under the lesson of "Circles" they render "Emerson's deepest disillusionment" a motive for a greater self-recovery.[4] Recent critics have continued this trend. Richard Lee Francis flatly reverses the trajectory of Emerson's thought: "Having found the 'Method of Nature' elusive, Emerson discovered instead the method of the self."[5] David Robinson, after an insightful discussion of the lecture, which *does* emphasize Emerson's radical attacks on the concept of Man and moral foundations, nonetheless dismisses Emerson's antihumanist turn by asserting that when he says Man is absent "Emerson means, of course, that there is no complete individual, no one who lives up to the potential which the intellect discerns." Given this dilution of the meaning of Man's absence, Robinson is unsurprisingly tentative in his conclusion that "out of the complicated entanglements of moral growth and mystical perception . . . Emerson is able to fashion a fragile synthesis, whose final result seems consistent with his earlier work."[6] Even Michael Lopez, in a work welcome for its detranscendentalizing intent, invokes as a critical framework for reading the lecture "Romanticism's 'anthropocentric conceit'" and endorses a Romantic conception of power wed to the individual's self-certitude, interpreting nature's erectness in terms of its use for Man, as "a reminder for [Man], in his fallen state, of his own original and potential power."[7]

Emerson's early work *is* founded on the potential adequacy of Man's accounts of nature, on the resolution gained through action and the use of nature, and on the potential this affords for self-recovery and authenticity. But it is precisely this adequacy and power that Emerson doubts in "The Method of Nature." Indeed, here, and still more emphatically in "Experience," he insists that Man's accounts cannot grasp nature, not even potentially. The middle period is characterized by Emer-

---

4. Whicher, *Freedom and Fate*, 97.

5. Richard Lee Francis, "The Poet and Experience," in *Emerson Centenary Essays*, ed. Joel Myerson (Carbondale: Southern Illinois University Press, 1982), 94.

6. David Robinson, *"The Method of Nature* and Emerson's Period of Crisis," in *Emerson Centenary Essays*, ed. Joel Myerson (Carbondale: Southern Illinois University Press, 1982), 83, 88. I disagree with Robinson's exacting analysis of the lecture principally because I believe he ignores the necessity Emerson attributes in the lecture to the opposition between nature's erectness and Man's belatedness.

7. Michael Lopez, "Transcendental Failure: 'The Palace of Spiritual Power,'" in *Emerson: Prospect and Retrospect*, Harvard English Studies 10, ed. Joel Porte (Cambridge, Mass.: Harvard University Press, 1982), 127, 126.

son's discovery that speech is *necessarily* belated and illusory, and so, therefore, are all of our descriptions of nature. There is no ambiguity in Emerson's words: Man, and all the value this figure earns in his early period, is absent. Emerson criticism needs to address the eloquence and necessity he recognized in this discovery, for Emerson's transitional period revolves around its effects and his later work responds to it. But instead, "The Method of Nature" has in large measure not been critically discussed at all, and an important opportunity to advance our understanding of the richness of Emerson's inquiry, which leads him out of the arena of Western humanism and into the still largely unmapped expanse of antihumanist nature, has been missed.

I want to begin, then, by emphasizing the difference between Emerson's critique here and in the earlier essays. His statements here should not be confused with his earlier critiques of rational subjectivity. He does not mean to emancipate further the individual, whose value he has already located in the destruction of institutions and whose nature he has shown to consist in the self-clarification possible for active reason. Emerson's purpose is to accomplish a more definitive revision, and not merely a revision of the individual.

He *contextualizes* the pluralist and emancipated activity that the self-reliant individual is taken to be, stripping that activity of its claim to universality and depth, its implicit claim to having no opposite. Yet he does so under the assumption of Man's privileged role as the medium of nature's presence. The description literally picks up the whole context of individual action, the entire gathering effected through labor—the *universe* as Emerson understands it during his early period— and displaces it. But to what? To what *could* Man be displaced in the wake of Emerson's radical humanism? Only to a nature now defined by the phenomenological power and failure of consciousness, which is to say, nature defined as the flux of appearance *and* disappearance, of coming to and passing from presence, the flux suppressed under the method of "Circles." And accordingly, nature's onwardness can no longer imply a teleological development: precisely the development and upbuilding of Man, understood as the uninterrupted and synchronic presence of nature. I will have said as much as I have to say in this chapter by stating that Man no longer situates the temporality of nature within his horizon and at the service of his growth, but rather is situated within a discontinuous temporality that manifests itself as nonhumanistic epochs of thought, as the no longer spiritual but now geological strata of intellect that Emerson describes.

Man does not pierce these strata; he does not call them up in the moment of presence as the constituents of his gathering identity. Rather, he floats on the surface of each alternately, and finds himself in the belated repetition of its law as the occasion dictates. The thesis of the lecture depends then on a realignment of the relation between will and thought. The passage cited above indicates that the contemporaneity of intellect enabled by its coincidence with will gives way to the belatedness of Man's thinking. In "Circles" Emerson assumes the individual's adequacy to nature: place him where you will, a Man cannot be outflanked, his intellect pierces to the core of nature and gathers it in a new generalization through a process comparable to the Hegelian *Aufhebung*. Emerson now recognizes "how tardily men arrive at any thought," and he remarks the disposition of the individual within the structure of a thought that exceeds him. That the authentic individual should arrive late to a thought is unimaginable in the early works: "[The] mind now thinks; now acts; and each fit reproduces the other," Emerson had written. Pulling apart the synthesis of thought and will, Emerson now renders individual thinking superficial: "All men's thinkings run laterally, never vertically." Individual action is viewed as reflecting, not the synthesis of thought for human identity, but surface alteration, ongoing displacement from one epoch of thought to another, a repetition that goes nowhere. "But as soon as he probes one crust, behold gimlet, plumb-line, and philosopher, all take a lateral direction . . . as if some strong wind took everything off its feet." The methodological premise that sets the individual as the end and purpose of life is undercut, and individuality is rendered finite, a superficial topos that can be picked up and shifted in its entirety to a new location in nature. The individual is deprived of authentic action, of rootedness in nature, and is rendered essentially ineffective.

Clearly, Emerson's language is directed at the very heart of what he had once taken to be the liberating capacities of the individual, the capacity of human intellect, invigorated by healthy will, to penetrate the depths of nature by overcoming structures of value, normative conventions of thought and action. He now ridicules the pretensions of such "great inquisitors." He directs his attack at precisely the characterization he had earlier in the year given of the reformer, who would "bore an Artesian well through all our conventions and theories, and pierce to the core of things." The individual, we are told, is no longer capable of such integration in nature, of owning nature: "We no longer hold it by the hand" (*CW* 1:123). We no longer are wed to nature; it no longer belongs to us. Emerson's imagery need not be taken to refer to an Edenic origin. It answers to his own conception of the essential reformer. He had once argued that our spiritual independence "is like the lovely varnish of the dew, whereby the old, hard, peaked earth . . . [is] made new every morning," but he now says, "We have lost our miraculous power: our arm is no more as strong as the frost" (*CW* 1:101, 123). The individual cannot place his or her arms around and rejuvenate the universe.

"The Method of Nature" is filled with statements that indicate Emerson's antihumanist insight, often, as above, by repeating and revising metaphors and images he had used to describe his humanist conviction. Thus, whereas in "The American Scholar" he wrote that the main enterprise of the world is the upbuilding of a Man, he now dismisses that goal: "That no single end may be selected and nature judged thereby, appears from this, that if man himself be considered as the end, and it be assumed that the final cause of the world is to make holy or wise or beautiful men, we see that it has not succeeded" (*CW* 1:125). He even personifies nature in order to let it speak the insignificance of Man: "I have ventured so great a stake as my success, in no single creature. I have not yet arrived at any end." And he employs the personification to identify human being as a function of nature: "My aim is the health of the whole tree . . . and by no means the pampering of a monstrous pericarp at the expense of all the other functions" (*CW* 1:126). The intellect will "still [ask] that a man may be born," and "we [will] not take up a new book, or meet a new man without a pulse-beat of expectation," but the fragile synthesis that enabled success has collapsed (*CW* 1:122–23).

Emerson's change in conception is not as simple as a mere reversal of his early thought. As I said, it does not occur along the line of a dualism that would allow a reversal of thought. It is better understood as a completion or clarification of what rests implicit in his earliest insight into the human capacity to presence nature through acts of will. Latent in Emerson's phenomenological conception of the relation between Man and nature is the necessity of withdrawal; that is to say, nature is brought to presence through an act that involves both expression and withholding. It is in the nature of phenomenological resolution not only to articulate nature but to withhold it as well, to inspire nature's love and fear by drawing a decisive mark around the field of natural presence that conceals nature as it gives it. Emerson's early essays emphasize, to the point of exclusivity, the expressive aspect of human phenomenological power and thus equally the conception of nature as the present. The only gesture made to the dynamic quality of presencing is the usurpation of nature's withholding for the definition of Man. As I indicated in the preceding chapters, Emerson can do so, or believes he can do so, in those writings, because he envisions the coincidence of vision and nature as the product of will. He is thus blind to what is withheld from decisive articulations of that coincidence. To be more precise, he identifies what is withheld as the soul, which is promptly rendered as the life power of will, and thus returns the value of what is withheld to the meaning of Man, reintegrating it in the spiritualist system that has expressivity as its only value. "The Method of Nature" indicates Emerson's growing awareness that nature consists of more than the present, that it consists as well of what is withheld in all acts of presentation, and that Man is inadequate to what is withheld in the phenomenological dynamic. This awareness leads Emerson to assert the superficiality of individual thinking, or, put otherwise, his assertion of Man's superficiality indicates his changed understanding of nature. In the citation above, Emerson still views Man as the expressive, phenomenological power in nature, the will that articulates the presence of nature. But he indicates that power is settled in what is withheld from speech: settled, therefore, in nature understood as the dynamic of a revealing activity that withholds itself in the very act of self-revelation.

Emerson's antihumanism consists in his recognition that authentic will, through its very activity of articulating nature's presence, withholds from itself the full dimensionality and power of nature and thus locates itself in the fluctuations of what is withheld. It stems from his awareness that the conception of that which is withheld in the phenomenological act derives from the insight into Man's central power to presence nature. The humanist synthesis, while it remains intact, is thus rendered partial—lifted up and moved laterally across the surface of nature to stress again Emerson's imagery. This is to say, of course, that it is destroyed in its essence. Far from reversing his position Emerson thus adheres exactly to the imperatives of his early method by recognizing, and clarifying for his readers, the conclusion implicitly demanded by the early essays: that is, the appearance of nature as the gathering of self, other, and the world entails the decentering of Man and the predominance of nature, and with these it announces the withering away of the humanist project and thus de facto the failure of all universal interpretations of Being in favor of a theory of nature as onwardness emancipated even from the decisive closure of authentic human will. "The Method of Nature" is an effort to show nature as the fluctuating power of presencing thereby released.

Along with Man, the first casualty of Emerson's antihumanist turn is the authenticity of speech. Emerson identifies the finitude of the individual with speech, thus opposing speech to nature. This reflects the initiation of a crucial development in his understanding of language. Speech had consisted, in its highest form, of primordial utterances, the issuance of authentic individuality in language. It had not predicted the individual, as I noted in Chapter 2, but it emerged out of the authenticity of the individual and was a means of presentation for authentic being-in-the-world. But in Emerson's new conception of it, nature is withheld from articulation. It is a dictation that eludes manifestation, that loves to hide, as he will make clear in "Experience." The primordial utterance of latent convictions that in the early essays marks the essential act of the individual is now characterized as "new words" for an old and repeated thought. Of course, Emerson is not denying that such "new words" presence nature. Rather, he is indicating the superficiality and speciousness of natural presence. The present obscures nature, for nature is now identified as the dynamic of which presence is an aspect. Decisive speech thus merely plays laterally on the surface of nature.

Emerson's new position refutes the central assertion of the "Spirit" section of *Nature*, the belief that the ascent to spirit through the dialectical steps of thought recognizes the omnipotence of individual will, that it answers the question of the whence and whereto of nature by indicating Man. Out of his new insight Emerson dismisses the individual's capacity to evaluate himself and nature: "It is true, he pretends to give account of himself to himself, but, at the last, what has he to recite but the fact that there is a Life" (*CW* 1:127). Emerson privileges without qualification the receptive capacity of the individual and the discontinuity of nature, rejecting as overstatement the turn through action to the recognition of Man and the continuous presence of nature: "There is the incoming or the receding of God: that is all we can affirm; and we can show neither how nor why" (*CW* 1:127). To be sure, Man remains the principal fact and the greatest phenomenon of nature, the terminal where nature is manifest, but it is no longer the depth and purpose of nature. Man remains the eyes of nature; but now decentered and partial, Man is a passive monitor: "He cannot read, he cannot think, he cannot look, but unites the hitherto separated strands into a perfect cord" (*CW* 1:128–29). Emerson views Man as a function of nature, a facet brought into existence to manifest nature's presence. Whereas action was essential to the humanist synthesis, there is nothing now for the individual to do but play the role assigned by nature. Rather than "affirm the power of the inspired will to re*make* the self and the world," as Whicher writes, Emerson now asserts—revising, it should be noted, his founding description of self-reliance as "not confident but agent"—that Man "is strong not to do, but to live; not in his arms, but in his heart; not as an *agent*, but as a fact" (*CW* 1:128, emphasis added).[8]

The turn from humanism can be further explained as Emerson's recognition that the process of willing, the labor of making, or production, can be viewed in two ways: either from within the activity of production, according to which, will acts *for the sake of* its product, and the unity of the product reflects the integrity and substantiality of will itself, or, as it were, from beyond the activity of producing—outside the paradigm of thought as teleological action—in which case it manifests itself as an activity that is used up in what it does and is thus partial, unguaranteed, and relative. This explanation needn't be imposed on Emerson's writings or treated as speculative. He cast the turn away from humanism in precisely this way. Evidence for this is found in the difference he asserts in "The Method of Nature" between two irreconcilable perspectives on nature, which he identifies as the platform of action and the platform of intellection. The "morals of self-denial and strife with sin," he says, "are in the view we are constrained by our constitution to take of the fact seen from the platform of action; but seen from the platform of intellection, there is nothing for us but praise and wonder" (*CW* 1:127). The importance of the distinction Emerson draws here, a distinction unprecedented by his early writings, where thought is construed on the model of human action, and arguably unprecedented in the metaphysical tradition, where thought is also construed on the model of human action, cannot be overstated. It inaugurates Emerson's mature theory; it carves off and renders superficial the performative ethics that Cavell most recently has demonstrated is at the core of Emerson's idea of self-reliance.[9] And accordingly, it provides a statement of the theoretical framework within which Emerson asserts the superficiality of Man. Emerson does not simply take the position that it is faulty logic to infer the substantiality of will from its effects. Rather, he makes the much more interesting observation that it is legitimate to do so only from one perspective, the platform of action. Only when we construe nature from the perspective of action—ac-

---

8. Whicher, *Selections from Ralph Waldo Emerson*, 179.
9. Cavell's insistence that a performative model of individuality is the common theoretical foundation of Emerson's works from "Self-Reliance" to "Fate" appears, therefore, to be explicitly at odds with the distinction Emerson draws in this lecture.

cording to a theory of action or by general analogy to action—is its activity properly teleological. Only then does the resolution of activity in a thing reflect the identity of the individual and thus institute the oppositions and goals that set in play value systems of accountability and responsibility—of purposiveness—both for the individual and nature. From the perspective of "intellection," nature is not constrained to the purposiveness of teleological action or limited to the final purpose of presence. The method of nature thus institutes a *moral reversal* of the process of nature's appearing, or of unconcealment. When viewed from the platform of action, this process occurs for the sake of what is brought to presence and thus assumes the operation of Man and will throughout the process, indeed, as the process. The platform of intellection, however, turns the temporality of unconcealment away from the moral articulation of presence as the final cause of nature and views nature as the movement of presencing in general, the flux of coming to and passing from presence. The result of this change in perspective is to overcome the teleological direction that the paradigm of thought-as-action imposes on the process of unconcealment and to recognize every presence of nature as equivocal, an appearance that implicates the withdrawal of nature. Nature emerges under this explanation as a force or power that speech invariably fails to articulate and that therefore remains concealed behind all articulations.

In the face of these two ways of looking at the primary fact of nature—Man or human will—Emerson was led to reconsider, just as he said, the topics of Man and nature. The change in thought evident in the statement above from "The Method of Nature" can be dramatized by asking what it would mean to think, to frame a manner of thought, distinct from the paradigm of human action, and thus distinct from the structure of teleology. It is in the context of this question, as an answer to this question, that Man appears as a relative and superficial phenomenon. Moreover, the question posed by the platform of intellection demands a reconception of nature outside of the constraining ethos of purposiveness inherent in the teleological structure. From the perspective of intellection, as Emerson understands it, nature is released from the temporality of human producing, to its own temporality. It "stands next" as the temporal flow of coming to presence. What this suggests, when put in phenomenological terms, is that presence itself is indefinite, that instead of being that for the sake of which nature is, presence is an aspect of nature's broader dynamic, a dynamic of appearing that is less a matter of unconcealing a true fact than it is a matter of un-closing the constraints placed on nature and thus dis-closing it. From the perspective of intellection, Emerson construes nature's disclosure, not as the self-evident fact of presence, of the "transparent eyeball," for instance, but as the essentially irresolute process of coming to presence, presence, and passing from presence. On the basis of the discernment of two possible ways of viewing the activity and effect of will in nature, and thus more broadly the activity and effect of human being, Emerson sets aside his faith in the power of will to draw nature within its horizon, in a sheer act of presence, and replaces it with the conception of nature as a dynamic, in which the presence of Man is disposed and secondary.

In general, then, Emerson's shift away from the primacy of Man derives from his recognition that thought and action are not reciprocal, as he had thought in his early period, that rather, thought and action represent two quite different ways of viewing and understanding the essential fact of human being in nature. Importantly, Emerson privileges the perspective of intellect, suggesting its greater eloquence for him, and holds it to be primary, whereas the active resolution of unified value he holds to be secondary, at least to the extent that he now refuses to credit any resolution of nature as definitive and instead places it under the sign of illusion. The change in approach inaugurated in "The Method of Nature" constitutes, then, only an adjustment of the intuition that motivated his early writings, but it is an adjustment that turns the emphasis in Emerson's early writings upside down. He reinterprets the metaphysical *dialectic* of revelation and concealment as an incessant *dynamic* in which every revelation of nature conceals nature as well, and in which the two moments of the dynamic refuse to be simply opposed to each other but are a part of the same process: the self-subversive phenomenological activity of will. There may be tentativeness and even confusion in "The Method of Nature," but if so, it is a tentativeness about how to deploy anew the images and figures of earlier essays, and it is the confusion that results from a profound unsettling of held beliefs. As such, the text dramatizes Emerson's turn from his early thought, and in at least one respect, the drama is complete.

It is essential to recognize that the decisive effect of the lecture is the critique of Man, for Emerson's work for the next two decades depends on it. In the above citation Emerson asserts in no uncertain terms that the depth and causality of the individual in nature is no longer: Man does not stand. The upright posture no longer defines the individual, and the individual's health must be reconceived. The boy's active eye, the innocence of which passed judgment on the world, is reduced to the terms of reception that Emerson finds in Zoroaster's statement: "If you incline your mind, you will apprehend it; not too earnestly, but bringing a pure and inquiring eye" (*CW* 1:132). Emerson's revaluation of the upright posture effects a renunciation of the method of Man, and the willfull presencing of nature thus gives way to the method of nature. Emerson wrote this lecture to identify nature, not Man, as the site of life and its universal term, and he says as much: "It seems to me, therefore, that it were some suitable paean, if we should piously celebrate this hour by exploring the *method of nature*. Let us see *that*" (*CW* 1:123).

Emerson's paean is to the nature that is not present, the nature given to Man's failed phenomenological centrality. To get at his new sense of nature it is useful to follow the lead provided by thinking through what nature's priority would be when developed out of this failure. It will consist, on the one hand, of presence or appearances. But it will also be thought in terms of what is not present. The hymn will not then praise the philosophical dialectic of presence and absence, which informs Emerson's early phase. In a metaphysical dialectic, absence has value as the negative potential for presence, and presence is given priority, precisely as that for the sake of which potentiality has a sense of Being. Emerson's revised conception of nature locates its principal value in neither presence nor what is not present, but in the dynamic of the play of *presencing*. Nature consists in the slippage of presence, the dynamic of the failure of Man's voice. It is conceived as a stream of appearances that lacks the capacity of the human voice to bring it to authentic presence, to resolution, and thus consists in the joyful play that precedes and is the condition for human articulations but that is at the same time the principle of the subversion of all human articulations. Nature is conceived, over and against Man's speech, as an irresolute succession, an essentially *silent* dynamic.

Emerson's elegant description of nature bespeaks the slippage implicit in the temporality of withholding and revealing, the slippage in language or in natural presence that always refers an appearance back to what is withheld, insinuating it into a cluster of relations and thus indicating that any presence is incomplete, is amid a larger constellation of forces that define the overall power of the gathering. It reflects Emerson's sense of the sovereignty and power of nature, as well as its inaccessibility for Man, and indicates his grasp of issues that continue to demand theoretical attention. Meaningful comparison can be made, for instance, to what Julia Kristeva in her critique of Lacan calls the "borderline" of language, "outside the transcendental enclosure within which we are otherwise constrained by phenomenology and its relative, linguistics."[10] The content of the method of nature put forward in 1841, nature understood as against Man, is the sheer flow of nature's unconcealment, which Emerson will describe in "Experience" as the stream of moods, and which he here depicts as the passing feelings of power. "How silent, how spacious," he writes of nature,

> what room for all, yet without place to insert an atom,—in graceful succession, in equal fulness, in balanced beauty, the dance of the hours goes forward still. Like an odor of incense, like a strain of music, like a sleep, it is inexact and boundless. It will not be dissected, nor unravelled, nor shown. Away profane philosopher! seekest thou in nature the cause? This refers to that, and that to the next, and the next to the third, and everything refers. Thou must ask in another mood. . . . Known it will not be, but gladly beloved and enjoyed. (*CW* 1:125)

This description of nature intersects with his revised conception of thought. Indeed, the description is as much of thought as nature. Accordingly, thought is no longer wed to the resolute acts of will, which place a stay on the succession of nature and thereby define its cause as precisely the limiting epoch of Man. Thought and nature are now given as a milieu that situates Man's power of articulation. In the final sentences above, Emerson anticipates the description of thought and nature that he will return to in "Experience." Thought and nature are given to feeling through the irresolution of moods. Thought and nature are *heard*, not spoken; are continuous, not discrete; are inexact, not conceptually clarified; are hidden, not revealed. "That well known voice speaks in all languages, governs all men, and none ever caught a glimpse of its form. If the man will exactly obey, it will adopt him. . . . If he listen with insatiable ears, richer and greater wisdom is taught him. . . . But if his eye is set on the things to be done, and not on the truth that is still taught . . . then the voice grows faint" (*CW* 1:130). The

---

10. Cited by Shuli Barzilai, "Borders of Language: Kristeva's Critique of Lacan," *PMLA* 106 (March 1991): 295. Kristeva's emphasis on borderline language as transgressively poetic is in the spirit of Emerson's view of the method of nature as the play of language related to and essentially transgressive and subversive of authentic speech, and suggests the extent to which Emerson's transitional period, characterized by *both* the release of nature and language from the humanist hold of will *and* Emerson's nostalgic linking of the method of nature to the subject, which maintains the subject deferred as the abstracted and largely empty principle of the inadequacy of all accounts of nature, *can* be apprehended through a psychoanalytic interpretation.

voice of nature does not speak from beyond the surface of appearances, from beyond language, as if from a metaphysical origin, but rather, he seems to say, it speaks from the borderline of language. That Emerson does not have in mind a metaphysical origin should be clear enough from his rebuke of those who would search for causes, and from his banishment of, not poets, but philosophers from nature's realm. No utterance captures nature's value; rather, each refers to something else; and in this dynamic of referral is found the silence and cunning, the metaphoricity that gives rise to the poetics of nature. Nature then does not consist in a hidden origin, or in the activity of a hidden origin becoming present, but in the ongoing incompleteness of presence. This recognition will lead Emerson in "Poetry and Imagination" to characterize nature in terms of metonymic displacements, and it is indeed a short distance from his assertions here to the later statement that "the value of a trope is that the hearer is one: and indeed Nature itself is a vast trope, and all particular natures are tropes" (*C* 8:20).

Emerson's new conception of nature is found in these statements, transforming nature into "second nature," or what is second in the metaphysical order of things (*CW* 3:13). Nature is appearance or presence made manifest through the work of the law, or the principle, which is to say, through the work of Man. If humanism ultimately realizes itself in the collapse of the distinction between the law and its expression, cause and work, then this explains much of Emerson's most perplexing language in the early essays, as for instance, his assertion in "Self-Reliance" that talk of reliance is a poor external way of speaking—poor and external because it implies a principle of reliance separate from its enactment. Speak rather of that which relies because it works and is, he says, indicating the meaning of Man: the identification of the law in, and as, the work of the individual. The law is the identity of the individual carried in every self-performance. Many of Emerson's readers accused him of merely immoral skepticism. But his early thought in fact develops and endorses the principle of practical self-identity and its attendant morality of accountability and responsibility; which is to say, it endorses the fundamental premise on which all humanist morals are finally based.

The reason for returning to this explanation of humanism now is not, however, to rehearse its moral implications but to recall that nature under the humanist scheme is a secondary phenomenon, a manifestation of the cause, the law, the work, of the individual, and to recognize that this is what Emerson means when he says nature is secondary. Thus, when he says Man is absent and nature stands next, he means it stands *in its secondariness*. The consequence of affirming the priority of nature as secondary, unanchored and equivocal, is to find nature in the sheer appearance of "the times," that is to say, the appearance of things separate from any explanatory construction, which would move synchronically from the passing of appearances to the "eternal." Emerson's second nature is not a metaphysical or esoteric reality; rather, it is a radical extension of the everyday reality he described in the early essays. It is "the times" as our lives open into them, prior to the clarifying work of active reason. Nature is the condition into which we are thrown, the milieu in which we find ourselves. It is our historicity evident as the immediacy of felt relations and possibilities that cannot be articulated through speech.

Second nature emerges in Emerson's thought at the point he realizes that reason cannot keep up with nature's onwardness, that the axis of vision cannot coincide with the axis of things, that active reason is always a matter of re-membering, of re-collecting nature and is barred therefore from an original relation to nature. Second nature consists in the "fast succeeding" thoughts that by degrees crowd out of the mind "the recollection of home" and that "obliterate" memory (*CW* 3:100). The terms of description may recall the early work, but in the early essays and lectures Emerson's criticism had been of retrospection, the tendency to follow convention in making our judgments. He had encouraged his listeners to replace that tendency with the reflective activity of reason. Reflection, he wrote in his journals of 1831, brings us face to face with God, because it actively gathers the conditions of one's experience. "Suicidal is this distrust of reason; this fear to think. ... To reflect is to receive truth immediately from God without any medium" (*JMN* 3:279). It renders reality. It settles us at home with our world. The remarks above, taken from the later essay "Nature," carry quite a different meaning. They dismiss the reflective activity that gathers and rounds out our reality, and in this respect they define a new sense of nature based on succession and irresolution: nature as a fleeting movement that resides nowhere, least of all in Man.

Emerson's second nature looks forward to the description of the staircase in the opening paragraph of "Experience" and backward to the description of the irresolution of nature in "The Method of Nature." However, it receives its clearest and, from the perspective of twentieth century thought, most prescient description in "The Poet," where it is characterized as language distinct from speech, a written text or system of signification neither natural nor arbitrary, but operating in the middle ground where it is determinant yet unceasingly figurative.

Emerson renews his call for an American poet but now sees in this the call for a speaker of his new yet unapproachable America, the America of "the times," of everyday reality that eludes, precisely, our speech.

"The Poet" provides a useful vocabulary for treating nature as the law. Emerson's seemingly romantic and somewhat inexact conceptions of the poetic capacity in fact predict recent attacks on logocentrism and specifically Derrida's distinction between speech and writing as figures of the medium of nature. The heart of Emerson's description begins early in the essay, when he writes, "The Universe has three children, born at one time, which reappear, under different names, in every system of thought, whether they be called cause, operation, and effect; or, more poetically, Jove, Pluto, Neptune; or, theologically, the Father, the Spirit, and the Son; but which we will call here, the Knower, the Doer, and the Sayer" (*CW* 3:5). One hardly needs a Freudian model to recognize the essential role of each figure in the process of thought. And as I have said, Emerson's identification of the poet as the sayer follows a long tradition in which the poet is viewed as articulating the law of the Father and thus reinstituting the Father. If on a first look Emerson's formulation is novel in any respect it is in his concise and compelling representation of this triplicity as fundamental not only to mythological accounts but also to logical accounts, not only to poetry but also to science. Emerson challenges his readers to speak whatever language they wish: logical, poetic, theological, or, as it were, Emersonian. No matter what discourse one chooses, Emerson says, thought has traditionally been construed to operate through such a threefold relation. The exhaustive scope he gives to the triplicity sets up the argument he will make for the meaning of the poet and the value of second nature.

In the paragraph that follows, having identified the poet as "the sayer, the namer," and certainly having thereby assured many readers that his position will fall well within the terms of a quasi-theological and overtly romantic humanism, Emerson proceeds to overturn the values he has set in place. "The poet does not wait for the hero or the sage," he writes; which is to say, the poet does not wait on the Doer or the Knower, the Spirit or the Father, the operation or the cause. Rather, "as they act and think primarily, so he *writes* primarily what will and must be spoken" (*CW* 3:5). The poet—the expressive capacity, the son, the effect—Emerson says, precedes its cause. And it precedes it as a written text of what must be spoken. Decisively, second nature is not identified with speech or what is spoken. Rather, it is the poet's writings that provide the condition for acting and thinking, the conditions for speech, the conditions for reason's activity. Should there be any doubt in the reader's mind, Emerson draws the conclusion: The poet "reckon[s] the others, though primaries also, yet, in respect to him, secondaries and servants" (*CW* 3:5). Emerson's poet emerges as the poetic and logical effect that precedes its cause, the theological son that precedes its father, the saying-that-is-writing that is never spoken, that precedes speech. Nature understood as the manifestation of the fact of the individual, the unconcealment of the individual's character, is exploded by this revaluation of the archetypes of Western onto-theology, and second nature takes shape as the irresolute and unapproachable dance formed by the antihumanist temporality of manifestation and withdrawal, or, as Emerson puts it, by the "admirable reserve and prudence of time" (*CW* 3:103).[11]

Apart from noting Emerson's exacting critique of the humanist tradition that under the label of logocentrism has received a more thorough attack in this century, and thus apart from wishing again to insist on Emerson's voice in the dialogue of Western metaphysical thought and its closure, I want to take advantage of his implicit depiction of second nature as written language, rather than as the speech that enacts humanist value in his early period, to get at the meaning he attributes to the method of nature. As the condition, the language structure, that predicts all possible experience, Emerson conceives of nature as both figural and historical. In the next chapter I shall show that "Experience" is developed around the premise of illusion at the source of all experience. What I wish to emphasize here is the historicity of second nature, its identity with what Emerson calls "the times," and thus his identification of the individual's historicity, call it his character, as met-

---

11. Emerson's argument anticipates Derrida's treatment of the relation of the Father and the Son in the logocentric tradition in "Plato's Pharmacy," and his "second nature" recalls Plato's description in *Timaeus* (52b, c) of the "third nature," which Derrida identifies with the text that precedes the dynamic opposition of the Father and *logos* ("Plato's Pharmacy," *Dissemination* [Chicago: University of Chicago Press, 1981], 160ff). Moreover, the imagery of the opening paragraph of "Experience" compares well with Plato's description and indicates, as I will show in the next chapter, that Emerson takes nature to be fundamentally illusory, situating the affirmations of will in the dreamlike play of illusions. The comparison is appropriate, for Emerson here takes up the topic, identified in "The Method of Nature," of the character of necessity, or that aspect of nature/Being that precedes and conditions the metaphysics of presence and thus cannot consist in the certitude enabled by the opposition of the Father and Son, i.e., the relation that defines truth as unconcealment. For related discussions, see Jill Fritz-Piggott, "The Law of Adrastia: Emerson's 'Experience' and Plato's *Phaedrus*," *American Transcendental Quarterly* 1 (December 1987): 261–71; Joseph Kronick, "Emerson and the Question of Reading/Writing," *Genre* 14 (Fall 1981): 368; and, for a contrary assessment, David L. Smith, "Emerson and Deconstruction: The End(s) of Scholarship," *Soundings* 67 (Winter 1984): 393ff.

aphorical or poetic—borderline—in structure and unavailable for univocal presentation. The conditioning constitution of human existence is thus enlarged beyond the epoch of Man, not, surely, as a positivist narrative of the past, which, as Emerson shows in "History," hardly exceeds the epoch of Man, but as the illegible inscription of the immediate world in which we find ourselves. "The times" consist in this inscription, the phenomenal language that rises to us from ahead as an unread script defining our possibilities. It comes to us as a fabric of relations that do not answer to our conceptions. If Emerson writes, "so persons are the world to persons," he also says this is "a cunning mystery" (*CW* 1:169). He means, I take it, that the texture of our world leads infinitely beyond our capacity to render it in causal explanations. It is the cunning superficiality, the cunning empiricism, of society and otherness that, rather than anchor value in our world, acts as the vanishing condition of self-articulation. Far from a world elsewhere, second nature is the immediate, ordinary world in which we find ourselves. But absent Man, it is this world absent the structure of the causal temporality of active reason. As long as nature, the appearing of the world, is structured on the model of causal action—the temporality of the movement from cause to effect, Father to Son—it gives itself to active reason, and the task of thinking is first and foremost to recognize the sovereignty and the claims of Man. Emerson's second nature, however, reflects a different temporal structure. It operates according to the fluctuations of coincident revelation and concealment. When Emerson writes that "poetry was all written before time was," he does not mean poetry speaks *eternal* truths, but rather that it consists in the text of immediate relations that resist presentation under the structure of active reason (*CW* 3:5). Poetry is written out of the "deeps of infinite time," he says, referring I take it to the ungraspable fluctuations of the here and now (*CW* 3:14). Poetry writes the "text in nature" as an effective scripture, evident in the joy felt in the relations with the ungraspable otherness of nature. Second nature consists in the play of withdrawal in everyday events, what Emerson will call succession and will describe as the impossibility of finding an anchor in the immediate world around us. Again, however, Emerson's revision of nature does not displace it from the immediate context or appearance in which we find ourselves—the everyday, finite world. Rather, it consists in the world's unwillingness to give itself up to its own presence or to the temporality of labor. The cunning of nature is the latent metaphoricity described by Emerson's "certain poet," the text given "wings" that fly from the *obfuscation and obstruction* of active reason's utterances

(*CW* 3:14). The poet characterizes second nature less as history or language, than as the historicity of difference, the condition of ordinary life's equivocations.

Emerson receives his insight into the metaphoricity of nature with a good deal of dissatisfaction and pessimism. In "Experience," he calls it the most unhandsome aspect of our existence, punning, as Stanley Cavell has noted, on his own figural equation of reason with the activity of the hand that manifests nature. In "The Poet" he simply concludes there are no poets. "We do not, with sufficient plainness, or sufficient profoundness, address ourselves to life, nor dare we chaunt our own times and social circumstance" (*CW* 3:21). The juxtaposition of plainness and profoundness indicates the poet Emerson calls for, as well as the difficulty of finding such a poet. He would be a speaker of "the times" that are lost in speech; he would sing nature's *aesthetics of disappearance*. "The path of things is silent," Emerson writes. And thus he rightly asks, "Will they suffer a speaker to go with them?" (*CW* 3:15). Emerson's answer predicts the direction his thought will take. A poet is possible, but "the condition of true naming, on the poet's part, is his resigning himself to the divine *aura* which breathes through forms, and accompanying that" (*CW* 3:15). The doctrine of fate will develop the idea of freedom and conduct in terms of the resignation he here calls for in the poet, and will recognize freedom in release to "the times." However, in this essay, and in the essays of this series, although Emerson can imagine what such a poet would be, he cannot yet formulate his "conduct." All conduct, all right action, he says, is lost to the recollective belatedness of active reason. Resignation then carries the sense of passivity here. And the essays of this period are characterized by the call for patience and passivity in the face of nature.

Emerson dramatizes this role in a remarkable dialogue near the end of "The Transcendentalist" between the world and the transcendentalist, in which the ascendant type of the speculator defends its inaction to the world.

> "New, we confess, and by no means happy, is our condition: if you want the aid of our labor, we ourselves stand in greater want of the labor. We are miserable with inaction. We perish of rest and rust. But we do not like your work."
>
> "Then," says the world, "show me your own."
>
> "We have none."
>
> "What will you do, then?" cries the world.
>
> "We will wait."

> "How long?"
> "Until the Universe rises up and calls us to work."
> "But whilst you wait, you grow old and useless."
> "Be it so: I can sit in a corner and *perish*, (as you call it,) but I will not move until I have the highest command. If no call should come for years, for centuries, then I know that the want of the Universe is the attestation of faith by this my abstinence.... Cannot we screw our courage to patience and truth." (*CW* 1:212)

As I suggested, this capacity will eventually be rendered again a mode of conduct, and indeed, the two types of transcendentalist Emerson describes, the actor and the student, will return under the doctrine of fate as the two modes of freedom. But at this point, the shift in Emerson's thought has unmasked as specious the activity of personal overcoming, of constant newness through individual labor, and has undercut even the transcendentalist's labor, leaving right action as its negation: patience.

"The Method of Nature" and the transitional works that follow from it depend on the conception of nature as a self-withdrawing dynamic, where revelation is aligned with the activity of reason and thus always bears in it the withdrawal and subversion of nature's presence. No action can be authorized. Under the doctrine of fate, Emerson will draw a distinction between fate and nature that he does not yet recognize. And on the grounds of this distinction he will legitimate a form of fatal conduct, a positive role for the individual. Indeed, he will describe "the timely man" he calls for in "The Poet," the man who would so "[fill] the day with bravery" that he would not "shrink from celebrating it," the individual whose actions would speak the fluctuations of his times (*CW* 3:21). But at this point Emerson's recognition of the metaphoricity of nature is debilitating, a fact reflected in his failure to distinguish fate from nature. Fate here has the meaning simply of the self-subversiveness of nature. It is written into the dynamic of presencing as nature's self-withdrawal, or the fatal inadequacy of reason to nature, its inadequacy to the fatal, constitutional presencing of nature. Eventually Emerson will conceive of nature as what we can do, what it is fatally given us to do, and will describe the positive conduct of the individual as both the affirmation of our fate and preparation to receive it. But here he conceives of nature as exactly what we cannot any longer *do*. The distinction will represent a reconception and revaluation of the method of nature that will transform it into the doctrine of fate and mark a decisive difference between, for instance, "Experience" and

"Fate." The meaning of the shift cannot, however, be clarified abstractly, by which I mean to say Emerson's reconfiguration of the method of nature has significance only in terms of how we live, what practice we actually bring to our everyday existence. Dismissed in 1841 is the practice of rationally clarifying our world through decisive action. In 1860 Emerson will embrace a new conception of fatal practice, or fatal conduct. During this transitional period, however—and characterizing the transitional period—he suffers under the conviction that no practice can be justified and thus forms the imperative of human existence, not around the activity of self-recovery, of finding as founding, but on the nonactivity of resignation and patience. The only positive value found here is that of being a sign, and it is as a sign that Man endures in Emerson's work. "A great man will be content to have indicated in any the slightest manner his perception of the reigning idea of his time" (*CW* 1:212). And so Emerson's transitional posture is one of sitting, Cratylus-like, as sign of "the times." In "Experience" he indicates most brilliantly the sponsoring ideas of his times. Precisely as such, however, the lords of life represent poetic suggestions that recede into the cunning metaphoricity of nature, their whence and whereto that Emerson will increasingly realize is not.

4

Experience Joy or Power

"Where do we find ourselves?" Emerson asks in the famous opening paragraph of "Experience" (*CW* 3:27). During his humanist phase, as I have shown, such a question would have been unnecessary: the individual stood at the center of nature, the horizon of its eye establishing nature's circumference, and to that extent the individual was manifest in every appearance of nature. But Emerson's turn from the humanist synthesis in the transitional lectures of 1841–42 upsets the organization of nature, making the individual's status and location a problem. I have articulated the problem in terms of the individual's inadequacy to nature and the superficiality of human presentations. The critique given in "The Method of Nature" cuts presence itself off from nature. Instead of being revealed through labor (and thus as essentially human), nature is understood in terms of concealment, as the power hidden behind superficial manifestations made present by human action. Nature comes to refer to the cunning dynamic of concealing and revealing, the liminal dynamic of coming to and passing from presence. In such a fluxional scheme, willful manifestations, though the sole means of presencing nature, are only moments, and more importantly, secondary moments. Human will lacks the power to dictate nature's authentic presence, for the field of presence itself has for Emerson lost authenticity. The will's presentations thus miss nature and remain superficial phenomena, floating on the surface of nature.

It is in the context of this altered conception of nature and Man that

Emerson asks and answers the question at the beginning of "Experience." The opening paragraph of the essay dramatizes the finitude of Man's situation in nature as the means of nature's appearance, thus emphasizing the individual's attempt to clarify nature from wherever he finds himself. Now situated in nature, the individual essays to see it. "Experience" follows sensibly out of the transitional lectures as Emerson's attempt to perform the work left to human being: to be the ambiguous figure of reversibility who overlooks nature and sees its "reigning idea" as it manifests itself in 1844, who looks on both the principles of the times and their finitude, and who looks on then and presences nature's self-concealment. In "Experience" Emerson takes the single role left for the transcendentalist: the role of indicator. When he asks where we find ourselves, he indicates the beginning of research into and an attempt to expose, as much as it is possible to do so, the situation of Man in the method of nature. He answers the opening question of the essay by locating the individual in a milieu defined by our finite and faltering vision:

> We wake and find ourselves on a stair: there are stairs below us, which we seem to have ascended; there are stairs above us, many a one, which go upward and out of sight. But the Genius which, according to the old belief, stands at the door by which we enter, and gives us the lethe to drink, that we may tell no tales, mixed the cup too strongly, and we cannot shake off the lethargy now at noonday. Sleep lingers all our lifetime about our eyes, as night hovers all day in the boughs of the fir-tree. All things swim and glimmer. Our life is not so much threatened as our perception. (*CW* 3:27)

Two sets of imagery intersect in this description of the milieu in which we find ourselves. The stair undoubtedly represents the discontinuous but unalterable succession in nature described in "The Method of Nature." The second imagistic cluster in the description is governed by the imagery of sight and blindness, given in conjunction with the figure of lethe—forgetfulness, or, as Emerson here uses it, the forgetfulness of sleep that blinds or conceals. Emerson has used the figure of lethe in conjunction with sight before. Toward the end of "Circles" he writes that we seek the forgetfulness that enables phenomenological resolution, the acknowledgment of the self and the enownment of nature within the horizon of the eye (*CW* 2:190). Here, however, the forgetfulness brought on by lethe clearly does not have the same value. Forgetfulness is now thrust upon us as a fatal reality. It does not initiate the dawn, establishing the omnipotence of the individual, but instead lingers at noonday. Rather than serve to set in relief the presence of nature through our actions, forgetfulness is mixed up in presence itself, in the experience of sight. Thus we find ourselves, not as the resolution of our vision but implicated in an indeterminate succession. Behind us on the stairway things pass from sight; ahead of us things seem to be coming to presence. And crucially, here where we are, things "swim and glimmer." It is presence that is troubled, our constructive perception that is threatened. The moment of crystalline transparency that describes transcendence and virtue in the humanist phase is lost to the insinuation of forgetfulness into presence. Whereas in the earlier essay forgetfulness enabled us to draw a new circle around nature, establishing the epoch in which presence is manifest and thus effecting the continuity of presence as the ecstasy of the individual, here fatal lethe robs us of clear perception and thus robs us of (self-) certainty.

There is no surprise then that Emerson writes "Experience," not as a "motto" for Kantian epistemology, but under the sign of Heraclitus's well-known assertion that nature loves to hide.[1] In Emerson's modern rephrasing of it, "Nature does not like to be observed" (*CW* 3:29). This is the fundamental truth of experience as Emerson understands it in 1844 and is the model for the rest of the essay. Indeed, experience replaces nature as the object of Emerson's inquiry because nature doesn't give itself to consciousness, and the world therefore lacks adequate presence: "Direct strokes [nature] never gave us power to make; all our blows glance, all our hits are accidents" (*CW* 3:30). Nature occurs as a fluid, hiding and coming to appearance but never as authen-

---

1. Cavell offers the Kantian comparison in *This New Yet Unapproachable America*, writing of the lines in which Emerson paraphrases Heraclitus, "here is another motto, in an Emersonian master-tone, for the *Critique of Pure Reason*, where perceptions, or say observations, without concepts are blind" ("Finding as Founding," 110). Cavell's identification of a Kantian comparison, and his effective suppression of the Heraclitean allusion, is significant because it preserves, for Cavell and for his inheritance of Emerson, a Kantian capacity for conceptual clarity that Emerson is here dismissing. This intention is clearer perhaps in Cavell's gloss of the opening paragraph of "Experience": "This is for me an image not alone of *the resolution in each step of a journey* and in each term of a series or of an expansive concept, but of the condition of a certain sociality or congeniality—a circulation—that seems to me distrusted and denied in deconstruction" (*This New Yet Unapproachable America*, 23, emphasis added). What is specifically not taken into account in this statement is Emerson's assertion that even here where we are on the staircase, here at the moment of presence, things "swim and glimmer." Cavell typically overlooks Emerson's turn from humanism and, as in this statement, indicates thereby his allegiance to a late, and admittedly radical, form of romantic humanism, which is more appropriate to Emerson's early synthesis than to his transitional works. See also Goodman, *American Philosophy and the Romantic Tradition*, 42.

tically present. Our perception does not achieve the univocity described in the early writings. All things show their dissolution; presence shows its default.

The opening lines of "Experience" indicate that Emerson has identified the "reigning idea" of his times as the superficiality of human will in nature and therefore the necessary speciousness of presence. He writes "Experience" in order to articulate the principles of the times that follow from this leading idea. Primary among them, of course, is the fact that all our experience is unrooted, cut off from the depth and certitude of nature. Our condition, the phenomenological experience of human being—and Emerson at no point questions that human experience is thematized phenomenologically—is situated in the field of passing appearances, the presence of which carries no authority in nature. Accordingly, first among the principles of experience is *Illusion*.

Illusion replaces sight or presence as the object of thought. In the early humanist essay, "Intellect," Emerson conceived of the power of thought as the capacity of spontaneous action that enabled the transparent presence of truth. The tension in the early works between reception and action is probably nowhere more apparent than in "Intellect," where Emerson writes of intellection both that "our spontaneous action is always the best" and "our thinking is a pious reception" (*CW* 2:195). As I showed in Part I, the reconciliation of reception and action under the idea of abandonment allows for the clarification of the world available to active intellect. "We only open our senses," Emerson had written, "clear away, as we can, all obstruction from the fact, and suffer the intellect to see" (*CW* 2:195). The turn in Emerson's thought in 1841 has, however, wrenched apart the reconciliation of thought and will that intellectual sight implies. It has divorced intellect from the resolution of action and forced a reconsideration of the object of thought, which is evident in Emerson's isolation of Illusion as the first of the lords of life. It is evident, as well, in his evocation of Heraclitus's fragment.

"Experience" is not the first essay in which Emerson has evoked Heraclitus. He refers to him at the beginning of "Intellect," as well, and his decision to call him up again suggests a conscious attempt to revise what he had said about intellect and thought in the early essay. In "Intellect" he had written, "Heraclitus looked upon the affections as dense and colored mists. In the fog of good and evil affections, it is hard for man to walk forward in a straight line. Intellect is void of affection" (*CW* 2:193). The power of intellect, this early statement indicates, is opposed to the teaching of Heraclitus, or, in any case, intellect is viewed as being mitigated by the play of feelings. Typically, it is simply cast in opposition to the subjection of thought under the coloring mists of affections, as is clear from Emerson's characterization of intellect as being "in the light of science, cool and disengaged" (*CW* 2:193). The use of Heraclitus in "Experience" principally reflects Emerson's embrace of Heraclitus's view that thought is sullied by "dense and colored mists." Heraclitus's imagery relates most significantly to the central role of moods in intellection, and I will return to it when I discuss Temperament below. But for now I want to emphasize Emerson's turn from the conception of intellect as the capacity to see clearly, to walk a straight line. Thought rather receives nature as the irresolute succession described in "The Method of Nature," and it thus receives nature as illusions.

Emerson builds "Experience" from his insight into Illusion as the leading idea of the times and as the first of the lords of life. In order to clarify the essay, however, it is important to emphasize that Illusion is not merely first of the principles of the times given in the essay, but also and more importantly, it is first logically; it is the principle that guides the other lords of life. Still, as the first principle of experience in the latter sense, Illusion nonetheless does not name a foundation of experience or a principle of its depth. Indeed, it acts in just the opposite way, and derives its logical priority from doing so. Illusion refutes the depth of *any* of the lords of life, determining all of them as superficial. It names the phenomenological difference indicated in every appearance by the dynamic of presence and coming to presence, the difference between what nature gives and what nature always refuses to give to sight. Put otherwise, it names the fact that nature always refuses to give itself to sight, and thus any appearance lacks depth and authenticity. Illusion is the principle of the times that contains the idea of nature's withholding itself as essential to every manifestation. No principle of experience, thus no experience, will move outside of the reigning idea of illusoriness, which is no more than to say that all experience is successive, consisting of appearances that dissolve in an enactment of nature's withdrawal.

However, as I noted in Chapter 3 and alluded to above, Emerson recognizes two fundamentally opposed perspectives in nature, the platform of intellection and the platform of action. And he distinguishes the posture appropriate to human beings according to them: the attitude of reception or of action, of wonder or of ethical teleology (see *CW* 1:127). In a moment I will show how "Experience" is organized around the opposition of thought and will, and will show that Illusion is clearly the primary lord of life *for* thought, just as, for instance, Reality is the first lord of life for will, or from the perspective of action. But before doing so I want to address what would appear to be the reasonable assumption that if so, that is, if Illusion is a lord of life only for thought, then it cannot rightly be said to condition all of the lords of life. Emerson, after all, writes at the end of the essay that the lords of life are sovereign and equal: "Illusion, Temperament, Succession, Surface, Surprise, Reality, Subjectiveness,—these are threads on the loom of time, these are the lords of life. I dare not assume to give their order, but I name them as I find them in my way" (*CW* 3:47). One might reasonably assume that Illusion is one among the lords of life and no more. In one respect this is true: Illusion can be posed as the opposite of Reality. But attention to Emerson's work since 1841 indicates that the times themselves, time itself, is settled in the flux of nature's hiding, in the milieu of the world as giving illusions. It is precisely this fact, the fact of nature's illusoriness, that disallows any ranking and hierarchy of the lords of life. The precedence I am suggesting be given to Illusion can thus be deduced from the contiguity and equality of the lords of life. It determines the epochalism and thus the superficiality of all of the lords of life, precisely inasmuch as it names the propensity of nature to withdraw itself. The perspective of will certainly has the power to give voice to nature's illusoriness—though not in a philosophically adequate way. Insofar as it does it articulates and resolves nature in moments of presence. It does not, however, overrule nature's hiding. On the contrary, it is conditioned by the withholding/revealing dynamic of nature, which gives rise to its fundamental illusoriness. Emerson's purpose in "Experience" is expositional; he seeks to expose the principles of the times. Such a task already indicates the finitude and epochalism of all principles and thus indicates the dynamic of withdrawal that underwrites the appearance of nature and predicts its illusoriness. Even the exposition in "Reality," in which Emerson seems to locate the depth of human existence in a binding will to unity, depends on nature's illusoriness. Illusion thus has the unique role among the lords of life of dictating the description of a world that lacks depth, a world founded on superficial principles that in turn reflect the reign of Illusion.

Thinking probably of the precedence of Illusion, Yoder rightly notes that there is in "Experience" "a sense of the old architecture ruined, of Emerson adjusting his art when he cannot drive down pilings," and that "no bare conclusion or frame can do justice to the texture of this work."[2] His conclusions seem to me especially convincing in respect to Emerson's sense of the sheer metaphoricity of language. But in regard to the philosophical content of the essay, the statements can be misleading, for it is possible to discern in the precedence given to Illusion a unified foundation in the essay and a coherent argument. It is, moreover, important to do so, not only to explain this stage in Emerson's philosophical development but also to preserve the awareness that his thought is developmental and follows a logic from *Nature* to the doctrine of fate. The method of nature, as I noted earlier, poses the most serious challenge to the integrity of philosophical discourse, and in order to maintain it, the organization of "Experience" around a discernible principle, the priority of Illusion, needs to be emphasized. Emerson's insistence on this principle indicates his allegiance to reason and his intention to provide not merely random descriptions of his experience but the highest account of experience available to him. His description offers two bare conclusions: the illusoriness of truth and the superficiality and exclusivity of the lords of life. And the structure of the essay follows in an exacting manner from these related conclusions, conclusions, it is important to note, that prohibit a dialectical reading of the essay. The structure of the essay reflects, instead, Emerson's discovery of the irreconcilable platforms of intellection and action. The perspective of thought yields the first three principles: Illusion, Temperament, and Succession; the perspective of action yields the second three: Surface, Surprise, and Reality. (For the time being I find it useful to leave Subjectivity out of the organization.) The transition from one platform to the other is, in fact, explicit in the essay. Following the discussion in "Succession," Emerson asks, "But what help from these fineries and pedantries? What help from thought?... Intellectual tasting of life will not supersede muscular activity" (*CW* 3:34). Obviously, he is not rejecting the three lords of life he has described. Rather, he means to differentiate the lords of life that typify the perspective of intellect and those that typify the perspective of will. Beginning with "Surface," Emerson describes the willful presencing of nature's desire to hide itself, the manifestation of nature's cunning. "Surface," "Surprise," and "Reality" describe the three principles that typify the effect of speech—the capacity to provide univocal expressions of nature's presence—when it is situated in the illusoriness of nature.

2. *Emerson and the Orphic Poet in America*, 44.

Isolating the structure of the essay in this manner allows me to approach the discussion of the first six lords of life through the terms of a question. Having identified the two groups of three principles, it is reasonable to ask what unifies the three, what the principle of each triplicity is. I have already said that the principle of all of the lords of life is Illusion, or nature's dislike of being observed. This essential doubleness is implicated in each description of a lord of life and primarily in the fact that each lord of life shows itself to be an epochal principle. Thus, insofar as each principle reveals nature, it reveals as well nature's slippage within any presentation. Within each triplicity, however, one of the lords of life seems to guide the other two and provide the terms for unifying the three as a group. It is clear from Emerson's statement, "The secret of the illusoriness is in the necessity of a succession of moods or objects," that although among the first three lords of life moods are emphasized, the three are unified under Illusion (*CW* 3:32). Thought is conditioned by affections, as Heraclitus had said, and thus there derives the necessity in thought of the principle of Illusion. Similarly, among the three principles of the second group, the description in "Reality" is emphasized inasmuch as it speaks the most powerful practical organization of nature and enables the appearance of Man. "Surface" and "Surprise" are linked to "Reality" as alternative and partial mediums of the appearance of Man, as practical power in the world or the presence of nature.

The distinction between the two triplicities could be summarized, then, by noting that the first, based on thought rather than will, does not broach the issue of the appearance of Man, but rather describes a world lacking presence and accordingly lacking the principle of individuality. The second triplicity, on the other hand, defined by the platform of will and action, describes the principles by which Man (and here as elsewhere Man is a trope for the humanist concept of unified, central individuality) appears in the world. Similarly, the illusoriness of thought describes a nonteleological relation and thus is opposed to "Reality," which describes the teleological relation that stands at the base of every representation of Being, inasmuch as the concept of Being depends, as Emerson had concluded in the early essays, on individual action, labor, work. The distinction beween thought and "muscular activity" thus depends on the basic relation assumed in the dynamic of nature. "Illusion" and "Reality" identify the two fundamental sorts of relation possible in nature: nonteleological and teleological. To the extent these lords of life are absolutely opposed, thought and action represent irreconcilable perspectives in nature, but insofar as both enter into the dynamic of nature's illusoriness, they are continuous and even converge: precisely, as alternate ways in which nature hides/reveals itself.

Identifying the structural features of "Experience" suggests how to proceed in a discussion of the essay. The first six lords of life will be discussed under the opposition of thought and will, or the opposition of the platforms of intellection and action. This opposition provides the guiding thread of my interpretation of the essay as a whole, on the assumption that Emerson's topic throughout the essay is the texture of inappropriable memory, the method of nature, and that experience consists in the apprehension of this texture first from the platform of intellection and then from the platform of action. The seventh lord of life, Subjectivity, which I have left out of the organization, brings the listing to a close.

THE PRINCIPLES OF INTELLECT

The overwhelming tone of the first section of "Experience" is of the loss of presence, the fact of Man in the world as fated to be out of touch with nature's presence, the sense of living in a world of things that are not present. It is this condition, "this evanescence and lubricity of all objects"—the fact that we cannot touch nature, or other people—that Emerson calls "the most unhandsome part of our condition" (*CW* 3:29). The dominant tone of the first three sections of "Experience" is that of lament, of the fall and failure of human being. Authenticity has no place in this world, and human being resides here in a condition of failed presence. The secret of illusoriness, nature's withholding of presence from thought, derives from the radical loss of the principle of permanence in nature. Emerson makes this clear in the statement from "Succession" partially cited above: "The secret of the illusoriness is in the necessity of a succession of moods or objects. Gladly we would anchor, but the anchorage is quicksand. This onward trick of nature is too strong for us: *Peri si mouve*. When, at night, I look at the moon and stars, I seem stationary, and they to hurry. Our love of the real draws us to permanence, but health of body consists in circulation, and sanity of mind in variety or facility of association. (*CW* 3:32).

Emerson's treatment of experience as versions of phenomenological temporality is reminiscent of Kant, but in a critical manner.[3] Kant's first analogy of experience is the principle essential to teleology, the notion of permanence in substance that binds together and unifies the appearance of nature, thereby giving it univocal value and progressive direction. Emerson's primary concern is to deny the fact of permanence in nature. Like the description of the method of nature cited in the last chapter, the above statement indicates that the Emersonian concept of Succession, or the form of thought's reception of nature, is not guided by a principle of permanence, is specifically opposed to the idea of permanence in nature, and, unlike the description in "Surface," cannot be construed as cause/effect relations.

If Emerson has Kant in mind, then it is to cast in doubt Kant's claim to have performed a "Copernican revolution" in thought. Indeed, the second half of the above citation strikingly evokes an astronomical metaphor, seeming to allude directly to Kant's description of his revolution. I have in mind the reference to Galileo's defiant remark, aimed as it was at the most powerful will-to-permanence of his times. Emerson situates himself in "Succession" just as defiantly against the love of permanence and suggests that *it* is our greatest illusion. Moreover, the remark sets in relief Kant's dependence on the category of permanence at the foundation of experience, showing that such dependence represents precisely a *refusal* of circulation, a refusal to embrace the implication of the comparison to Copernicus: that is, the moral displacement of Man from the static center of the universe. Far from effecting a revolution, Kant only moves laterally, changing his language but still maintaining the basic "Ptolemaic" centrality of Man in nature. Interestingly enough, a later pragmatist develops the very critique implicit in Emerson's remarks. In his Gifford Lectures of 1929, John Dewey arrives in explicit terms at this assessment of Kant's supposed revolution: "The endeavor to make the known world turn on the constitution of the knowing mind, seems like a return to an ultra-Ptolemaic system. . . . That the consequence was Ptolemaic rather than Copernican is not to be wondered at. In fact, the alleged revolution of Kant consisted in making explicit what was implicit in the classic tradition. . . . [Kant's] 'revolution' was a shift from a theological to a human authorship; beyond that point, it was an explicit acknowledgement of what philosophers in the classic line of descent had been doing unconsciously be-

---

3. See Cavell, "Thinking of Emerson," 126ff., for a discussion of the relation between this section of "Experience" and Kantian philosophy.

fore him."⁴ A true "Copernican" revolution would reject the humanist centrality of Man, and would do so in part by denying the centrality for thought of the category of permanence.

Clearly, Dewey's remarks could as well be directed at Emerson's early synthesis, and they serve the second purpose then of indicating the extent to which the argument of "Succession" critiques Emerson's own early humanist position. If Emerson's early essays complete the humanist project in more radical terms than Kant, inasmuch as his early theory already departs from Kant's adherence to a logical foundation of reason, there can be little doubt, and I urged this point in Chapter 1, that Emerson is working in his early writings, at least in broad terms, within the same tradition as Kant, and for that matter within the same humanist tradition that governs Western philosophical thought from Plato to Hegel. Like Kant, he finds permanence, unity, and purpose in nature, if not in the knowing mind then in the self-acknowledgment available to an individual who sheds the false order of normative and theoretical conventions and engages the spontaneity of art and thought to realize the phenomenological transcendence of the individual. Acts of intellect, choice, thus enable the individual to bring nature's flux around to unity. The argument of "Succession" reads as a direct repudiation of the humanist assumption that the individual provides the permanent substrate that gives unity and direction to the appearance of nature. It is reasonable to conclude that if the argument of "Succession" is aimed at Kant, then inasmuch as Emerson's early thought not only departed from Kant but also extended Kant's transcendental project, it is also aimed at Emerson's own early position. Simply, it takes aim at the fundamental presumption of humanism, the centrality and depth of Man in nature.

The dismissal of any principle of permanence, and especially the permanence of Man, shows that "Illusion" speaks to the fundamental question of ontology. Emerson does nothing less than expose the dissociation of the origin of presence from appearances and describe the subsequent reduction of appearances to counterfeit. The important point is that he does this in response to his early claim for the humanist origin of presence. The principle of his early thought, the desire and labor of Man, is drawn into the system of illusions, manifesting illusions through its lateral activity as repetitious surfaces. In order to grasp the meaning of "Illusion," it is necessary then to distinguish Succession

---

4. John Dewey, "The Copernican Revolution," in *The Quest for Certainty* (New York: G. P. Putnam & Sons, 1980), 287–88.

even from the counterfeit and repetition of appearances that describes nature's manifestation in "Surface." To be sure, "Illusion" and "Succession" prepare the way for the treatment of appearances as surfaces, but it should be kept in mind that the first three lords of life describe the principles of the times for intellect or thought, not as seen from the platform of will or Man. For that reason, Illusion does not refer directly to the manifestation of nature as the repetition of discrete surfaces. Resolution, however superficial, is a function of will. For thought, the flow of nature is continuous and unresolved, the occasion of joy but not power. Succession does not name the presence of one object after another in a series of appearances, a series that would imply an agency of resolution capable of detaching and naming each object. Succession instead names the flow of nature when it lacks such an agency—again, when it lacks the power of will. For this reason, Emerson aligns Succession with the dynamic flow of nature in "The Method of Nature" and repeats the idea again in the image of the stair at the beginning of "Experience." For thought, experience is not a sequence of resolute presences, but a flow that is as much of disappearing as it is of appearing, an undirected power, a string of passing feelings the experience of which is, precisely, like a dream. It is received by thought, listened to in its indeterminacy and boundlessness, not seen, resolved, or uttered. Only from the perspective of will or action is this flow resolved into the repetition of discrete surfaces.

Emerson's argument in "Succession" is, then, more radical than might at first be supposed. It denies the permanence of any appearance, to be sure, but it also, and more fundamentally, denies even the principle of permanence that allows for the authentic resolution of a discrete presence in nature. Succession implies circulation, an unending flow of nature unapprehended under the will of Man, and it thereby represents both an alternative and a compelling critique of the superficial perspective on life given through the will. The importance of the distinction rests in the suggestion it makes that the intellectual reception of nature cannot be redeemed from illusoriness. The feeling of loss that characterizes our experience of nature is not a contingent reality for Emerson, but rather is an abiding sense of reality. And the attempt to read progression in the order of the lords of life, from loss and illusion to self-recovery and reality, is futile, as the section on subjectivity will also make clear.

Emerson reflects this futility here through the celebrated remarks about his son's death. But if he uses his son's death to represent the "philosophical abyss" he has reached, then, as Yoder says, "intellect had prepared for this crisis, and perhaps it was Emerson's prior attention to appearances that made him write in 1843 that grief taught him nothing of reality."[5] What Yoder emphasizes is that Emerson's subject in "Experience" is the philosophical shift that occurs in "The Method of Nature" and not the psychological trauma of his son's death. His philosophical development resonates, much more, I would say, than the illustrative use of Waldo's death, in the structure and themes of "Experience." Especially in the first few pages of the essay Emerson characterizes the situation of the individual after the failure of the humanist principle that founded the early works. His characterization of the dissociation or disjunction, the sense of loss, at the core of our experience of life is less a psychological reaction than the result of a philosophical meditation that has its origins in the line of thought first explored in the lecture, delivered six months prior to Waldo's death.[6] Emerson's remarks on his grief at Waldo's death serve the themes of his emerging antihumanism, and I do not find in these remarks any assertion of the redemptive power of grief.

When Emerson writes, "Grief too will make us idealists," one should neither ignore nor exaggerate the limits of his reactions to tragedies and losses in his life (*CW* 3:29). He could just as well have written this statement after the death of his first wife, Ellen, which he also could not get close to himself. But he didn't. Instead, he went on to embrace the idea of spirit and its transformative method, an idea that *can* be aptly figured as the power of grief to initiate self-recovery. Important here, then, is what Emerson does not say about grief; he does not write that grief will make us *spiritualists*, that the sense of loss motivates the work of mourning. Rather, his remarks reflect his dismay at the impotence of

---

5. *Emerson and the Orphic Poet in America*, 43–44. Yoder's identification of Emerson's crisis as in part philosophical is untypical of Emerson criticism. The source of Emerson's crisis is usually located in grief over the son's death. Sharon Cameron is representative of critics from Whicher and Bishop to the present. In her subtle treatment of "Experience," she states flatly, "The grief occasioned by the death of the child is the essay's first cause" ("Representing Grief: Emerson's 'Experience,'" *Representations* 15 [Summer 1986]: 26).

6. David W. Hill adds textual support to my contention, writing, "the time at which various journal sources were written also calls into question oversimplified identifications of Emerson's initial grief at his son's death with the problematic nature of the essay. The 'Illusion' and 'Temperament' sections of 'Experience,' darker in tone than the rest, are the most highly synthetic, drawing material from almost all of the journals Emerson used between 1838 and 1844. . . . the history of the essay does not amount to a simple progression from grief in 1842 to attenuated hope in 1844. The essay taps in a complex way veins of feeling which stretch back to the journals of the 1820s" ("Emerson's Eumenides: Textual Evidence and the Interpretation of 'Experience,'" in *Emerson Centenary Essays*, ed. Joel Myerson, [Carbondale: Southern Illinois University Press, 1982], 111).

grief. Recalling his critique in *Nature* of the limits of idealism, its inadequacy to the whence and whereto, that is, the teleology, of nature, it is clear he means to say that grief will turn us to the illusoriness of nature, to the ideality and immateriality of nature that he here calls its lubricity, *unredeemed* by spirit. In his early work Emerson had conceived of grief as bringing us in contact with our essential self; it had thrust us up against the fact of our finitude and framed our existential condition in the world. Grief, dread, anguish, and fear are the terms of self-reliant freedom. Initially, it is to the "brink of fear" that the transparent eyeball extends, and, as James M. Cox says, it thus "displaces" fear.[7] Reality is rendered by the process of thought that in tracing our finitude, confronting the awesome sense of the world without God or external foundation, is turned back on itself to find in dread the terms of its power and joy. In the early writings, spirit emerges through the recognition of Man as the self-regenerative principle of permanence in nature, hardly a conceptual or logical construct for Emerson but, as in "Circles," an earned self-empowerment: enownment. But here in "Experience" Emerson explicitly denies that grief carries out the work of spirit. His remarks on his son's death figure, instead, a new thought, deeply at odds with a romantic thematization, a thought that is insinuated in the brink of fear: the abysmal thought of the brink itself.

The unsettling description of the "moods in which we court suffering, in the hope that here, at least, we shall find reality, sharp peaks and edges of truth," captures the sense of our disposition in the brink of fear (*CW* 3:29). We court consciousness of death, attempting to fix an account of the world upon the anchor of this fact, but its redemptive power eludes us. The world consists of the experience of objects, even the experience of death, that are not gifted with the depth, integrity, and originality that derives from an earned identity with the soul. "Souls never touch their objects," Emerson writes (*CW* 3:29). Our experience of the world is of objects that embody no life, hold no truth. Here is Emerson's vision of grief that does not touch us and thus robs us of the last fact and certitude, the last anchor in our existence: the redemption of pain's assurance that we are. "The only thing grief has taught me, is to know how shallow it is" (*CW* 3:29).

Emerson's remarks on grief are best taken as a critique, by which I mean he draws the limits of grief's activity and terminates them short of any capacity for self-regeneration. It is not the work of the self that any longer concerns Emerson, except in the negative sense of the limits of that work's efficacy. Indeed, Emerson now views attention to

---

7. "R. W. Emerson: The Circles of the Eye," 59.

the work of the self as an obstacle to thought, a texture of surface interpretations that positively veil nature and impede thought's reception of nature. The work of mourning, by which the sense of loss is turned to presence, when thematized through the self, or say consciousness, obscures nature precisely to the extent it presumes resolution; for as Emerson has recognized since 1841, nature does not give itself resolutely. Saying this should not be taken to suggest, however, that the work of mourning does not occur—or to state it more properly, that we cannot thematize the always interesting topic of Man's relation to nature in terms of the work of mourning. Rather, Emerson severs the work of mourning from individual self-consciousness and decisiveness. A passage from his 1842 journal speaks to this point, intimating the work that goes on unavailable to consciousness:

> When a friend has newly died, the survivor has not yet grief, but the expectation of grief. He has not long enough been deprived of his society to feel yet the want of it. He is surprized and is now under a certain intellectual excitement . . . this defends him from sorrow. It is not until the funeral procession has departed from his doors, and the mourners have all returned to their ordinary pursuits, & forgotten the deceased that the grief of the friend begins. In the midst of his work, in the midst of his leisure, in his thoughts which are now uncommunicated, in his successes which are now in vain, in his hopes which are now quickly checked & run low, he sees with bitterness how poor he is. As it is with the mourner so it is with the man of virtue in respect to the practice of virtue. The evil practice of the country & the time is exposed by some preacher of righteousness and after some time the land is filled with the noise of the reform. Men congratulate themselves on the great evil they have escaped and on the signal progress of society. But it is not until after this tumult is over, & all have, one after another, come into the new practice, & the reaction has occurred, and great numbers are disgusted & have gone back again, not until then, does the true reformer, the noble man, begin to find his virtue and advantage. Through the clamor he has said nothing,— he embraced the right which was shown, at once & forever. Now society is back again where it was before, but he has added this beauty to his life. (*JMN* 8:284)

The entry is important for a few reasons, but first of all because it indicates Emerson's view that what we do in reaction to loss, what we construe as *our* work of mourning, is superficial and formal. That is to say, it shows that Emerson viewed actual mourning as something that happens to us, not something we do, and, decidedly, as something we cannot take as our own. The parallel between this treatment of mourning and Emerson's general turn away from the capacity of Man to recognize his centrality in nature and own his world is clear enough, I think. Insofar as we thematize Man's power through the concept of mourning, we suggest a self-conscious capacity to grieve our losses and thereby turn them to gain. If this formulation of the matter echoes some of Emerson's early remarks on the opportunity to be found in loss, it ignores his revision of the work of mourning in an antihumanist direction.

Two more things can be said about the description in the journal. It indicates secondly that the work of mourning goes on, absent our consent or knowledge, at the interstices of our everyday actions. Mourning is written into the way we live our lives. The sense of loss does not, then, initiate a process of self-recovery that would lead to, precisely, the recovery of a univocal identity. Rather, the description suggests that the sense of loss is an abiding aspect of our reality, written into and in large measure defining the events of our life. When Emerson writes that grief will make us idealists, he does not deny the place of grief in our lives; he radicalizes it. He recognizes our condition as always invariably implicated in loss and mourning. Correspondingly, he defines nature now as hiding, withholding itself in its presentations, giving itself to us as already lost, as a feeling that defies our attempts to grasp it, as the powerful "tension between what is visible and invisible."[8] Such a representation of the work of mourning establishes it as an irredeemable quality of human existence and deposits Man's power within its conditions. From the vantage point of nature, the posture from which Man is, as Emerson calls himself in "Lectures on the Times," an indicator, a sign that points the way of nature, from the vantage point then that will later be identified as fate, humanistic interpretations and assertions of present value merely obscure nature's mournful activity—its dynamic dance of self-giving loss. Moreover, insofar as Emerson's enduring ethic is the disclosure of nature through thought, he is compelled to renounce Man's assertions and to seek a mode or manner of thought that manifests nature as it is, *things as they are*. Such thinking had been Man Thinking, but, as I have shown, Man Thinking presupposes the clarity and univocity of intellect and is thus inadequate to nature's dynamic. To think, Emerson now suggests, is to receive na-

---

8. Cameron, "Representing Grief," 40.

ture's irresolution and to tally the revealing/concealing dynamic, to figure what is lost into every account of nature's revelation. What is lost, principally, is the redemptive guarantee of the speaker behind the account. As "indicator," the speaker is exhausted in each account of the lords of life; he is lost, that is, to the eloquence of the statement. And the duty of the reader is to suffer that eloquence as a sign of the times, without presumptive recourse to the eternality of the self, to concede that the cost of reality is an expenditure of the self that runs beyond our accounting methods.[9] Toward what end then? Emerson dismisses the question as deriving from a "paltry empiricism," but I would suggest that the end he obeys is the path of eloquence itself, leading not to a speaker but to the power of statements.

The significance of Emerson's identification of moods as the medium of thought, and, by extension, of action, emerges in the context of this description of the content of thought. If thought in its essence consists in the inscription of loss in what is present, then its content is nature's turning, and it will not be manifest as a concept or an idea, but, as Emerson aptly suggests, as a mood.[10] Moods carry the continuity of life as the circulation of illusions: "Dream delivers us to dream, and there is no end to illusion. Life is a train of moods like a string of beads, and as we pass through them, they prove to be many-colored lenses which paint the world their own hue, and each shows only what lies in its focus" (*CW* 3:30). Moods are the vehicle of thought and the medium of nature's hiding. They determine both the withholding of presence from any object of thought and the limits of the possibility of moral resolution. We should understand by moods the irresolute medium of feeling that governs what we may attend to but refuses our ownership of it. Emerson evokes the sullying influence of affections that, for Heraclitus,

---

9. For a contrasting view see Gertrude Reif Hughes, who describes the position of the narrator or orator of "Experience" as a ventriloquist speaking through a dummy, and who warns against confusing the beliefs of the ventriloquist with the eloquence of the statements made by the dummy and of thus overlooking the redemptive "overtone" of the essay enabled by the speaker's endurance behind the dummy (*Emerson's Demanding Optimism*, 45ff.). Hughes curbs her remarks, however, when later she concludes: "But it is the right to speak that Emerson seems to be disclaiming, rather than the rightness of what is being spoken. . . . Emerson has moved from his position of speaker and ventriloquizer into the position of listener, [and] . . . enacts that he, no less than any member of his audience, is 'too young yet by some ages to compile a code' that will reveal order and unity where there now is lethe and fragmentation (*W*, III, 83). Meantime, Emerson can wait" (64)

10. For discussions of Emerson's philosophical use of moods, see Stanley Cavell, "An Emerson Mood," in *The Senses of Walden*, and Anthony Cascardi, "The Logic of Moods: An Essay on Emerson and Rousseau," *Studies in Romanticism*, 24 (Summer 1985): 223–37.

assures that nature remains hidden in every manifestation of itself. Moods determine what we can think and what we can see and assure that all thought and sight is mitigated by the sense of loss, by nature's withholding. They provide the succession of nature that our will can act on, can animate, and thus can know: "We animate what we can, and we see only what we animate" (*CW* 3:30). The "Surface" section of "Experience" will show, however, that when we do act on moods, we enter into a radically mechanistic causality that eludes the closure of knowledge, and the resolution of moods gives rise, then, to anarchic action that defies teleological accounts.

The change that occurs in Emerson's conception of the role of moods, from his early work to "Experience," affects their scope and status. Moods are now taken to be the *fundamental* medium of thought and experience—indeed the principle that defines the human condition as experiential rather than real—whereas in the early essays our creative will was fundamental and moods served will, returning the plurality of moods to the ecstasy of the individual. Emerson sought in the early essays to indicate the plurality of the world manifested by the creative will, and he included the flux of moods among the mediums of omnipotent will in order to reflect the nonrational content of the world. In "Experience" he reverses the priority, describing moods as preceding and situating the activity of will. We receive nature as feelings in accord with the metaphor of listening, rather than will's figure of sight. Moods then are not articulated as our perception; rather, they carry the power of nature's withholding and frame resolution in its self-refusal, thus determining both what we can see and the status of what we see. Emerson could have answered the opening question of the essay by saying that we find ourselves amid the flux of our moods, which we cannot control and order and which delimit our perception.

It is crucial that moods not be hypostatized. Moods come upon us, they take us; thinking consists in passing from one mood to the next. But moods have no depth; they name no principle of interiority. Moods, that is to say, are not the name of freedom and do not describe the infinite capacity to see an ever-richer world. Moods are the medium of our reception of nature, and that reception consists for the most part of repetitive illusions. Moods themselves may always arrive as seemingly new, but "Temperament," Emerson writes, "is the iron wire on which the beads are strung," and because rooted in Temperament, moods reveal themselves in the long run to be nearly systematic in their regularity (*CW* 3:30). They are a power fatally limited by Temperament. Not the name of human freedom and enrichment, moods are the medium through which nature gives us the limits of our possible self-manifestation. They are tautly structured but severed from presence, originality, and authenticity: "Temperament also enters fully into the system of illusions, and shuts us in a prison of glass which we cannot see" (*CW* 3:31). When we listen to nature and follow its dictates—and however much will enlightens our world with its spiritual light, Emerson would have us recognize that we are always listening to and following the dictates of nature—when we think, Emerson would say, life appears to us written broad in the forms of our Temperament. As the verse at the beginning of the essay notes, Temperament has no tongue with which to articulate onwardness as our own. To be sure, if freedom is to be found, it will be found in this milieu: the fatal succession of moods. And of course, Emerson will recover freedom in later essays precisely here in the felt event of thought that carries the affect of command in a situation. From an antihumanist perspective freedom can carry no other value, surely no metaphysical value. But that recognition awaits Emerson's formulation of the doctrine of fate. Here his nostalgia for a metaphysical—or at least humanist—referent to freedom constrains his thinking, necessitating the conclusion that the irresolution of moods disallows the clarity and resolution he has long attributed to freedom. Mourning itself suggests this humanist nostalgia. It is for Man that nature's hiding represents a loss. Under the doctrine of fate, mourning will be replaced by the joyous affirmation of power, by education in the art of power, set free from the perception of loss. Humanist loss will be replaced by fate as the prolific source of value that refuses the status of origin but subsists as the cunning of power that draws it on. And, as I show in Chapter 5, it will be replaced in virtue of a severing of nature and fate that is nowhere to be found in the description of "Experience."

But in this essay nature's hiding is construed as Man's loss, and we are barred from the power of origination or self-recognition. Nature instead gives us the perpetual succession of the same, and life resolves itself in the repetition of the same. To assume originality in people, impulse, willful creation of the world, is mistaken. "In the moment, it seems impulse; in the year, in the lifetime, it turns out to be a certain uniform tune which the revolving barrel of the music-box must play. . . . the temper prevails over everything of time, place, and condition, and is inconsumable in the flames of religion" (*CW* 3:31). The loss of self-certitude renders our experience of the world belated and repetitious and casts us into a world that appears "almost all custom and gross sense," where there are "very few spontaneous actions" (*CW*

3:28). Emerson does not deny novelty to our experience, any more than he retreats from his conviction that nature appears in relation to the individual's constitution. What he rejects is the ability to *earn* authenticity, to will it. When novelty or newness does make itself evident in the world, its origin cannot be located, much less enowned, but only inferred from appearances that become manifest as already a part of the world's repetition.

Emerson is both metaphorical and literal when he writes that novelty and spontaneity do not occur in history. Insofar as history unfolds along the line of teleological temporality—for Emerson, the temporality of the individual's labor—new value always occurs for us outside of history. The genealogy of a new utterance cannot be traced; appearance in time is cut off from nature. "'Tis wonderful," Emerson concludes, "where or when we ever got anything of this which we call wisdom, poetry, virtue. We never got it on any dated calendar day. Some heavenly days must have been intercalated somewhere" (*CW* 3:28). By saying that our relation to the value of our world originates beyond history, Emerson indicates that our relation to it is necessarily secondary. There is no mysticism implied here, but rather a condition of life. The world that appears, that would be present, is a repetition for which we cannot locate the original, a simulacrum. The world comes to us as "scene painting and counterfeit" and resists our best attempts to turn its images to reality (*CW* 3:29). "'Tis the trick of nature thus to degrade today; a good deal of buzz, and somewhere a result slipped magically in" (*CW* 3:28).

What has been lost, subverted by nature's dance, is the possibility of authentic success. Previously rooted in the will's labor and now displaced to a nature that is for us all moods and illusion, success is reduced to a superficial show: "There is no adaptation or universal applicability in men, but each has his special talent, and the mastery of successful men consists in adroitly keeping themselves where and when that turn shall be oftenest to be practised. We do what we must, and call it by the best names we can" (*CW* 3:33). Authentic success, true circulation and health—which Emerson always holds as the meaning of virtue—is nature's ecstasy, consisting of the dynamic of appearance and disappearance that involves but does not serve Man and cannot be owned through individual toil. It is given to the individual as the limitations of Temperament and moods, aspects of nature's success, but for Man the names of fatalism and defeat, the tricks that nature has us play. "But is this not pitiful?" Emerson asks. "Life is not worth the taking, to do tricks in" (*CW* 3:34).

The movement of Emerson's theory during these transitional years is toward a redescription of thought. The first three sections of "Experience" represent a step in the passage, a moment of passage. He passes from the conceit of Man's capacity to resolve nature under his willful gaze, and thus he concedes to nature its prolific duplicity. From this passing emerge the twin problems that I take it consume him in the years to come: the problem of the task of thinking in the absence of an anchor and the problem of action, intimately related to thought, in the absence of an anchor. The doctrine of fate and the essays in *Conduct of Life* represent his response to the question of thinking and right conduct after the fall of Man. But in "Experience" Emerson's tone is descriptive and resigned: thought's irresolution gives itself here as the loss of Man.

In the sections that follow "Succession" Emerson describes the manifestation that is possible for will situated in antihumanist nature. He describes what reality and what individual self-account can be within the terms of antihumanist methodology. It is the retreating voice of Man that at the beginning of "Surface" queries: "But what help from these fineries or pedantries? What help from thought? Life is not dialectics." Emerson thereby turns the discussion of experience from the platform of thought to the platform of will (*CW* 3:34). But if the principles depicted in "Surface," "Surprise," and "Reality" describe the experience of nature's trickery from the platform of action, they fit, still, utterly within the contours of the trick. In no respect do they unravel it.

THE PRINCIPLES OF ACTION

The human world, the world of effects forged through muscular action and articulated in the structure of the teleological relation that follows from the omnipotence of will, is the unifying theme of "Surface," "Surprise," and "Reality." The three sections are tied together as an exposition of the principles that govern the possibility of individuality in nature. One can trace the emergence of this theme from the statement in "Surface," "Man is a golden impossibility," to the assertion in "Surprise" that the miracle occurs, "Every man is an impossibility, until he is born," and finally to the claim in "Reality" that the indeterminacy of nature will be ordered and bound together under a single will. In these three sections Emerson pulls apart the qualities he had in the early writings lumped under the power of human will: the capacity to render the world transparent before the causality of the will, the spontaneity of will, and the depth of will. The three principles share their derivation from the will's perspective on life, a turning away from the nonteleological structure of thought to human purpose in nature.

"Surface," "Surprise," and "Reality" do not, however, merely restate the early humanist synthesis, now opposing it to the antihumanism of thought's perspective on life. The opposition of thought and will has the crucial effect of rendering human activity and identity superficial in nature, and this is reflected in the radicalization of the value of action and work found in the description of these three lords of life.

The antihumanist turn of thought first of all affects the principles of action by rendering each finite, no more or less than an epochal lord of life. It is especially important to bear this in mind when reading "Reality," which evokes the idea of metaphysical depth but raises it, as I have said, as only one among a number of finite principles of experience. The antagonism of thought and will is further reflected in the fact that each of these principles is settled in, and an articulation of, nature's illusoriness. This is most evident in "Surface" and "Surprise," which together give voice to the two aspects of nature's illusoriness: the disjunctive superficiality of the appearance of life and the ahistorical emergence of new thought. Inasmuch as they do so in and through action, they define modes or principles of (human) presence. Only in "Reality," however, do these principles reach their completion in the full articulation of will unifying the world.

"Surface" is the most emphatic section of "Experience," the most powerful section, because it describes the bare manifestation of the world possible for a finite will. The section articulates the sheer unrootedness of human presence and the indifference of nature. As the principle of this function, Surface consists in radically unreflective action: "Do not craze yourself with thinking, but go about your business anywhere. Life is not intellectual or critical, but sturdy. Its chief good is for well-mixed people who can enjoy what they find, without question. Nature hates peeping, and our mothers speak her very sense when they say, 'Children, eat your victuals, and say no more of it.' To fill the hour,—that is happiness; to fill the hour and leave no crevice for a repentance or an approval" (*CW* 3:35). What is striking about "Surface" is that its most famous lines express the quantification and delimitation that overtakes the imperative to live in the present tense when it is placed in the context of the method of nature. "To finish the moment, to find the journey's end in every step of the road, to live the greatest number of good hours, is wisdom" (*CW* 3:35). Indeed, as these lines indicate, "Surface" returns resolution to nature, the resolution of the present tense lost to thought in the first half of the essay, but resolution is now settled in the context of Man's superficiality: "We live amid surfaces, and the true art of life is to skate well on them. . . . Let us be poised, and wise, and our own, today. Let us treat the men and women well: treat them as if they were real: perhaps they are" (*CW* 3:35). The system of Illusion, the radical indifference and hiding of nature, does not allow us to know that men and women are real, but neither does it allow us to know they are not. The jury is still out; thought has not yet given us an answer and presumably won't for some time. "Surface" fills the breach. In the meantime, Emerson suggests, it is for us to treat the world we have as real, to live well amid its surface appearances, without questioning their truth. If nature denies us depth and authenticity and casts us in the flux of succession, of coming to and passing from appearance, then we should ignore the indeterminacy, limit our vision to the midworld of the present we bring around through our actions and that we can therefore know with certainty. Emerson evokes the imagery of "Illusion" to set a contrast to what he is here describing as precisely the proper activity of the individual and the proper response of human being to thought:

> Men live in their fancy, like drunkards whose hands are too soft and tremulous for successful labor. It is a tempest of fancies, and the only ballast I know, is a respect to the present hour. Without any shadow of doubt, amidst this vertigo of shows and politics, I settle myself ever the firmer in the creed, that we should not postpone and refer and wish, but do broad justice where we are, by whomsoever we deal with, accepting our actual companions and circumstances, however humble or odious, as the mystic officials to whom the universe has delegated its whole pleasure for us. (*CW* 3:36)

"Surface" represents Emerson's first significant response to the problem raised by his turn to antihumanism, the problem and question of action, of what we should do. His answer still reflects the vast affirmative seemingly inexhaustible in his soul. We should accept without comment, he suggests, the texture of the world as we will it. If nature is illusory, then it is impossible to gauge or rank appearances, impossible to determine depth and superficiality. Value and worth are found only in what is present to us, and we should take the attitude of emancipated will free from reflection (and deflection from the present), an attitude that speaks the presence of surfaces as the manifestation of healthy will (*CW* 3:36). Emerson is well aware of the consequences such an approach has for society and culture. He knows specifically that if it describes a manner of social interaction, it does not describe any possible culture. Culture, as I noted in Chapter 2, meant for Emerson a reflective posture that can judge and discern good from bad. From the perspective of "Surface," which is to say the fundamental perspective of will in antihumanist nature, such culture is not only illegitimate but repressive: it is dyspeptic and life despising. "Surface" accordingly describes the presence of nature freed of the reflection that enables cultural judgment and value. The America Emerson predicts in "Surface" is life affirming, nonreflective, superficial, and, as such, anticultural. "Culture with us," he writes, "ends in headache" (*CW* 3:34). Even the radically humanist culture described in "Man, the Reformer" under the doctrine of the farm remains within the fold of reflective thought to the extent it distinguishes the depth of ownership from the superficiality of the second heir. Here cultivation gives way to the indifferent manifestations of a people that skate across the surface of life, a people that can accept *any* companions and circumstances as the mystery and end, the fundamental value of the universe. Emerson does not distinguish between the Transfiguration and the Last Judgment, between "the Bible, Homer, Dante, Shakespeare, and Milton"—a fair rendering of the high points of Western culture—and the everyday events of life (*CW* 3:37). All are brought before the superficial vision of the ordinary person. "I find my account in sots and bores also" (*CW* 3:36). "Everything good is on the highway," on "the equator of life," on the line of the will that moves laterally across nature, never achieving depth and, more importantly, never reflecting on that as a failure or a diminution. Will on the line of the equator takes nature as it comes, "eating and drinking and sinning," and does not impose its conscience on nature (*CW* 3:37). Similarly, Man in "Surface" knows no conscience, being a function that presences nature's onwardness, but lacks the power of synthetic thought, the presumption of moral rectitude, and the imperatives of conscience that dominated the early essays. Emerson is explicit, too, about the amorality of "Surface," writing that "if we will be strong with [nature's] strength, we must not harbor such disconsolate consciences, borrowed too from the consciences of other nations. We must set up the strong present tense against all the rumors of wrath, past or to come" (*CW* 3:37). Unlike the action of will in the early essays, in "Surface" will reflects no substantiality that places a stay on nature and thus appropriates nature for cultural or moral judgments, for authenticity.

"Surface" gains its power in the essay, especially in relation to "Reality," because it describes the dispersal of the principle of causality in effects. This essentially pragmatic revaluation of causality is the condition for the exhaustion of the dynamic of production. It renders every first cause itself a product and thus represents all value as external effects or surfaces, untraceable to an origin or First Cause. The revaluation is brought about by carrying to its limit the logic, the externalizing dynamic, of teleology. For teleological thought, the articulation of value consists in *production*, precisely in bringing around the externality of a thing's *telos*, its end. The fundamental dynamic of teleology is directed outward, from origin to end, from cause to effect, under the governance of a purpose. But the effect is taken to express the cause—in Neoplatonic terms, to be an emanation from the origin that returns to it—and thus to embody the purpose predicted in the cause. Similarly, products of will are assumed to express and carry the presence of the will. And to be sure, "Surface" derives from the teleological dynamic. Insofar as it describes actions and operations of the will, it *implies* a depth of will beneath its externalized productions. The principle of Surface enables the univocal manifestation of nature, its presence, and the linear temporality of the movement from cause to effect that defines the essential structure of teleology. It assumes a teleological conception of time and the relation of appearances based on the relation of cause and effect. For these reasons Emerson will later refer to the realm of Surface as the "kingdom of known cause and effect" (*CW* 3:39). In each of these respects, "Surface" predicts, or is of a fabric with, the effective depth of will that emerges in "Reality," and represents the first stage of Emerson's descriptive development of will in nature.

Clearly, though, the principle of Surface itself does not admit such depth and, in fact, retains its epochal unity in virtue of refusing to do so. This fact warrants reflecting on for a moment. Rather than embrace the teleological depth implicit in the relational structure described in "Surface," Emerson instead uses the section to depict the fact that the teleological dynamic of causality moves away from cause and toward effect, and thus locates value solely in effects or surfaces. Fixed absolutely in the present tense, Surface marks the endpoint of causal relations and of the teleological relation in general. As a representation of the last stage of the teleological relation, its most bare manifestation, "Surface" contains both its final affirmation and its self-refutation and internal destruction. Depicting the utter externalization of will, it is Emerson's vision of the collapse of the long hegemony of teleology in

Western thought.[11] If it predicts the depth of will in "Reality," then it does so retrospectively from the perspective of its fatal endpoint, a fact that is notable in view of Emerson's overtly historical presentation in "Reality," or as one might say, the epoch of Reality.

"Surface" indicates the failure of teleology in relation to two general effects: First, it subverts moral depth and thus dismisses the issue of the moral value of action. Second, it dismisses metaphysical depth, or rootedness in nature, and thereby renders the world radically exterior.

As the secret of illusoriness is succession, or the lack of permanence in nature, so the secret of Surface—and the anticulture it describes—is the disposition of the individual as an uprooted phenomenon on the narrow belt of the equator of life (*CW* 3:36). This condition, of course, is not limited to human being and does not merely imply a romantic vision of the alienation of Man from nature. It reflects the reigning idea of the times, the fabric of nature itself: Illusion. This is why Emerson says "the exclusion" reaches all of nature: "the climbing, flying, gliding, feathered and four-footed man" (*CW* 3:37). None have any "root in the deep world," and all aspects of nature are, like human being, "superficial tenants of the globe" (*CW* 3:37). Unrootedness is the condition of nature in general, of presence, not merely of Man, and therefore nature reveals itself only as exteriority: "The new molecular philosophy shows astronomical interspaces betwixt atom and atom, shows that the world is all outside, it has no inside" (*CW* 3:37). Here then is the principle of Surface, consequent on its effective dismissal of teleology. The sheer exteriority of nature is both the consequence and the condition of human action. It dictates that the significance and action of Man will consist in skating on the surfaces of life.

"Surface" portrays the broad field of concrete human existence as Emerson understands it. He has conceded that we find ourselves situated in the flow of illusions, that "life is a bubble and a skepticism, and a sleep within a sleep," and we therefore have no authentic terms or criteria for distinguishing rightly value in nature (*CW* 3:38). "We are encamped in nature, not domesticated," he writes, explicitly recalling and reversing the terms through which he had cast the revolutionary claims of self-reliance (*CW* 3:110). Still, in the face of this withering

---

11. The best modern emblem of the unmitigated logic of effects is technology, and "Surface" well describes the essence of the technological age. Man is understood solely in terms of his effective productions, external effects or technology in general. The principle of Surface provides no alternative conception of Man but as his productions, and thus situates Man in and as the fatality of his technology.

skepticism—a skepticism inscribed in nature, not merely in reflective thought—Emerson does not dissolve into the melancholy of pessimism, into the specious vision of the failure of individuality and the paralysis of human will, into the decadence of nihilism. To do so would be dishonest to our lived experience. "Grant [skepticism], and as much more as they will," he writes instead, "but know that thy life is a flitting state, a tent for the night, and do thou, sick or well, finish thy stint" (*CW* 3:38). "Surface" maintains Emerson's affirmation of action, however local and merely tactical, amid the failure of all criteria of right action. The affirmation is not logical but natural. It does not yet define conduct, for conduct will require a legitimating interpretive context that awaits *Conduct of Life*. Here Emerson insists only on an expository point, an indication, the sign of Man: we act, inasmuch as we are human beings; we do. And if so, our actions give voice to the world. "Surface" characterizes the presence of the world that is possible for a will cut off from depth and truth, and thus it describes the embrace and manifestation of the shadowless exteriority of life on the line of the equator.

Undoubtedly, much of the discussion in "Surface" reminds us of aspects of Emerson's early essays. The idea of immediate justification in the present tense in particular resonates with the thesis of "Compensation." In language that, if anything, even more strikingly anticipates Nietzsche's discussions of the spirit of revenge, ressentiment, master and slave morality, nature's love of the beautiful and the strong, and the error of conscience, as well, of course, as the general argument for immediate justification, Emerson describes the fundamental argument for exteriority beyond the spirit of revenge. The repetition is unsurprising. Emerson's earliest intuition predicts the essential thesis of "Surface": simply, that value is found in manifest effects detached from any first cause and, thus, that the "Last Judgment" of nature, its final cause, occurs every moment and is found in the present. Clearly, however, a crucial distinction between "Compensation" and "Surface" exists. The distinction derives from the context in which each conception is set forward and thus finally from Emerson's turn to antihumanist thought. For "Compensation," surface exteriority did not imply a finite, epochal principle but served a universal end, the possibility of human identity through phenomenological resolution. Indeed, it is precisely on this point that Emerson's use of the figure of revenge in "Compensation" diverges from Nietzsche's.

Through the discussion in "Surface" Emerson accomplishes two crucial revisions of his early intuition of compensatory exteriority. First, he detaches exteriority from its service to phenomenological resolution and thus can present it as a sovereign and amoral principle of the appearance of nature. Second, and much more importantly, he relocates his early intuition, clarifying its place among the principles of nature's appearance, as well as within the history of ideas. In the early essays, the doctrine of compensation and the thought of exteriority, in their relation to self-reliance, stood at the center of a humanist doctrine that was taken to be absolute in nature. Emerson now clarifies the epochal status of justification and Surface, showing their place within the teleological relation and the essential thought of human identity, but as the internal critique of that structure and effect. That is to say, in "Experience" Emerson recognizes that the thought of surface exteriority—and thus the pragmatic thesis of his work—stands at the logical endpoint of the way of thought that takes human action and identity as its purpose. "Surface" situates the early thought precisely where it belongs: at the endpoint of the tradition of humanism, founded on the teleological relation. But then far from serving human identity, the depiction of a world of pure surface effects determines that "a man is a golden impossibility" (*CW* 3:38). "Surface" turns a retrospective glance on the self-destruction of individuality that is the fate of the teleological relation. It expresses the subversion of teleology (and, thus, of Man) that was always implicit in the doctrine of compensation but that is avoided in the earlier essay by virtue of the withdrawal of the Oversoul. If "Surface" resonates with phrases from the early essays, then each one shows the difference that the antihumanist turn causes. The play of surfaces remains compensatory in the Emersonian sense and predicts the meaning that the doctrine of compensation will come to have in Emerson's later writings. But the doctrine now refers to the inhuman play of superficial causal relations, the sheer display of power relations.

Man is impossible under this principle inasmuch as the individual consists of the miracle of depth that the principle of Surface cannot provide. "Surface" engages the rhetoric of affirmation, consisting of the wholesale affirmation of the shifting causal play of power in the present tense; but with respect to logical or final unity it is a negation, negating precisely the presupposition of teleological depth that enables the appearance of Man. The individual's value becomes nomadic, it flits across the surface of nature as a tent for the night. Look for the continuity and depth of an individual, Emerson suggests, and it is nowhere to be found. The principle provides no foundation for the individual's stability and endurance. Indeed, properly speaking, it doesn't provide the principle of the individual's presence. The midworld consists in partial expressions, fragmented utterances, bound together by no more than the bare law of causality: this causes that, and that the next, and so on, to paraphrase Emerson's description of succession in "The Method of Nature." It articulates the anticulture of a world of repetition, lacking the possibility of newness and novelty. The superficiality of will described in "Surface" disallows the finality and ultimacy of the will's presence necessary for the appearance of Man. What will be required for the "real" presence of Man is a principle that gives will the potential to articulate nature's presence as other than the surface relations of cause and effect, as anomolous disruptions of the law of surfaces, or precisely as surprise.

"Surprise" begins by indicating the inadequacy of life lived only in the "kingdom of known cause and effect" (*CW* 3:39). "Presently comes," Emerson writes, "a day—or is it only a half-hour, with its angel-whispering—which discomfits the conclusions of nations and of years!" (*CW* 3:39). If "Surface" represents the causal transparency of the moment, the present state of affairs, disregarding the stairs that stretch out below and above the present, then "Surprise" describes the effect of the intercalated days that in "Illusion" Emerson says account for newness in the world. The first is a matter of choice—we will the superficiality of the world—but Surprise, while still an aspect of human action, is related to the receptivity of thought. It is "the kingdom that cometh without observation" (*CW* 3:40). The principle of Illusion does not allow us to trace the superficial value of our world. "God delights to isolate us every day, and hide from us the past and the future. We would look about us, but with grand politeness he draws down before us an impenetrable screen of purest sky, and another behind us of purest sky" (*CW* 3:39). New value can only come, then, as an unprecedented presence that is an index of an opening in the closed economy of our willed calculation of the world, a power, to be sure, but one that "keeps quite another road than the turnpikes of choice and will, namely the subterranean and invisible tunnels and channels of life" (*CW* 3:39). Emergent out of the work of one's constitution and given as the principle of the rearrangement of the world, this lord gives life to the kingdom of surfaces.

Emerson's purpose in this section is to indicate that Surprise is the manifest effect of the reception, through thought, of the power of nature. It is, then, a spontaneous action that is dictated by listening to nature. He makes this especially clear by describing the class of people that represents the value of Surprise in terms that repeat his description of thought and Illusion, thereby indicating that "Surprise" describes the embodiment or presence of the power of thought: "The most attractive class of people are those who are powerful obliquely, and not by the direct stroke: men of genius, but not yet accredited: one gets the cheer of their light, without paying too great a tax. Theirs is the beauty of the bird, or the morning light, and not of art" (*CW* 3:39). The statement repeats images from some of the most important passages in the first three sections of the essay. Moreover, the opposition between this class of people and the artist implies again the shift that has occurred in Emerson's thought and the resituation of aesthetic detachment and choice that has occurred. In the early writings aesthetic detachment was central to the power of Man to presence the world. Spontaneity, inasmuch as it had served the clear vision of intellect, also served the decisive capacity of art. Here spontaneity—Surprise—is divorced from aesthetic choice. Emerson still thinks of spontaneity in terms of a poetic capacity to utter authentic truths. He identifies it as the point "where Being passes into Appearance, and Unity into Variety," and refers to this moment of surprising articulation as "the secret of the world" (*CW* 3:9). Similarly, in "The Poet" he writes that "the birth of a poet is the principal event in chronology," and there can be little doubt that the birth of the poet corresponds to the moment of surprising intervention in the causal existence described by "Surface." But here Emerson indicates that the poetic capacity is *not* linked to the depth of human will, as it had been in the early writings, and is thus not an aspect of human causality in nature. If the poet certainly speaks, the poetic capacity is nonetheless not properly represented by speech, but by listening. Poetry does not articulate the truth of human being so much as the fatal power of nature, which again operates as an index of the limits of human power. A poet is the type of human being that represents nature's power as the form of history in language irreducible to will's speech. Poetry is the surprising language of thought that Emerson describes in "The Method of Nature" and that, he suggests, is uncommon in a world of surface speech.

Emerson does not devote a very large section of "Experience" to the discussion of Surprise, and even within the section, he moves quickly to his principal assertion that Surprise is the moral sentiment. "The moral sentiment is well called 'the newness'" (*CW* 3:40). Having said that, he goes on to dismiss the relevance of human will to the moral sentiment: "I would gladly be moral, and keep due metes and bounds, which I dearly love, and allow the most to the will of man, but I have set my heart on honesty in this chapter, and I can see nothing at last, in success or failure, than more or less of vital force supplied from the Eternal" (*CW* 3:40). He indicates the dependence of Surprise on thought and the genealogy of the moral sentiment in nature rather than Man. Beyond this, the moment of newness offers little more to be said: "The path of things is silent," and no description of it can be given (*CW* 3:15). Any description is finally of the effects of Surprise, and those effects are worked through in "Reality."

The importance of Surprise should not be underestimated, however. It enables Man. In a world of surfaces Man is an impossibility. He is unrooted and fleeting, and therefore cannot be identified. The terms of surface causality manifest a world in which the individual has no place. What is required for the appearance of Man is a surprising effect in the system of causes and effects, the presence of unprecedented power, of newness in nature, around which the individual gathers as the articulation of the unity and order of nature made possible by the new effect. Man is impossible until a surprising sentiment enters nature and motivates a new interpretation of nature. Man, then, is the principal surprise: "Every man is an impossibility, until he is born" (*CW* 3:40). Individuality, the expression of the moral sense, the affect of unity and depth, shows itself as a surprising effect. Surprise fills the role necessitated by a logic of effects—a radical pragmatism—by enabling change, which precisely is impossible in terms of the willful calculation of the kingdom of known cause and effect. By including Surprise among the lords of life, Emerson reveals from a different direction the exhaustion of the teleological dynamic of Being.

The value of Surprise is evident not only retrospectively in relation to "Surface," however, but also when Emerson takes up the transition from "Surprise" to "Reality." The movement between these two lords of life is the most complicated of the essay. Up to this point Emerson has followed the principle of Illusion as it dictates the manifest world of presence. He has thus described the superficiality of the world and the presence amid that superficiality of surprising effects, indices of nature's power of hiding. But neither of these principles of life can fully explain the appearance of human individuality. That is left to "Reality," which names the appearance and principle of teleology, the unification of the world under the authority of a will and the identification of the individual with that will. "Reality" thus completes the explanation of the principles of Man, begun, as I have said, in "Surface," and it completes it by locating the principle of teleology, or the principle of the will's unification of the discrete appearances of the world. Bear with the clangor and jangle of contrariety in the world of surface presence,

Emerson says, for surprisingly "[the distractions] will one day be *members*, and obey one will" (*CW* 3:41).

But it is reasonable to ask how the emergence of a unifying will to reality, as opposed to the partial exertions characteristic of human action in "Surface," is possible in Emerson's exposition. What justifies it? Put otherwise, how does Emerson make the transition from "Surprise" to "Reality," from the impossibility of Man and the surprising and inexplicable appearance of Man, to the principle of Man as the will that unifies the world and thus draws from the superficiality of presence the human experience of the reality of the world deriving from the depth of will? One can trace Emerson's transition to "Reality" in two movements, which together consist in a sort of deduction of reality. For Emerson describes the experiential emergence of reality, the fact that the human experience of time does show the unification of discrete appearances under one will. Both movements of the discussion derive from "Surprise," the first limiting the thesis of "Surprise" and the second drawing out its consequences.

If "Surprise" marks the limits of "Surface" as an adequate representation of the presence of the world, then Emerson begins "Reality" by rejecting the deification of Surprise: "The ancients, struck by this irreducibleness of the elements of human life to calculation, exalted Chance into divinity, but that is to stay too long at the spark,—which glitters truly at one point,—but the universe is warm with the latency of the same fire" (*CW* 3:40). The assertion is not arbitrary; it follows from the logic of the argument in "Surprise." "Surprise" recognizes chance in its effect, and that effect is itself a surface phenomenon, or an aspect of nature's presence. It cannot then be traced to its origin, and therefore we cannot expound, or take as an aspect of experience, the origin of surprising new elements in life. Emerson's purpose is to show the *experiential* falseness of the assertion of a discrete origin of value or existence and, thus, to imply the multiplicitous origin of will. However true the notion of a chance origin of human existence may be, it is not to the point with respect to the reality of human life. "The miracle of life," Emerson therefore goes on to explain, "will not be expounded, but will remain a miracle" (*CW* 3:40). Emerson refuses the irrationalism of privileging chance and asserts instead that life—which is to say will—proceeds from a plurality, not an essential unity, and that will, therefore, is not an entity, certainly not a faculty of the individual, but an event that comes together out of the elements of life. Life lacks an origin—or at least "has no memory" of an origin—and proceeds from three or more points. To put the matter somewhat differently, Emerson here indicates that life and will are settled in and derive from the only milieu available in antihumanist nature, the dynamic of nature's hiding that dictates a world of partial and conflicting powers. Thus, will emerges from the interactions of power in the world, from the milieu of nature's revealing/concealing dynamic, which includes not only the sensuous presence of surfaces but also the surprises that restructure our conception of the relations of sensuous surfaces (*CW* 3:41).

Having barred the reduction of the principle of Reality to a singular or original cause, Emerson sets the ground for his treatment of Reality as oriented toward the future, specifically, as the teleological relation of emergent unity in the world. Reality will not be found in memory, but will be realized through the emergence of a governing will that synthesizes Reality out of the disparate pieces of experience. Reality will consist in the feeling and awareness of forward directionality—the universal sense—or tendency in life. In both respects it is the gathering of nature manifest in "Surface" and "Surprise," but in neither case does it encroach on the irresolution of nature for thought. Thus, speaking of Surface and Surprise, he indicates that it is exactly tendency in life that these principles are inadequate to reveal: "That which is coexistent, or ejaculated from a deeper cause, as yet far from being conscious, knows not its own tendency. So it is with us, now skeptical, or without unity, because immersed in forms and effects all seeming to be of equal yet hostile value, and now religious, whilst in the reception of spiritual law" (*CW* 3:41). Neither surface dispersal nor the sheer affect of surprising unity is adequate to the real because neither contains the quality of tendency that predicts the unity of the world. Reality consists for Emerson in the power of will to bind together "the coetaneous growth of the parts" described in the preceding two sections (*CW* 3:41). Reality is the synthesis of surfaces and surprises, of causal experience and the affect of unity, and as such it is the very essence of his early humanist thesis: "On that one will, on that secret cause, they nail our attention and hope. Life is hereby melted into an expectation or a religion. Underneath the inharmonious and trivial particulars, is a musical perfection, the Ideal journeying always with us, the heaven without rent or seam" (*CW* 3:41).

Still, up to this point in the essay it would be too much to say that Emerson has done anything more than assert that the emergence of unity does occur. The principle of Reality requires more than that; it requires an exposition of how it emerges.

The second movement of "Reality" addresses this issue and consists in a description of the manner of our apprehension of newness in the world. It indicates that if Surprise is inadequate in itself to the real, the exposition of the principle of Reality nonetheless depends on the experiential effect of Surprise, on what Emerson calls the "latency" of chance in the universe, which, as I have suggested, institutes a new interpretation of nature. The miracle of life, though it will not be expounded, "introduces a new element" that *initiates* the emergence of the unity and order of nature, that is, Reality. The event of Reality is not, then, a surprising dispensation. Rather, it is the endpoint of a process, motivated by the sentiment or feeling of a surprising effect, that gathers nature together into a unified presentation.

> Do but observe the mode of our illumination. When I converse with a profound mind, or if at any time being alone I have good thoughts, I do not at once arrive at satisfactions, as when, being thirsty, I drink water, or go to the fire, being cold: no! but I am at first apprised of my vicinity to a new and excellent region of life. By persisting to read or to think, this region gives further sign of itself, as it were in flashes of light, in sudden discoveries of its profound beauty and repose, as if the clouds that covered it parted at intervals, and showed the approaching traveller the inland mountains, with the tranquil eternal meadows spread at their base, whereon flocks graze, and shepherds pipe and dance. But every insight from this realm of thought is felt as initial, and promises a sequel. I do not make it; I arrive there, and behold what was there already. I make! O no! I clap my hands in infantine joy and amazement, before the first opening to me of this august magnificence, old with the love and homage of innumerable ages, young with the life of life, the sunbright Mecca of the desert. And what a future it opens! I feel a new heart beating with the love of the new beauty. I am ready to die out of nature, and be born again into this new yet unapproachable America I have found in the West. (*CW* 3:41)

The process of thought, motivated by the moral sentiment, the affect of still merely potential unity, brings the individual to a sense of self and the world that is as old as the feeling of unity and as young as what the context of action allows. Emerson locates America in this decidedly local and superficial instantiation of the One, the order and organization of nature that shows itself in the desert of thought and shows itself there by virtue of the moral sentiment that arises out of nature's dynamic cunning.

Emerson's description of the ideal is not unique. Indeed, he seems intentionally to have called up the worn phrases of the idyllic and the pastoral to place his conception of the ideal in the long tradition of metaphysical thought, emphasizing that illumination occurs as a process. Emerson writes, "Every insight from this realm of thought is felt as initial, and promises a sequel." The ideal does not consist in any quantity or content, but in a quality, here described as the quality of promise, of hope raised by the power of a surprising event. The ideal is described as principally a feeling: the feeling of possible unity that promises the resolution of the world in an identifiable order. The ideal is the affect or sentiment of unity—the affect of an omnipotent will—that is raised by the appearance of a new element. Every surprise gives hope of a unifying order, and that hope is present as the feeling of unity, what Emerson above called the moral sentiment, which propels us "to read or to think" and thereby to slowly bring to resolution the order enabled by the surprising element. The ideal Emerson describes is no more or less than the promise carried in the affect of the moral sentiment, the feeling of hope, of possible unity. Surprise emerges in the world as the implication of order, a new order, and from this emerges the will to a new order, concretely to be realized in the organization that transforms our conception of the order of things motivated by the surprising element.

However, if the description of the ideal fits the archetypal patterns of Western metaphysics, there is nonetheless something quite new in Emerson's treatment. For Emerson is less interested in following the articulation of a new order than he is in describing the genealogy of a will to order. His emphasis rests therefore on the derivation, in every case, of the will to unity from the appearance of a surprising element in the world, on the emergence of will out of thought. The promise of order is given to us through thought. What is new in his treatment of the ideal, and what Emerson certainly wanted his readers to notice, is the eventlike or adventitious nature of the occurrence of the ideal. We do not make the ideal; we do not make the new order that emerges in the world. Rather, as he shall say in "Fate," it makes us. We arrive to a new order as at an inexplicable oasis of possible structure in the desert of irresolution, or surface repetition. The confusion of reception and action—the genesis of will from thought, and the resolution of thought as a new willed order—is aptly reflected in the imagery of the description, mixing as it does the new with the old, the East with the West, Mecca with America, the repetitive with the novel, death with life. Reality emerges under the principle of Illusion then as the surprising resolution of thought.

The complication of Emerson's transition from "Surprise" to "Reality," his deduction of Reality, is evident here. For if the ideal is given to us through a surprise, and if our will is not involved in the appearance of the ideal, then it would be logical to expect the ideal to participate fully in the system of illusions and thus to be consistent with the flux of moods. And yet Emerson writes to the contrary: "If I have described life as a flux of moods, I must now add, that there is that in us which changes not, and which ranks all sensations and states of mind" (*CW* 3:42). The question raised is how it is possible for a function of thought to anchor the flux of moods and, thus, to rank all states of mind. And, of course, the answer will be found by recognizing that surprises bring more than a possible new thought to experience; they also bring the affect of unity that demands the new thought be realized. But before getting into this it is well to note that the very question raised here is how humanism is possible on the premise of antihumanism. How is it that Man appears in nature? Emerson's answer is crucial, not only for his discussion of experience in general but even more so for the fatal synthesis he will develop in *Conduct of Life*. Indeed, it predicts the question and the solution Emerson will arrive at in "Fate," when he turns his attention to the problem of human freedom in an antihumanist theory. For if the unwilled nature of the ideal follows from the logic of antihumanism and comes as no surprise at this point in Emerson's writings, it nonetheless should be stressed, because Emerson's late conception of fatal freedom will consist in nothing but the event of will in nature.

Without wishing to understate the difference I will draw in the next chapter between Emerson's approaches in "Experience" and in "Fate," it can still be said that here in "Experience" Emerson provides an important description of the genealogy of will in nature and thus an initial response to the question of the derivation of will under the terms of antihumanist method. The answer to the question I have raised—the question of how a new element and a new possible thought can move out of the realm of intellect and into the realm of will and thus anchor a presentation of reality—relies, as Emerson's description makes clear, on the fact that Surprise carries with it, as it were, not only a possible new thought but also the moral sentiment or the affect of the desire that our thought should prevail. From this the will to anchor the flux of thought emerges. The affect, or sentiment, the passion, of surprise raises the will that ranks our consciousness, anchors the slippage in consciousness, and determines, for a time at least, the value of our world. "The consciousness of each man is a sliding scale, which identifies him now with the First Cause, and now with the flesh of his body; life above life, in infinite degrees. The sentiment from which it sprung determines the dignity of any deed, and the question ever is, not, what you have done or forborne, but, at whose command you have done or forborne it" (*CW* 3:42). From sentiment emerges the motive that identifies us with the ideal—and brings together the world beneath the power of our causality—or reduces us to living in our senses, the motive that determines the location of our world on the spectrum between the real and the display of surfaces. No act is intrinsically good or evil, then; no act is more or less valuable. An act's value reflects the sentiment that motivates it. Emerson stresses the passionate and moral root of this formulation, but one should not overlook its intersection with his conception of the role of eloquence in determinations of truth and reality. It should simply be noted that the affect that ranks consciousness and discerns the real from the apparent will be the sentiment that speaks most eloquently to our condition. On this poetic relation Emerson pins the hope for the real.

The reception of thought, of feeling, is variable; eloquence is uncommon and eventlike. Most of what we receive is "a good deal of buzz," the repetitive and "uniform tune which the revolving barrel of the music box must play" (*CW* 3:30, 31). Inasmuch as such feelings sponsor consciousness, we live in a world of sensation and uprooted surfaces. When, however, the sentiment dictating our lives is moral and our listening warrants conviction, that is to say, when our reception is of newness—arriving through the "door which is never closed, through which the creator passes," as Emerson put it at the end of the "Temperament" section—our consciousness is identified with the First Cause, and the world is unified under the will forged from the moral sentiment and the thought it carries. The perspective of action predicts such moments of unity; which is to say, it predicts the emergence of order around a surprising event. But for that very reason unity is possible only because of the place of Surprise or the moral sentiment in the world, which is to say, only because of the emergence of new thought and the feeling that it should be, from the emergence of thought under the force of the perspective of will.

The location of the moral affect at the center of Emersonian reality indicates how Emerson's conception of experience can be understood. Affects, or feelings, operate continuously throughout the various principles of experience. The principle of Illusion derives from the insinuation of feelings—moods—into intellect, and Emerson's characterization of reality is ultimately based on sentiment, or affect, as it produces will in the world. In both respects, it would seem, the essential affect of human being—*the feeling of power, the body*—is, in the language of "Reality," the "unbounded substance," the "ineffable cause" of the world (*CW* 3:42). This substance, however, when viewed from the opposed perspectives of thought and will yields a quite different value. In the first case, the life-power that flows through the world, the play of feelings and moods, entails the impermanence and inhumanity of Succession. It dictates the irreality of Illusion, an irreality generated precisely by the impossibility that this perspective should see the tie between human feelings and the appearance of what is. Rather, human affects sully the clarity Emerson once thought possible for intellect—a clarity that had also illuminated the centrality of Man in nature—and define the world as illusory, containing no principle at all. They define nature as sheer and cunning play, not yet resolved even in surface causal relations: a milieu of revealing and concealing. From the perspective of will, on the other hand, human affects arrive as eloquent and compelling sentiments, enabling a recognition of Man's centrality in nature, as well as the determination of the gradations of consciousness that take form as reality. The first half of "Experience" privileges the expression of the fundamental affect of humanity dictated by thought's perspective and thereby privileges Illusion and the repudiation of Reality, presence, and unified human being. The second half of the essay alternatively describes affects from the perspective of will. That there is nothing metaphysical about Emerson's description should be clear enough, all the more so in view of his reminder at the end of the essay that he does not rank the lords of life and thus certainly gives no precedence to Reality. Rather, when he identifies the fundamental affect of human being as Being itself, substance, the First Cause "which every genius has essayed to represent by some emphatic symbol, as, Thales by water, Anaximenes by air, Anaxagoras by (Nous) thought, Zoroaster by fire, Jesus and the moderns by love," he is doing no more than following the logic of the perspective of will (*CW* 3:42). All of these symbols, of course, share the sense of process and interminability that is now, as in the early essays, central to Emerson's conception of omnipotent will. Will understood as the "vast-flowing vigor," as Being, is the process by which the moral sentiment carries us to new descriptions of the world, and thus to new worlds. From the perspective of will, the affect of human being is the essential moral principle that is indistinguishable from Being, which is to say, indistinguishable from the principle by which the universe is created, the transitory power that brings the world to resolution before the eyes. Consistent with his theory of eloquence, Emerson identifies this power as the impulse to belief: "So in accepting the leading of the sentiments, it is not what we believe concerning the immortality of the soul, or the like, but *the universal impulse to believe*, that is the material circumstance, and is the principal fact in the history of the globe" (*CW* 3:42–43). The First Cause in the world, and thus the first name of reality—substance and Being—is the will to believe, the power of desire and hope, the religious sentiment that promises unity and wholeness in the world and certitude and integrity to the individual.

The deduction of Reality from surprising events recapitulates the basic argument of the early humanist synthesis. "Reality" describes the very heart of the human capacity to will the world into existence, and it is this causal power embedded in human will that Emerson names Reality, or Being. The cause of causes, the center and purpose of the world, and the interminable potential that propels history forward and assures the perpetuation of joyous affirmations is Man, or, more specifically, it is the will to believe. Being is no more or less than tendency, direction in nature, sense, which predicts an account of things. The "vast-flowing vigor" is language, to be sure; but more than that, it is the energy that coincides with language and realizes it in speech, the moral sentiment of unity that consists in the articulation of an account of the world. It is poetic language at the instant of becoming history, as it comes to resolution in a discrete utterance by Man. Reality is both the feeling that attends the poetic conditions of experience becoming Man and speech, the sense, or affect, of unity that is evident in the feeling of gathering directionality, and the account of unity. Nurture this feeling, bear with it, and the parts will be unified in a whole; it will yield an utterance that resolves the world, brings it to ownership under the eye of Man. "Nourish it correctly," Emerson quotes Mencius saying, "and do it no injury, and [the vast-flowing vigor] will fill up the vacancy between heaven and earth" (*CW* 3:42).

"Reality" completes the discussion of the teleological relation begun in "Surface," drawing from the fact of will in the world the feeling of tendency, the sentiment to unity, that gives the sense of depth to the individual. It consists in the feeling of will's power to unify the world and in many respects repeats the fundamental faith of the early essays. But it would be incorrect to suggest that it revitalizes the humanist synthesis. Rather, the interrelations of "Surface," "Surprise," and "Reality" draw apart and articulate the conception of Central Man put forward in the early essays and by so doing indicate the dependence of will on a reception of nature's power, on a surprising sentiment. That is to say, they indicate the contingency of will's appropriation of the conditions of experience and thus denote the situatedness of the relation of teleology in the antihumanist play of relations. It is from the interactions of power that reality emerges, whether one construes that play through thought as the flux of moods or through will as surface causality.

Nonetheless, the will to believe is hardly incidental, nor is it a fleeting and superficial phenomenon in nature. Emerson's description and explanation of Reality indicates, on the contrary, that the will to believe is a fundamental value of nature: is Being. The will to believe marks the intersection of nature and human being and is the sentiment that Emerson earlier asserted as the grounds of the godliness of Man. The convergence of thought and will described in "Reality" indicates a depth to will that cannot be ignored and that suggests "Reality" is implicitly posed against "Illusion" as an alternative exposition of nature. The irreconcilability of "Illusion" and "Reality" is evident in Emerson's remark, cited above, that if life is a succession of moods, then there is also that in life that does not change and that, precisely, anchors all appearances. What does not change is the effect of the moral sentiment, the will to believe; what does not pass away is the existence of the platform of action. That the moral sentiment depends on thought hardly diminishes its fundamental value, but rather indicates, as I have said, the convergence of thought and will and provides what support can be found for dialectical readings of the essay.

Emerson finds himself in "Reality" within the very contradiction that stands beneath his mature thought: the contradiction between freedom and fate, between the moral sentiment and the fatality of the world of illusions, between conviction and despair. He does not here reconcile this contradiction. But he does make clear that it is not a contradiction between Man and nature. Rather, the opposition is between two ways of viewing or seeing life: that defined by intellection and that defined by action. Neither is given priority. From the perspective of thought, life is illusory, the passing of irresolute moods. Most importantly, from the perspective of thought, life or nature has no direction, it is pure succession. Whereas the perspective of will—"muscular activity"—enables the sentiment of tendency, or direction, which is the purest manifestation of will in the world, and supports teleological interpretations of experience. From the perspective of thought, life is without a tongue, irresolute, the passing of moods. From the perspective of will, life is fundamentally the will to believe, or the sentiment of life as direction. Simply put, it is the sentiment of will. As I have indicated, the articulations of the vast-flowing vigor take shape as a world of surfaces, surprising events, and the promise of order. From the perspective of this principle, which is to say, "in liberated moments," we feel the infinite potential of human will, "we know that a new picture of life and duty is already possible; the elements already exist in many minds around you, of a doctrine of life which shall transcend any written record we have" (*CW* 3:43). The will to believe is the essence of the human reality of the world as Emerson conceives it in "Experience," and accordingly it is what endures of his humanist faith. Specifically, it is the noble will to believe in a world that preaches indifference, an irreconcilable will to unity and wholeness of presence situated in a nature that does not like to be observed.

SUBJECTIVITY

The final section of "Experience," on "Subject, or the One," which I have so far left out of the organization of this chapter, is most striking for the insistence with which Emerson distances subjectivity from the unified will described in "Reality." That there is no progress or unity among the principles described in the essay is attested by the fact that Emerson begins "Subject, or the One" with a repudiation of the faith of the early writings and, by extension, a repudiation of its reaffirmation in "Reality." His famous assertion that we have discovered our fall certainly responds both to the Edenic myth and to his early belief in the centrality of Man. But it is directed as well at the discussion in the preceding section of the essay. On the principle of Reality, were it universally effective, we would again "live in what we saw," the world would again surround us as the articulation raised by our will to believe. Emerson has doubted all such articulations since 1841. The fall of Man signifies much more than the enabling precondition of our self-recovery, then; it refers to the failure of presence described in the essay's first paragraph, to the recognition of the superficiality of our will in nature, the antihumanist recognition that our eyes do not penetrate nature, that nature hides behind our manifestations. And Emerson accordingly introduces the idea of the subject in language that repeats the descriptions in "Illusion" and "Temperament": "We have learned that we do not see directly, but mediately, and that we have no means of correcting these colored and distorting lenses which we are" (*CW* 3:43). It still needs to be said that epistemological readings of this statement misunderstand Emerson's point. The distortion that concerns him is moral, a trembling and warp along the teleological line of evaluation. Emerson brings "Experience" to its conclusion by posing the principle of subjectivity outside of the teleological development that culminates in "Reality," and by so doing he delimits and diminishes the enthusiasm expressed in "Reality."

This needn't imply there is no continuity between "Reality" and "Subject." What continuity there is consists in the representation of human being as affective. But in "Subject" Emerson rejects the defining idea of Reality, the premise that the affect of subjectivity is moral and entails the organization and unity of the world. Whereas Reality builds on the sentiment that gauges our deeds and commands our action or forbearance, and thus builds on the sentiment that determines our attention and our world, Emerson's conception of subjectivity consists in that which endures through the effects of attention. Reality is reducible to the operation of will, and as such, it acts on its impulse and measures the world accordingly. In "Subject" Emerson is intent on reminding the reader that such action, which he summarizes here, as earlier, in terms of love or the absence of love, is superficial and suspect. Speaking, pointedly enough, of the fixation of Jesus at the center of our cultural attention and as the exemplary Man, and thus directly invoking his description of reality and Being in the modern period as preeminently Christian love, he writes: "But the longest love or aversion has a speedy term. The great and crescive self, rooted in absolute nature, supplants all relative existence, and ruins the kingdom of mortal friendship and love" (*CW* 3:44). Far from completing or extending the concept in "Reality," subjectivity destroys it, rebuking love. One must draw the conclusion then that the Emersonian subject in 1844 stands on grounds other than that of Being.

Equally, I am led to conclude the subject has no terms to provide for the moral judgment of an act. Moral judgment depends on the will to believe and the organization of the world it implies. In "Reality," as in the early works, conscience consists in the imperative to see clearly the disposition of things in the world, and that possibility itself depends on the will to believe, the essential faith that our sentiment of unity will organize the world through our actions, creating a rank order that enables judgment. In "Subject" the principle of organization is absent, and so, therefore, is the possibility of moral judgment. For this reason Emerson poses the subject outside the conditions of crime, beyond good and evil: "We believe in ourselves, as we do not believe in others. We permit all things to ourselves, and that which we call sin in others, is experiment for us" (*CW* 3:45). Whereas the moral sentiment in "Reality" had been an anchor that ranked the sliding scale of consciousness, this subject is amoral. It is for conscience—for will understood as the will to belief, to unity, to order—to ascribe good and evil to actions, to draw the parts of the world together in a whole, to act and through action organize the world. Emerson is explicit on this point, and he renders it in precisely the terms I have been using, terms that suggest again his guiding recognition of the incommensurability of the platforms of thought and will. "Saints are sad, because they behold sin, (even when they speculate,) from the point of view of the conscience, and not of the intellect; a confusion of thought. Sin seen from the thought, is a diminution or *less*: seen from the conscience or will, it is pravity or *bad*. The intellect names it shade, absence of light, and no essence. The conscience must feel it as essence, essential evil. This it is not" (*CW* 3:45). Intellect attends to the phenomenological fluctuations of nature without resolving them as values, whereas conscience or will convicts this play to a moral claim. This opposition has been evident since "The Method of Nature"; what's important here is to note that the subject is placed on the side of thought and thus sees the world as a fantastic display, an interwoven texture of light and shade, a play of images. The subject does not think through action, has no conscience, and is thus defined otherwise than according to the moral sentiment that defines will in "Reality." Need it be added, the subject cannot be explained through the traditional terms of metaphysical subjectivity or individuality?

The subject is explained rather by attending to the overall logic of "Experience," viewing it in the context of the development I outlined in the last section. There I showed that the logic of "Experience," the organization of the essay, stresses the different shape nature takes depending on its mode of presencing. When presencing occurs from the perspective of thought, nature presences itself as a succession of moods, as the world of illusions perpetually in a state of becoming and withdrawing from that which it becomes. Thought presences the primordial affect of nature as a stream of irresolute illusions. Only when viewed from the perspective of will does nature take the form of Being or reality. Figured through muscular activity, the feeling of nature's succession reveals itself in causal surface interactions and in the unity of reality.

Emerson privileges neither of these perspectives, although the very distinction between them depends, as I said, on a recognition of the contingency of the affect of human being, an indeterminacy that reaches even, and precisely, to its own self-recognition. My decision to leave "Subject, or the One" out of the organization of the essay put forward at the beginning of this chapter is guided and justified by Emerson's refusal to privilege either platform, for withholding "Subject" until now from my interpretation emphasizes the perspectivism of both the nonteleological and the teleological presentation of nature, the perspectivism of thought and will, Illusion and Reality. It implies that subjectivity sponsors both perspectives, that the subject is the very contingency of the affect of human being that insistently dissolves articulations of the moral sentiment into illusions of experience.

Read in this way the organization of the essay reflects the foundation of experience in the unsteadiness of affects, which I take to be the essay's leading idea. It suggests moreover that the final principle of experience is the very principle of life itself, the pure Oneness of the primordial affect of human being. The meaning of "Subject" is found here in the indication that subjectivity refers neither to Being nor to the withdrawal of Being, but rather to the principle of the human power that shows itself as nature alternately for thought or will and thus shows itself as illusory succession or reality. Emerson's decision to call this principle subjectivity certainly reflects the consolidation of nature under human being that occurs in the modern period, and thus indicates his historical disposition. In broad terms it reflects the externalization of the humanist synthesis, which characterizes both Emerson's own early writings and the epoch in which he writes. By ending the essay with "Subject" Emerson gestures to the eloquence of the modern account of nature. But this needn't lead one to confuse subjectivity with the principle of nature's presence. Emerson's conception of subjectivity in no way corresponds either to the modern notion of an epistemological or rational subject or to the principle of direction and unity described in "Reality."

Indeed, the nature of subjectivity can best be explained by opposing it to the unified will described in "Reality": "The subject is the receiver of Godhead, and at every comparison must feel his being enhanced by that cryptic might. Though not in energy, yet by presence, this magazine of substance cannot be otherwise than felt: nor can any force of intellect attribute to the object the proper deity which sleeps or wakes forever in every subject. Never can love make consciousness and ascription equal in force" (*CW* 3:44). As in the previous citation, the subject described in these lines is the sheer affect of awakening power. It is a potency that carries no teleological value of unity or belief, no teleological *tendency*, but rather is concentrated at a single point, as dissociated *intensity*, the feeling of human power that is the condition for illusions and reality. Emerson develops the idea of the detached intensity of the subject by alluding to an opposition between energy and presence, terms that are typically coincident in the Aristotelian tradition. Energy calls up the idea of a power that acts with direction toward an end or purpose, whether that end is defined or not. Energy is impulsive, a force of directionality; minimally it implies action, which has no choice but to define a direction. Energy thus implicates the definitive fact of life viewed from the perspective of will or action: teleology. Emerson's substitution of "presence" for the affect of energy in his characterization of subjectivity does not here suggest a moment of phenomenological resolution, but rather the unprecedented nature of the affect of subjectivity. It indicates that the subject is not felt as a tendency or will to believe. The subject is not energy, not the capacity to gather parts into a whole, the teleological power of love that, when nurtured, fills the distance between heaven and earth. It is, on the contrary, a fragmentary feeling, implying no direction or sense, but only the sheer and intense affect of nature's succession. The subject is a pure affect of force or intensity that promises nothing, knows no fruit. It is the pure feeling of human being, prior to any definition, a feeling that thus consists in the power of the unanchored succession in nature. It is the undifferentiated "thing" at the center of experience.

The consequences of Emerson's characterization of the subject are far-reaching. The description indicates the essential solitude of the individual in the world, a solitude that not only extends to but is defined by the simulated nature of all manifestation. The subject is in the world with a single object: nature that consists in images, sense without meaning. "Life will be imaged," he writes, "but cannot be divided nor doubled. . . . The soul is not twin-born, but the only begotten, and though revealing itself as child in time, child in appearance, is of fatal and universal power, admitting no co-life" (*CW* 3:45).

Emerson develops the subject out of his conception of a nature that does not like to be observed and a life that, therefore, shows itself only as images. "Subject" completes the development of experience and the human condition, of human being in a world set within the parameters of the principle of Illusion. If our will to believe enables the energy necessary to draw the world together in a unified order, then Emerson here affirms that the order is counterfeit, a masquerade, mere images. Surprising effects seduce us; they call us *as if* from a deeper nature, *as if* from beyond the superficiality of our world. They draw us away from the direct path of cause-effect relations and promise us the universe.

And insofar as we believe them, we rank and gather our world in an ethical totality. But "Subject" makes clear that our gathering, too, enters fully into the system of illusions and consists in images that carry no sovereign value:

> Do you see that kitten chasing so prettily her own tail? If you could look with her eyes, you might see her surrounded with hundreds of figures performing complex dramas, with tragic and comic issues, long conversations, many characters, many ups and downs of fate,—and meantime it is only puss and her tail. How long before our masquerade will end its noise of tambourines, laughter, and shouting, and we shall find it was a solitary performance?—A subject and an object,—it takes so much to make the galvanic circuit complete, but magnitude adds nothing. What imports it whether it is Kepler and the sphere; Columbus and America; a reader and his book; or puss with her tail? (*CW* 3:46)

This short narrative goes beyond the pragmatic skepticism of *Nature*, where Emerson had dismissed the problematics of epistemology by questioning what difference it makes whether Orion is in the sky or in the mind. His only purpose then was to show it matters little whether the order of the world, the hierarchy and ranking we give it, is ideal or real. What is important, *Nature* affirms, is the unity of nature, the fact that nature does cohere and have purpose. The citation above makes quite a different point. The hierarchy in which we take ourselves to live shows itself to be counterfeit, arrives for us as a masquerade. The subject is alone in the world, its only object is a nature that reveals itself to be no more than a specious image of the subject.

"Subject" puts forward a lord of life that carries the structure of the succession of illusory representations, subverting the power of will. It is in order to characterize the topos of nature, not the principle of its organization, that Emerson writes, "Thus inevitably does the universe wear our color, and every object fall successively into the subject itself. The subject exists, the subject enlarges." Thus he adds, "I am and I have: but I do not get" (*CW* 3:45–46, 48). The movement described in "Subject" is not, as in "Reality," outward to determinations of the world, but inward to fragmented moments of intensity whose expression is found in the succession and prolific interplay of illusions. "Subject" describes human being in antihumanist nature, the sheer and radical solitude that is left to human being in the wake of the failure of humanism, an affective solitude that expresses itself solely in a world of illusions, including the illusion of reality and Being. Our integrity is limited to our solitude, to the sense of ourselves that Emerson grasps as the single virtue left to advocate: the "capital virtue of self-trust" (*CW* 3:46).

But the fall from self-reliance is marked. Self-trust is now situated in a world of images, where indifference is written into the fabric of things and society is predicated on illusions. It no longer gives voice to the universal sense, no longer articulates the world as an expression of love. Emerson adheres nonetheless to this value, and his persistence bears fruit in *Conduct of Life*, where self-reliance returns to prominence, coming to have for Emerson the value of a narrowly focused will manufactured in nature by the forces of fate. Although not yet applicable as conduct, at this point, too, self-trust names the most powerful attitude left to human being, an attitude consistent with Emerson's own posture as a writer, an attitude defined by narrow attention to its solitude, a glance that turns back from the images of the world to the affect of force that defines the subject, a turn thus back away from the specious diversions of the world to a posture of reception that can listen and point to, if not yet adequately articulate, nature's dictation.

From the vantage point of the end of "Subject, or the One" it is possible to see with some clarity what Emerson has accomplished in "Experience." On the basis of his antihumanist insight into the split of thought and will, and the consequent superficiality of Man, he draws apart the constituents of his early humanist synthesis, revealing each one to be a sovereign lord of life in its own right. Initially, this means drawing apart thought and will and explicating the principles of thought. In the process of doing so he indicates the priority of Illusion as the reigning idea of the times. "Illusion" also describes one perspective on life, set against the perspective revealed in "Reality," but it underwrites the entire enterprise of explicating finite and epochal principles of life. Even the subject is the affective power of the interplay of illusions, the reception of ourselves as a prolific feeling of nature's potency.

The most compelling sections of the essay remain the sections on will and the subject, for these speak to the fate of human being in nature, they speak to the principles that govern the human presencing of nature. Emerson draws out the power of presencing nature in the final four lords of life. Each one depicts an independent principle of presence. I have emphasized the interrelations among them not least of all because doing so indicates the disposition of the separate principles in comparison to the unity the four held under the humanist synthesis, where reception and action were coincident. Emerson accomplishes in these sections the representation of the finitude of the principles of Being that sponsor the humanist synthesis. He situates such crucial concepts as teleology, Being, will, and presence, showing their limits along with their power. The exposition contained in "Experience" is in this respect consistent with the project of deconstruction carried out by recent thinkers. Emerson makes no claim for the exhaustiveness of his deconstruction, and neither will I; but an attentive reading of "Experience" indicates that it broaches many of the most cherished and privileged concepts in the tradition of Western metaphysics, locating them in the context of antihumanist thought.

As important and profound as his anticipation of the critical turn on humanist metaphysics is, however, it is overshadowed (though, of course, complemented) by his identification of the mutual exclusivity of thought and will. The primary significance of the essay is its exploration of the consequences of this opposition, which can be summed up by Emerson's recognition of the fatality of joy and the superficiality of power. The bare presence of subjectivity amid the masquerade of life fittingly articulates this destiny. There is little use in suggesting that we need to get behind the masquerade, find the truth of the world; there is no behind the masquerade, least of all the fragmented force of the subject, which is as elusive as nature and expressed only in the images that successively tumble into subjectivity and mark its fragmentation. The only thing we might imagine to be "behind" the presence of the world is thought, thought's presencing of nature's dynamic, but thought in this respect is precisely the source of the counterfeit world. Emerson's vision is of nature that loves to hide and that hides most then when we think we have it in hand. We can view it from the perspective of thought, as the passing of moods, or from the perspective of will. In either case it eludes us. "Life wears to me a visionary face," Emerson thus concludes. "Hardest roughest action is visionary also. It is but a choice between soft and turbulent dreams" (*CW* 3:48). We have the ineluctable choice of letting life pass by us or missing when we reach out for it. The essay indicates the futility of all action, and thereby it robs any human action of legitimacy. Finally, it is "Surface" that depicts the common sense of this world, summed up in the assertion "There is no longer any right course of action, nor any self-devotion left among the Iranis" (*CW* 3:34).

Emerson finds himself in this unfounded position: having discovered that Man is the cause of the presence of the world, having returned the power of divinity to Man, and having then discovered the fall of Man.

The power of the first thought coupled with the power of the second leaves no room for progress or escape. Nature stands now, and Man can only wait for nature to speak a new truth. In the interim Emerson says we will live in a world of surface repetition. The only role left for individuals who reject this fate is to seek to clarify nature as it is, to expose its principles, Emerson's project in "Experience." There is no more to be done than await nature's call. "Patience and patience, we shall win at last" (*CW* 3:48–49). The victory, of course, will be nature's. But it will be a victory nature accomplishes through Man. For the one affirmative implication of "Experience," the affirmation that Emerson will develop under the concept of freedom in the second half of "Fate," is that nature is manifest only through Man, that Man is of nature and has, moreover, the crucial function of presencing thought. Nature, indeed, consists in the dynamic of coming to presence and presence, of thought and will, of genius and power. Thus, even if only secondarily for Man, still "the true romance which the world exists to realize" will be accomplished. The possible will become actual, because nature exists as "the transformation of genius into practical power" (*CW* 3:49). In the following chapter I will explain how Emerson traces this fatal transformation and thereby renews the possibility of conduct, drawing praxis out of the experience of unanchored *poiêsis*.

Part III

WHIRLING

The man of the world bows with a vertical movement of the head, up & down. My Stoic used a horizontal Salutation, as if always saying No.

Thought is nothing but the circulations made luminous. There is no solitary flower, & no solitary thought.

'Tis the receptivity that is rare, 'tis this I value, the occasions I cannot scientifically tabulate; the motive or disposing circumstances I could never catalogue; but now one form, or color, or word, or companion, or book, or work, & now another strikes the mystic invisible string, I listen with joy.

There is a Columbia of thought & art which is the last and endless sequel of Columbus's adventure.

—Emerson, *The Journals and Miscellaneous Notebooks*

Emerson's critique of the discourse of nature and Being can remind us of subsequent poststructuralist critiques emanating from Heidegger's writings. I have tried to emphasize this point without doing an injustice either to the independence of Emerson's inquiry or to the differences in style, vocabulary, and, to some extent, content that intervene between writers separated by an unusually long century. Emerson did not write in the context of a culture that had experienced, for instance, two world wars, the Holocaust, or the development of nuclear power and weaponry. He did not, for the most part, even write in the context of the United States' own Civil War, the greater part of its industrial development, or the social upheaval of waves of immigration. And most significantly he did not, as later writers do, write in the context of the advanced technology of the twentieth century. The ready, and sometimes misleading, complementarity of poststructuralist theory and postmodern culture reflects the twentieth-century development of technological expertise that has brought it closer to parity with the developments of reason. But Emerson's thought experiments were carried out largely in the absence of a corresponding technological culture. If "Surface" reminds one of descriptions of postmodern culture, as it does me, then it operates not as actual cultural critique, but rather as prophecy.

It can do so, however, because of the determinative and thus predictive power of reason, and it is in virtue of the developmental nature of reason that Emerson's transitional writings can be compared to poststructuralist writings. He certainly looked on different applications for his thought, but Emerson traced the same path of reason in his middle essays and lectures as these contemporary thinkers. And, as I showed in the last section, he traced this path to a generalized assault on the substantiality of Being, coupled, to be sure, with a nostalgia for substance that largely determines the tone of the period. He recognized the destructive element of dialectical overcoming, its endpoint in incessant self-overcoming that refuses to warrant a stay on nature and thus produces a world of illusions and images. Some of Emerson's descriptions seem curiously understated, even homely, such as the short narrative at the end of "Experience" of the kitten chasing her tail. But he can also be strikingly exact, as in his description of the method of nature, which emphasizes the temporality of the horizon of nature and thematizes it in terms of language. He can be philosophically precise in his terms and phrasing, as he is in a later treatment of the topic in "Illusions," where he writes, "There is the illusion of time, which is very deep; who has disposed of it?" (*C* 6:302). Emerson, just as well as poststructuralist writers, saw the threat reason's motility posed to the discourse of Being. He followed reason to its presentation of a technocratic vision of the world and recognized in it the threat thus posed to the humanity and dignity of the individual.

What one can hope to find in his later writings, then, if not relevant criticism of material culture, is a response to the threat reason seems to raise against its longtime ally, philosophical discourse. One can, that is, follow Emerson as he tracks reason beyond the humanist nostalgia and pessimism implicit in the method of nature, to the doctrine of fate and its recuperation of philosophy as an affirmative practice. The movement from the method of nature to the doctrine of fate can be seen as marking a philosophical development, a development of philosophy, that guards and preserves, if not Being in the technical sense, then at least this practice. I find the fundamental significance of Emerson's later writings in this development and preservation. The writings present an angle of vision, to use one of his own metaphors, from which reason shows its advance beyond the destructive dialectic of self-overcoming, which still figures decisively in philosophical and antiphilosophical discussions, and shows its redefinition of philosophy as the practice of life.

In essence, this advance is the movement, predicted in "Compensation," from an interior to an exterior focus of mind. Emerson puts his final thinking on the matter in these terms, writing in "The Natural History of Intellect," "I share the belief that the natural direction of the intellectual powers is from within outward
. . . but a study in the opposite direction has had a damaging effect on the mind" (*C* 12:12). The difficulty in understanding what this shift in focus consists in and what it entails, what becomes, then, the content of reason, is quite real. For Emerson's shift from an interior to an exterior focus of mind is earned and has significance in the context of, precisely, the history of his own intellectual development. An internal, introverted focus of mind comprehends both his humanist and anti-

humanist phases, both fixated on the mind's action as the object and telos of thought. Emerson's typically understated call for an external direction of mind amounts to no less than the rejection of interiority and the abandonment of dialectics as that for the sake of which we stake our existence. He thus casts his net wide indeed, for dialectics takes in for him any conception of life based on a potentially obtainable principle. As he had from his earliest writings onward, he would therefore include materialism, Lockean empiricism, Platonic and modern idealism, Christianity, indeed all systems of thought, as symptomatic of a dialectical pretension. But he would also include their negation. An internal direction of mind refers to any way of thinking (and acting on thought) that does so for the sake of a principle. Thus the idea of conducting one's life on the foundation of a telos, whether it is grasped by the individual through authentic action or perpetually eludes one's grasp, is what Emerson turns attention from. Such a turn of mind requires the discipline of abandoning any hope of finding a foundation for one's life. And equally, it requires turning from either the nostalgic torment of a withdrawn source or the ironic pleasure of manipulating its withdrawal. The external direction of Emerson's later thought is then characterized by the "terrible earnestness" of taking life as it comes, as it gives itself, without hope, nostalgia, or ironic detachment (*C* 7:93).

Emerson's embrace of an exterior orientation of mind responds to his discovery that the interior logic of humanism, which for him is the endpoint and domestication of the logic of Western metaphysical thought, turns on itself, overcomes and destroys itself, and in so doing casts suspicion on its origin. The writings of the transitional period, linked still to the humanist project but now by nostalgia and a sense of irrecoverable loss, are characterized by this suspicion. Emerson's advance on this position consists in the recognition that suspicion is a product of the interior logic itself. An exterior orientation gains its power and eloquence by setting itself as an alternative, indeed an antidote, to the suspicion raised by the dialectic of interiority. But it should be added, it does so, at a practical everyday level, by upholding the critique the transitional writings contain, for it is this critique that demonstrates the futility of pursuing a moral or epistemological source or origin of existence and thus opens up the meaning and value of an exterior direction of mind. Put otherwise, the transitional critique is maintained in Emerson's later writings as a regulative bar on reflective introspection and seems oddly to mimic (toward different ends) the use Emerson earlier made of the idealist "hypothesis." If idealism had, as it were, said, Suppose truth is immaterial, what then? and *Nature* had answered with a humanist doctrine, then Emerson now seems to be saying, Suppose truth is an illusion, what then? Indeed, in an 1850 journal entry Emerson very nearly asks just that: "*The Times*. That is to say, there is Fate; Laws of the world; what then?"[1] His answer, the doctrine of fate, arose at the point he put the critique in the transitional writings to use.

Because most readers of his later works would grant their continuity with the writings of the 1840s, it is more important to emphasize the difference between the two phases. Their difference consists in the shift from an interior direction of mind to an exterior direction. Emerson's antidote to interiority is to turn from a questioning and dialectical attitude that casts suspicion on "the source," and to preserve and guard it by taking instead a pious attitude toward its *difference*. "Yet what we really want," he writes elsewhere in "The Natural History of Intellect," "is not a haste to action, but a certain piety toward the source of action and knowledge" (*C*, 12:9). "Fate" renders that piety doctrinal. The signifying move by which it does so is the withdrawal of fate from nature, the unprecedented determination of an *absolute disjunction* between fate and nature. The sovereignty of fate indicates, and renders methodological, Emerson's belief that the proper direction of mind is external. It does so by setting as its first premise the radical disjunction of fate and nature: that is, the disjunction between the *source* of what we do and what we do.

The evolution of Emerson's philosophy is completed by the determination of this fundamental difference and the exterior orientation of mind it prescribes. He stressed the active foundation of value from his earliest period, of course, and the pragmatic nature of his thought has been explored on that basis. But his relation to the tradition of American pragmatism seems most convincing to me in these later writings, where it is rooted in his articulation of a method of thought that systematically precludes the turn inward to an abstract reflection on the source of action, maintaining piety toward that source, instead, by observing the effects of the source in the everyday practices of life. The doctrine of fate thus has two overt philosophical consequences. The first, earned through Emerson's exhaustive reflection on and ultimate disposal of interiority, is the identification of the practices of the individual—"the world as it is," Nietzsche writes, "without subtraction, ex-

---

1. Cited by Phyllis Cole, "Emerson, England, and Fate," in *Emerson: Prophecy, Metamorphosis, and Influence*, ed. David Levin (New York: Columbia University Press, 1975), 92.

ception, or selection . . . the eternal circulation:—the same things, the same logic and illogic of entanglements"—as the field in which the source of Being shows itself, and thus as the proper object of philosophy.[2] This identification affects his understanding of conduct by privileging sheer, unreflected-upon behavior.[3] The second is the characterization of thought in the epochal terms of an event, utterly at odds with the Cartesian tradition that assigns a necessary relation between the subject and thought. In this respect, too, Emerson predicts Nietzsche, who writes similarly in *Beyond Good and Evil* that "a thought comes when 'it' wishes, and not when 'I' wish. . . . *It* thinks, but that this 'it' is precisely the famous old 'ego,' is, to put it mildly, only a supposition, an assertion, and certainly not an 'immediate certainty.'"[4] More significantly, I think, he also anticipates Heidegger, whose later work is characterized by his sense of thought as "das Ereignis."[5] "The event of appropriation," as it is usually translated, refers to the occurrence of an appropriating law that gathers, Heidegger says poetically, in "a *primal oneness* the four—earth and sky, divinities and mortals."[6] Similarly, Emerson refers to the emergence of an insight that will "fill up the vacancy between heaven and earth" (*CW* 3:42). For both writers, thought could not maintain its function of preserving Being while coincident with the activity of will. Through that reciprocity, as one can see in Emerson's development, thought became the vehicle first of exclusionary power and then by extension of a life-denying dialectic that threatens thought itself. Part and parcel, then, of Emerson's rejection of interiority is his identification of thought as an event outside the province of our will and his preservation of the content of such moments of insight.

2. Friedrich Nietzsche, *The Will to Power*, ed. and trans. Walter Kaufmann and R. J. Hollingdale (New York: Vintage Books, 1967), 1041.

3. Hughes makes a similar point in *Emerson's Demanding Optimism*. Although she is not concerned directly with the philosophical content of Emerson's later writings, her discussion of *Conduct of Life* begins with a convincing account of the fatality of eloquence and impressively draws out the central importance of "Behavior" as representative of that fatality.

4. *Beyond Good and Evil*, in *Basic Writings of Nietzsche*, ed. Walter Kaufmann (New York: Modern Library, 1966), 214.

5. Heidegger develops the idea of "das Ereignis" in many of his later works, but a good discussion of it can be found in "On Time and Being," trans. J. Stambaugh (New York: Harper and Row, 1972).

6. "Building Dwelling Thinking," *Poetry, Language, Thought*, trans. Albert Hofstadter (New York: Harper and Row, 1971), 149.

5

The Fatal Event and the Birth of Agency

Conduct of Life confronts and, at least to Emerson's satisfaction, resolves the problem raised by the antihumanist thought that he developed in the 1840s: the problem of what to do, what authentic action can be, in view of the delimitation and critique of human action contained in the transitional lectures of 1841–42 and "Experience." The transitional essays and lectures do not, of course, deny the possibility of human action; rather, they subvert its claim to authenticity. Emerson's delineation of the seven lords of life in "Experience" completes the exposition he would give of the human experience of antihumanist nature. It speaks to the failure of humanism, to the reduction of Man to superficiality and repetitive action, and to a world of counterfeit and masquerade, cut off from originality and authenticity. It puts forward subjectivity as a sheer affect, an intense force that lacks any power to organize the world and thus gives rise to a world of successively subverted images. "Experience" privileges the irresolution of thought, posing will as a surface phenomenon and lamenting the collapse of the humanist synthesis. It completes the developments that began with "The Method of Nature," and in the final section, the essay makes clear that Emerson has made no progress on finding a foundation of right human action. On the contrary, he has left conduct out of his exposition of experience.

It is in this context that I read his well-known lines at the beginning of "Fate":

> It chanced during one winter a few years ago, that our cities were bent on discussing the theory of the Age. By an odd coincidence, four or five noted men were each reading a discourse to the citizens of Boston or New York, on the Spirit of the Times. It so happened that the subject had the same prominence in some remarkable pamphlets and journals issued in London in the same season. To me, however, the question of the times resolved itself into a practical question of the conduct of life. How shall I live? (C 6:3)

Directing attention to conduct, these lines indicate that for Emerson the times consist in practical action, a rather surprising emphasis given his premises in "Experience." But although the citation presents action and conduct as a problem and a question—How are we to live? What can right conduct be? Is freedom any longer possible?—the fact that it introduces the essay, and the book in which it is found, suggests some advance from "Experience" to a new stage of thinking.

The issue of conduct has of course been Emerson's central concern from his earliest writings onward. Throughout his writings he has understood proper action in terms of the metaphor of vision, in terms of seeing truly by willing the presence of nature. As I noted in Part I, conduct initially depends on the practical imperative to abandon normative forms of thought, and it yields the universal sense of authentic individuality as phenomenological resolution. In the early writings the eye stands, upright and face to face with nature, manifesting nature through a decisive act. It manifests the constant soul, the essential "I," as the constancy of presence. Phenomenological resolution is enabled by the conflation of sight and will, which allows the appropriation of nature's appearance by the individual, the enownment of self and nature figurally through the act of vision. Authenticity consists of this self-enownment, but it consists thereby as well of the ownership of nature, or articulating the universal sense of nature. Nature appears in the epochal unity of the horizon of the eye. When Emerson later laments that we are born to unity but see only parts, it is the unity of phenomenological resolution—of the self- and nature-possessing eye—that he has in mind. We are born to, our will gives us, the unified revelation of nature as our own. We are born to create the world anew with each turn of the spade that organizes and ranks the world. This is the fundamental faith of the early essays, and it is at bottom a faith in the capacity of human will to manifest nature, to make the world appear.

As I have shown, Emerson's critique of humanism subverts that capacity, indicating that Man itself is a finite possibility, and thereby destroying the centrality and universality of phenomenological resolution. Acts of will are scattered across the surface of nature. But the most important consequence of the critique, reflected in the structure of "Experience," is that will or Man is situated in the broader ecstasy of nature and placed at odds with thought, which emerges as the capacity to receive nature's flux. Will is, conversely, diminished to partial and essentially false acts. "Experience" has the effect of posing against each other, as the basic terms of humanism and antihumanism, the very powers that through their reconciliation enable the early humanist synthesis. By virtue of its completeness, moreover, the essay leaves Emerson's theory straddling the gap between the irresolution of thought and will's promise of freedom and univocity.

So if Emerson certainly never questions that we act, he does question whether we act freely and effectively. Written into the fabric of the exposition in "Experience" is the belief that our action is ineffective and in a fundamental sense not even our own. In one respect the doctrine of fate emerges simply as a clarification of that belief, a recognition that fate is fundamental. But as the above citation suggests, it also takes shape as a renewed affirmation of freedom and conduct, as in some way a response to the question how we are to conduct our life, how we are to live it rightly. Certainly, Emerson does not abandon the critique in "The Method of Nature" or the exposition of "Experience." But in "Fate" he *revalues* his understanding of human experience. In order then to understand the final stage of Emerson's thought, represented in the essays in *Conduct of Life*, and by extension to understand Emerson's justification of conduct, it is essential to discern the terms of the clarification the doctrine of fate works on the transitional theory. The question is not so much what fate adds to the exposition, but how it reconceives nature and human experience, and how it thus allows for a description of not just action but freedom, not just Man but conduct.

My reading of "Fate" really begins, then, with a return to the transitional works, aimed at locating the difference between the premises of the two periods. My principal assertion is that the crisis of conduct emerging from the turn to the method of nature in 1841 results from the manner in which Emerson conceptualizes the method of nature during the transitional phase, and that his initial conceptualization is contingent, not necessary. Simply put, Emerson continues in the transitional period to identify nature with human experience, as he had in the early humanist phase. The turn to antihumanism has pressed on his conception of nature suspicion of presence and thus the demand that nature include a withdrawal. As I showed in the last chapter, Emerson responded to this demand by asserting nature's illusoriness, its tendency to hide itself, and thus by implicating in nature the dynamic of revelation and concealment. Insofar as this dynamic is identified with experience, it shows its self-subversion. Because nature remains inextricably linked to presence, and thereby to human experience and Man, the human activity of presencing is shown to be settled in the milieu of its failure, the milieu of nature given as thought's irresolution. The articulations of will that presence nature have their origin in and must recede to the fact of nature's hiddenness and illusoriness. Or conversely, nature consists in the dynamic set in play by the failure of human causality and offers no terms for principled action.

Here then is the aspect of Emerson's initial conception of antihumanist nature that leads to the crisis of conduct: the primordial thing, which consists in the revealing/concealing dynamic of nature, is simply identified with human experience, given in its two modes as thought and will. The crisis in the transitional phase stems from the assumption in "Experience" that nature consists in nothing but the interrelation of thought and will, that thought—life seen from the platform of intellection—is the manner of the thing's irresolution. This assumption represents the interrelation of thought and will as a totalizing discourse that contains within itself the necessity of its own dissolution. Because Emerson's conception of the primordial thing in "Experience" only goes so far as to indicate the superficiality of presence, its illusoriness up against the hiddenness of nature, the essay in effect dictates the perpetuation of Man's failure. The essay is limited to the opposition of the promise of reality and the inevitability of its slippage and falsity, and thus to the exposition of superficial principles of the times. What should be clear is that Emerson's transitional conception of the method of nature betrays the latent nostalgia for human centrality, which marks the tone and in this respect even the content of "Experience." For insofar as nature emerges only through the perspectives of thought and will, the thing remains essentially human. Indeed, given the priority of thought in "Experience," nature is construed utterly in terms of intellect, intellect that now bars conduct. Thought's double gesture both sponsors and debases willful actualizations of nature's power.

The point I want to emphasize is that this result is necessary only given the interpretation of the method of nature put forward in the essay, an interpretation that continues to construe the dynamic of revelation and concealment in terms of human being, and thus in terms of a *single* discourse. Human experience, contained in the movement of thought to actuality, can only be poetic, as it were. It is destined to be the actualization of nature's slippage and becoming, but never, for Man at least, to be practical and effective. But this conclusion depends on the prior assumption that the interrelation of thought and action universally defines the scope of nature. Practicality, reality—pragmatic conduct, in short—is only thus situated in the poetic slippage of nature-as-thought and rendered inauthentic. Under this conception of the method of nature the only value fate—human destiny—can have is the negative or failed dialectic of Man's self-subversion. If Emerson is to develop the doctrine of fate in distinction to the method of nature, it will be by recognizing the contingency of his conceptualization of nature in the transitional writings and by recasting the topic precisely in respect to the universality he accords to the dynamic of revelation and concealment. Earning the contingency of this dynamic—the very motility of nature—tasks the imagination, to say the least, but it is, I would suggest, the challenge Emerson responds to in "Fate" and the basis on which he raises the problem and question of conduct in its opening paragraph. The paragraph represents a new beginning of sorts, a rethinking of the issue of antihumanist nature, and an effort to conceptualize antihumanism in such a way as to account for the conduct and the dignity of human being.

FATE AND NATURE

The change in Emerson's thought expressed in "Fate," and the principal manner in which "Fate" departs from the transitional works, resides in the distinction Emerson draws between fate and nature. This difference is unknown in "Experience," where fate is indistinguishable from nature, consisting in the failure of Man's phenomenological power. The overall argument of "Fate," however, describes a severing of nature from fate and a disposal of nature within fate. Indeed, the distinction between the two ideas is evident in the very fact of Emerson's isolation and development of the doctrine of fate, a doctrine that would be unnecessary were the single fact of Emerson's thought still understood in terms of the method of nature. The doctrine of fate can be seen then to replace the method of nature as the central fact of Emerson's thought. Throughout the essay, fate is described as the limit or parameter of nature, the fundamental value that circles round and makes possible the appearance of nature. No corresponding value is included in the explanation of the method of nature, where, instead, Man is the horizon of nature's presence, but, as I noted, an horizon that Emerson makes tremble. The method of nature consists entirely in the dynamic of revelation and concealment, where each pole of the dynamic is implicated in the other and where appearance derives from this coimplication and consists, thereby, in illusions. The doctrine of fate reconceives the essential dynamic of nature and introduces the value of fate as distinct from presencing itself.

As I said, this is expressed in the essay as a whole, which traces the effects of fate in nature. It is indicated explicitly, however, early in the essay, when Emerson writes, "The Circumstance is Nature. Nature is what you may do. There is much you may not do" (*C* 6:20). Emerson's meaning may seem vague at first, but it becomes clear in the context of the development and trajectory in his thought, outlined in the preceding chapters, and specifically in the context of the definitive relation between nature's presence and Man's action or doing, a relation that endures from the early humanist synthesis through its failure and now into the final period of Emerson's thought. Bearing that relation in mind, the statement reflects the distinction between fate and nature that is implied by the rest of the essay. Nature is precisely what it has always been for Emerson: what may be done, enacted, caused, brought to presence. It is the circumstance, the horizon of presence, that gathers around and defines the individual and the world. In the early period of his writing Emerson held that the circle of presence overruled circumstance and described the universal sense of nature. In his transitional writings he denied its presence, reducing it to illusions. Here he recovers nature in a new way: as the circumstance or actuality that it is given to Man to enact. Nature is given as what we may do and is set against what may not be done. The statement indicates fate's dual dictation of what may and may not be done, showing thereby a difference between nature and fate. What is crucial here is the suggestion that the essential *thing*—the concealing/revealing dynamic—is therefore not exhausted by nature; which is to say, it is not exhausted by the intersection of Man and nature and the illusory presences given rise to through that intersection. Rather, fate carries the revealing/concealing dynamic, the giving and withholding that enables nature. And nature takes the status of what fate gives to be done. This revaluation releases nature from its self-subversive dynamic and predicts Emerson's later description of it as an event.

But what then is fate? It is easier to say what fate is not, for the simple reason that fate is not nature, and nature is what appears, is enacted, and thus can be seen and known. In this respect one could say fate is nothing at all, an assertion I don't take lightly. From the perspective of phenomenological method, which guides Emerson's thinking—and indeed guides it to the overthrow of phenomenology itself—fate marks no space. It has no place in the field of nature's presencing dynamic. Rather, fate is the limit that stands around the presencing activity that is nature—stands around nature *as* what we may do. Properly speaking, fate has no existence. It is not. Fate is the condition of presence and Being and the limit of the dynamic of revelation and concealment. It is the limit of phenomenological efficacy. Construing fate conceptually as historical, social, or cultural determinacy—linguistically, for instance, as Cavell does, or, on the other hand, naturalistically or biologically: racially, in the case of Cornel West—misunderstands the most essential aspect of fate: that it precedes and predicts the appearance of nature but is not of nature.[1] Any effort to name fate, to locate it among the relations of which nature's appearing consists, indicates a passing over from fate to nature and, as one could predict, from fate to potentiality and freedom.

Whereas "Experience" had described the aspects and possibilities of human experience—the illusoriness of thought and the willful nature of reality—"Fate" situates human experience in a wider movement or motility. Emerson begins "Fate," as it were, behind the treatment of human experience. Fate is the fact of limit that has not been passed under thought, that has not been articulated or resolved in any way, not even as illusions. As such, fate is the pure fact of limit within which the dynamic of coming to presence and presence is played out as the possibility of human experience. Fate should be interpreted on the principle of phenomenological method, as it were, by following the clue of Emerson's early phenomenology. When thought of in this way, human experience remains in the fold of the phenomenological dynamic—of nature—but fate exceeds it.

This is a helpful way to think about fate, for two reasons. First, it makes clear that fate is not nature. But second, and more importantly, it shows that fate implies a perspective that is for nature, not for Man. Here, I think, terms emerge for expressing the revaluation Emerson makes in "Fate" of the method of nature. The revaluation can be simply put: it amounts to Emerson's recognition that the method of nature, the dynamic of coming to presence, presence, and passing from pres-

---

1. See Cavell, "Genteel Responses to Kant," and West, *The American Evasion of Philosophy*, 31ff.

ence, is subversive only insofar as we maintain a desire for the unity and depth of Man. Under the burden of that nostalgia, the intellect's recognition of the superficiality of Man is desperate indeed. *From the perspective of nature's dynamic itself*, however, the appearance of Man as a surface phenomenon—the superficial event of will in nature—far from being mistaken, is inscribed in nature's process of unconcealment and is thus inevitable, destined, fatal. Moreover, it is to that extent the legitimate manifestation of power. The doctrine of fate announces then a reconsideration of the dynamic, or method, of nature, which views the play of appearing and disappearing without concern for the moral terms of humanist thought and thus fully embraces the platform of intellection Emerson identified in "The Method of Nature," no longer posing it against the platform of action, as was the case in the 1840s. The ethos of action is given as subordinate to fate, and for that reason as fatally legitimated. The dynamic of coming to presence, presence, and passing from presence is seen, not as one way of viewing nature, but as nature's sole activity, as nature's destiny. The doctrine of fate indicates that fate *necessarily* gives nature; it is, indeed, nothing more than the necessity of the giving of nature. Equally, it thereby affirms Man's superficial appearance as the destiny of nature, as what nature is fated to do.

The distinction Emerson draws between nature and fate is crucial because it indicates his completed rejection of metaphysical thought, a rejection that reaches completion only at the point he sets aside the *habit* of thinking in terms of final causality. To the extent fate is not a principle of nature or Being, but rather is posed against nature, it names a force beyond the limits of the metaphysical tradition and its guiding question of the cause of Being. To be sure, Emerson had described the method of nature as the milieu of nature's acausal appearing in his 1841 lecture. But at that time, and continuously through the writing of *Essays: Second Series*, the acausality of nature's appearing operated as a privation on the depth and authenticity of Man. It established a world of essentially ironic illusions. In "Fate" Emerson literalizes, as it were, the world of illusions, recognizes its reality, or, rather, recognizes that it is illusory (or not) only from the perspective of humanist thoughts and pretensions. He revalues nature, then, by letting pass the opposition he had first seen between the platform of intellection and the platform of action and by asserting, as he does in "Fate," that there is only one continuous view, or doctrine, of nature, and that is the doctrine of fate. The doctrine of fate embraces the acausal motility of the method of nature as nature's destiny and recognizes its destiny thereby in the activity of appearing. It is, moreover, this very notion of the destiny inscribed in nature that gives rise to the doctrine of fate and to the distinction between fate and nature—a distinction, I should add, that is not absolute but precisely a gesture to the sense that there is a destiny inscribed *in* and understood as being *for* nature.

To ask once again, then: What is the doctrine of fate? What is the destiny inscribed in nature? It is the very *fact* of an acausal condition of nature's appearing, a condition, therefore, that cannot be construed in terms of teleological relations, that cannot be accounted for or held responsible, and that thus demands another kind of apprehension. Fate has no existence within the limits of the humanist logic of nature's presence. It is nothing at all insofar as it is never anything we *can do*, insofar as it is never present and therefore ascertainable as a cause of what appears: either directly or as the displaced implication of a cause. Fate is the thought of an unprincipled condition of nature withheld from nature; and as such it is nothing at all. But it gives rise to all things—to nature. Fate is the destiny of nature to come to presence. It is nature's self-giving. Here is the profound change that occurs between "The Method of Nature" and "Fate": nature's temporality, the illusoriness of time, is disposed under fate and thus reconceived and affirmed as self-given.

It cannot be overstated that by distinguishing fate from nature Emerson indicates the severing of nature's destiny from human interpretations and moral evaluations, both humanist and ironic. It indicates that nature is neither the handmaiden of Man nor the irresolute medium of his fall. Nature is fatal, and as such is dictated to Man as what we may do.

That the fatal affirmation of Man is settled in a deeper sense of the finitude of Man is evident in the use Emerson makes of the theory of evolution. Needless to say, he appeals to evolution, not in order to voice an empirical interpretation of fate, but, as with the geological transfiguration of the humanist method of circles, in order to figure the situation of Man in nature's destiny, both as fatally dictated and as the possibility of freedom and conduct:

> The book of Nature is the book of Fate. She turns the gigantic pages,—leaf after leaf,—never re-turning one. One leaf she lays down, a floor of granite; then a thousand ages, and a bed of slate; a thousand ages, and a measure of coal; a thousand ages, and a layer of marl and mud: vegetable forms appear; her first misshapen animals, zoophyte, trilobium, fish; then, suarians,—rude forms, in which she has only blocked her future statue, concealing under these unwieldy monsters the fine type of her coming king. The face of the planet cools and dries, the races meliorate, and man is

born. *But when a race has lived its term, it comes no more again.* (*C* 6:15, emphasis added)

Emerson's final cautionary note is directed at the pretensions of Man, inscribed in the history of metaphysical thought. Man is not the end and purpose of nature, or its limit and horizon, as he made clear in "The Method of Nature." Man is, however, the current destiny of nature geologically situated, as Emerson's description emphasizes. To be sure, nature is destined to manifest Man for the simple reason that it consists in a dynamic made possible only insofar as human being exists to articulate horizons of presence. This fundamental fact of the relation of Man and nature is constant throughout Emerson's writings. It is the significance he gives to this fact that changes, and changes profoundly from 1836 to 1841, and then again from 1841 to 1860, when "Fate" is published. Only in his final manifestation of it does Emerson view the dynamic of nature affirmatively as that which fatally gives Man as the event of freedom.

Fate then names an unprincipled and anarchic condition of nature and Being. It is not a cause to be known and pursued, to be indicted and accused, or finally to be held responsible in any sense. The identification of fate as the destiny of presence written in nature releases nature from responsibility for and to what is concealed, and releases it too from the subversive dynamic that characterizes the transitional period. In the broadest sense, of course, Emerson continues to view nature and fate as identical. As he writes, "The book of Nature is the book of Fate." His point, however, is that the book of nature is therefore fatal and gives presence to the inevitable and spreading destiny of nature. As such, the book of nature is neither rooted nor uprooted, neither hidden nor revealed. It moves along horizontal trajectories that, showing no synchronic cause, are sheerly manifest, given in gathering and dispersing networks of relation. The book of nature is the book of fate inasmuch as the dynamic of nature is destined to presence, and destined to precisely the presence it has taken. The implication of concealment held in the activity of presencing shows its fatality; or put otherwise, it shows that we did not cause nature, shows that nature has no causality, not even the causality of its own withdrawal to hiddenness. Nature's first activity is fatal—the giving of presence, the very image-making activity of which nature consists and in which Man is situated.

On this foundation, set in a revaluation of the method of nature that legitimates nature and Man as a spreading network of effective relations, Emerson develops his revised understanding of conduct. His reconsideration of the method of nature, and his identification of fate's distinction from nature, serves to enable freedom, to regain what he will call the sovereignty of power in the essay "Power." In "Fate" power emerges as an autonomous capacity. In a general sense, Emerson means by this that Man is necessary, that fate gives rise to Man. That Man, freedom, and action are fatal dictations has two consequences: it delimits Man as it also calls for recognition of what nature dictates when it speaks Man. The age of Man is finite and inessential but destinal, a destiny of nature, an epoch that fate prepared for, if also one that fate will overcome.

Emerson's transformation of the book of nature into the book of fate indicates a further complication in the topic of Man and nature. His description of the evolution of nature through various epochs to the age of Man implies an awareness of the significance of fate for itself— its self-understanding—in the age of Man. Indeed, he writes, "But if there be irresistable dictation, this dictation understands itself" (C 6:4). Fate's giving of nature as the power of presence is traceable to this moment of self-understanding. That is to say, fate gives nature as the presence that is gathered together in virtue of a fatal reflection on fate, by virtue of fate's self-reflection. Emerson's language here can be misleading. By introducing the vocabulary of self-understanding he invites a humanist reading of fate's reflection, or at the very least an interpretation of fate that locates it within the horizon of human thought. And to a certain extent this is true; fate's self-understanding occurs insofar as fate is brought under thought. It is not surprising, then, to find readers who impose a humanist reading on the text, often by insisting on ironic interpretations. Emerson goes to some length, however, to avoid presenting fate's self-reflection as humanistic, or, in any case, as something Man does, and only a refusal to address the very possibility of his antihumanism would force one to read irony in his claim that we do not cause reflection, but rather it occurs. His point is clear and follows from the logic of his late work: thought is itself fatally given—it approaches us—and Man too is given, precisely as that which does the reflecting. But Man is introduced into this explanation decidedly after the fact, as the name of the fatality that reflects and thus as the vehicle of fate's self-understanding. If he is the "criticism that pries into the matter," Man is far from a whimsical creator deploying fate as one more turn of the screw, a description that once again employs a decidedly poor and external way of speaking (C 6:26–27).

Emerson's description of fate's self-understanding complements the reading of fate as that which gives nature and Man, and the overall critique of Man according to which since 1841 Emerson has not recognized the efficacy of Man. It sets in place a fatal reflective capacity that is consistent with the sense of destinal nature. When Emerson writes that fate understands itself, he indicates the destiny of nature, the fact that fate is destined to give nature. It does so through an act of self-understanding—an act that is no more than fate's turning back on itself and gathering itself within a circle of presence. That the cause of this act is left out of the explanation—though troubling from a humanist perspective, from the platform of action—is nonetheless in keeping with the doctrine of fate.

If Emerson develops his conception of conduct on the basis of the doctrine of fate, then he accordingly develops it without reference to a principle of action and without responsibility to accountable effects. As alternative and opposition to the seductive call to mastery, conduct occurs in and through fate's innocent giving of nature and, as such, occurs as what we may do. Emerson talks about conduct in two general ways, perhaps risking some confusion by calling them freedom and fate, the two poles of the double consciousness he speaks of toward the end of the essay. In the following section I will show that both of these general sorts of conduct are fatal and that they are in fact continuous with each other, emerging in the single fabric of nature's power relations. The distinction between them, of which so much has been made, does not suggest an escape from the dictates of fate—which is the last thing Emerson would advocate—but rather two manners in which fate gives itself, and thus two sorts of conduct. Both, I would now emphasize, consist in the enactment of fate and derive from attention to what fate makes possible. Emerson's theory in "Fate" is in no respect dualist, a fact that should be obvious enough from his assertion that freedom is necessitated. It bears repeating, nonetheless, that fate is not posed against the noble essays of freedom, and this is the case notwithstanding some of Emerson's less precise descriptions that might imply just that. Rather, fate gives conduct in alignment with the power relations of nature, and the only conceivable dualism it admits is that between the conduct that obeys and the conduct that commands. Both of which are given functions within fate's powerful calculus.

FATAL CONDUCT

The meaning of conduct becomes clear when viewed in terms of the distinction between nature and fate, which itself depends on the fatal preeminence of Man in nature. Fate shows itself as the limit of the activity of presencing, and nature is the process of human experience—the process of presencing, or what we may do. Fate is the limit that defines the contours of Man, within which Man is situated. Man remains the activity of vision, the process of presencing thought, but remains this as situated within fate's limits and as given rise to by fate. This suggests that conduct will consist in the activity of presencing nature according to the fatal definition determined by what we may do, by our circumstance or context of action: in being the medium of nature's manifestation or, indeed, being fate considered from the side of nature.

Emerson's actual characterization of conduct in "Fate" follows this description by identifying the conduct of the individual as the presencing of nature in and through the enactment of fate's limits. That is, it describes conduct as the process of presencing the power dictations of fate, of enacting the power made possible by one's circumstance. In essays like "Power" and "Wealth," as before in the "Surface" section of "Experience," Emerson develops the sort of conduct associated with this fatalistic description. In the broadest sense, he describes right conduct as the enactment of the organization, or law, of the circumstance in which one finds oneself, that is, in doing what it is given one to do and thereby disclosing power. Conduct in this sense operates as rigorously and as determinately as the laws of nature. Indeed, for Emerson, the situation of the individual is essentially no different than the interaction of natural forces; the situation of the individual is governed as much as any object by the force relations defining the situation. The development of Emerson's thought out of a critique of the humanist philosophy of will yields this conception of nature as a field of externalized forces, which admits no final gathering will. Thus Emerson characterizes nature as a plane of spreading forces in an 1856 journal entry: "Blessed wonderful nature," he writes, "without depth, but with immeasureable lateral spaces,—has only the thickness of a shingle or a slate. . . . Nature itself is nothing but a skin" (*JMN* 14:46–47). Nature, he suggests, is a tissue of force relations that show no origin or end and indeed no progress beyond increasingly complicated constellations of power. His approach to nature has shifted from the early period's attempt to find in nature evidence of Man's centrality, to his later conception of nature as an infinitely extended board on which the network of forces is the condition for playing games of power. "Some play at chess, some at cards, some at the stock exchange; I prefer to play at Cause & Effect" (*JMN* 14:57). Power, causality, and thus *conduct* enter nature as something to do.

The relations of cause and effect are for Emerson a power game, then, with no metaphysical repercussions. His field of interest is the interaction of forces into gatherings of power, and it is here that he finds conduct, *praxis* that consists in adapting to the fatal direction, the destinal drive of nature. So far I have spoken of this movement principally in the broad terms of the activity of presencing, but it should be clear that presencing has its concrete reality in discrete relations of cause and effect—in what we may do or effect, in the practical power we realize. This is the significance of nature under the doctrine of fate: the power given as what we do and defined by action. Conduct, then, consists in action that accords with the fatal direction of nature, that listens to fate's dictations, releases to them, and enacts them. Emerson's use of naturalist metaphors is not simply tropological. Certainly it implies no materialist thesis, or in any case not such a thesis as it would be construed under the terms of modern dualism. But it does imply the accordance of action with the laws of fate and, *through such accordance*, the instrumentalization of fate. "The right use of Fate," he writes, "is to bring our conduct to the loftiness of nature. Rude and invincible except by themselves are the elements. So let man be. Let him empty his breasts of his windy conceits, and show his lordship by manners and deeds on the scale of nature. Let him hold his purpose as with the tug of gravitation. No power, no persuasion, no bribe shall make him give up his point. A man ought to compare advantageously with a river, an oak, or a mountain" (*C* 6:28). The description loses a merely metaphorical quality and some of its seeming imprecision when placed next to Emerson's remarks on the thinness ("oh so thin") of nature. Then it becomes clear that relations in nature are for Emerson the indices of the play of power, and if his purpose in the above statement is to set aside the conceit that the individual has any essential depth or final referentiality, then it is also to endorse conduct as the enactment of the power given in the circumstantial relations of nature. At stake for conduct is neither moral goodness nor religious justification, but the use of power.

First of all, fatal conduct is utterly divorced from motives extraneous to the situation in which one finds oneself; its motives are nothing but the finite terms of one's circumstance. Fate is not a universal cause, and conduct, therefore, is rigorously circumstantial. Any appeal beyond the context of possible action, the constellation of force relations that define the individual's situation and capacity, is, as described above, a "windy conceit." Like those pragmatists who come after him, Emerson has little patience for conduct and action that locates its origins beyond the real situation in which we find ourselves or that identifies its value as anything but the power, the pragmatic effect, realized by action. But perhaps even more stringently than some of them, he insists that conduct is nothing but the sheer enactment of one's power. He construes ethics in mathematical terms, as the calculation of the intersection of forces in a situation, as the science of power. The "morally" right is that which exposes the organization of a scene by enacting its power. Right conduct is natural, it is doing what we may do, and Man is thus a natural function. Emerson reads Man back into nature, affirming that his conduct is governed by the forces of nature, the circumstance of power. There is little place here for Man that is self-motivated or self-reflective. Emerson posits Man, conduct, as a function in the larger machinery of nature. Even his metaphors tend now to characterize nature technologically, as powerful machinery.

Inasmuch as his theory of conduct is founded on the realization of the necessity and power inscribed in the law of any circumstance, I see no alternative but to assume that he views conduct as consisting often in obedience to the forces that command one. Moreover, such obedience is of necessity blind, in the sense that Emerson says we blindly obey hereditary tendencies and bodily limits. The will that commands these actions is not our own, and we conduct ourselves as a force within its gathering. In this respect, too, and perhaps in this respect primarily, fate dictates our conduct and, again, dictates it as nothing more than acquiescence to the motility of nature. Nonetheless, Emerson does not restrict the sense of conduct to obedience to a greater will, nor does he emphasize this sense of conduct. His purpose in "Fate" is, instead, to show that from this model of fatal conduct it is possible to affirm free action. Free action or conduct occurs when we *do* identify with the commanding will in a situation, or, to put it more properly, when it is fatally given to us to identify our force with the will that gathers and commands a scene and thus to know its power. Nothing in this description of freedom separates it from the doctrine of fate and the subsequent interpretation of nature as a field of force relations. On the contrary, Emerson views freedom utterly within the terms of nature's power game. Freedom is the occurrence of knowing ourselves as the commanding will in a situation.

The second half of "Fate," which focuses on freedom, explores this explanation of the fatal occurrence of freedom. Emerson develops it in terms of the relation of thought, affect, and will to the doctrine of fate. His discussion is prepared for by his earlier assertion that fate understands itself. As I said before, that self-understanding is given; it suggests no philosophically significant human power or foundation. Emerson's remarks on thought attest to his confidence in the fatality of reflection and, thus, of freedom, and he accordingly alters the traditional sense of thought and intellection as a capacity of Man, as something that we do. Consistent with his assertion of the superficiality of human thought, of Man Thinking, he here presents thought outside the boundaries of human power, showing that we do not so much think as thought comes over us, that thought is, as in Heidegger's later writings, an *event* that happens to us, and, moreover, that freedom derives from the event of thought, from the fatal appearance for thought of unity and order in nature, which, as above, gives command over a situation.

The awareness given in thought does not exceed the limits of fate, nor does it enclose fate. Rather, it is precisely the thought *of* the limits of our circumstance. Importantly, this indicates that thought is not manufactured or willed, or defined by our utterance; we in no way are accountable for thought. Rather, thought arrives for us as the appearance of the law of nature. It comes to us, as it were, inexplicably, overcoming us and revealing the necessity governing nature. We do not clarify the order of nature, and any willful rationalization of nature's order remains superficial under the critique carried out in "The Method of Nature." Equally, therefore, thought is not continuous, at least not in the sense that it provides an effective reflection on the law of nature. Moments of fatal reflection that yield awareness of the limits and order of nature are given to us sporadically, and the law of nature itself is finite and contextually limited. It arrives, Emerson states, as events that give us an illumination of the unity of nature. In the absence of such events of thought, our conduct is limited to the obedience described above, and it is therefore through the event of thought that Emerson says we realize freedom:

> The revelation of Thought takes man out of servitude into freedom. We rightly say of ourselves, we were born and afterward we were born again, and many times. We have successive experiences so important that the new forgets the old, and hence the mythology of the seven or the nine heavens. The day of days, the great day of the feast of life, is that in which the inward eye opens to the Unity in things, to the omnipresence of law:—sees that what is must be and ought to be, or is the best. This beatitude dips from on high down on us and we see. It is not in us so much as we are in it. If the air come to our lungs, we breathe and live; if not, we die. If the light come to our eyes, we see; else not. And if truth come to our mind

we suddenly expand to its dimensions, as if we grew to worlds. We are as lawgivers; we speak for Nature; we prophesy and divine.

This insight throws us on the party and interest of the Universe, against all and sundry; against ourselves as much as others. (*C* 6:25–26)

If the giving of nature and presence, and ultimately of freedom, occurs for Emerson at the point when fate gives itself as thought, thought itself is presented as larger than the individual, an occurrence in which the individual is situated. Emerson's theory began as a philosophy of will, for which will articulates thought within the epoch of the individual, but he here describes thought in an entirely different way. Thought is something that comes over the individual, not something he causes or articulates. "It is not in us," he says of thought, "but we are in it. It is of the maker, not of what is made. . . . This uses and is not used" (*C* 6:30). Neither does human freedom have its origin in anything we do, but rather in what is done to us. Freedom, too, is received. The clarity of thought occurs to us, beyond our power to control it. It comes as an event that we are born into. When thought happens it makes us, gives us power that is posed against even our sense of ourselves, gives us power *as* a lawgiver to the world. Still, the occurrence of thought, though it resolves nature's law for us, remains distinct from the humanist conception of thought as phenomenological resolution, inasmuch as Emerson describes thought as coming to us, as effective. We experience such thought, when we do, by listening to fate. Emerson here reveals his conviction that the completion and closure of the metaphysical epoch releases thought from principial structures in general and from the hegemony of will in particular and gives it as an *event* that dictates us.

The full extent of Emerson's conception of freedom is, however, only implicit in his description of the event of thought. As he writes, the insight thought gives us carries with it the recognition of what must be. The event comes, then, not only as a vision of nature's law but, as importantly, as a command to carry the law out in action. For Emerson, the insight given by thought and the will to carry it out are inseparable. "Our thought . . . affirms an oldest necessity, not to be separated from thought, and not to be separated from will. They must always have coexisted" (*C* 6:31). The reconciliation that he could not locate between thought and will during the transitional period is here realized under the doctrine of fate, but it is realized by the subsumption of will under fatal thought. Emerson makes this point explicit by showing the genealogy of will in the coimplication of thought and affect. So if his later thought renovates the activity of will subverted in the transitional works and presents freedom as the birth of agency in nature, reaffirming it as "the one serious and formidable thing in nature . . . will," it is a will that no longer reflects human interpretations of nature or human foundation (*C* 6:34).

Following the form of his deduction of reality in "Experience," Emerson asserts, "If thought makes free, so does the moral sentiment. The mixtures of spiritual chemistry refuse to be analyzed. Yet we can see that with the perception of truth is joined the desire that it shall prevail; that affection is essential to will" (*C* 6:32). Will emerges in nature out of the clear perception of the law that defines the relations of forces in an event and the intense feeling of directionality, the moral sentiment toward action, that enacts the perception. If thought entails will's realization of the relations of an event, then Emerson notes that to that extent it carries with it the feeling that motivates its enactment. An event thus arises through the complicity of thought and affect. "Insight," Emerson writes, "is not will, nor is affection will. . . . There must be a fusion of these two to generate the energy of will" (*C* 6:29). The event is more than a moment of illumination; for Emerson, it is the order put in action through thought realized as practical power in the world. In this respect it is as much will as thought, and finally, for Emerson, it is power. The event returns the power of Man but, Emerson insists, at the price of individual self-possession: "There can be no driving force except through the conversion of the man into his will," Emerson writes, "making him the will, and the will him" (*C*, 6:29). The cost of freedom is the reduction of Man to his will, which is to say, the surrender of human interpretations and release to the power of nature, to the fatality given rise to through thought, release to the finite articulation of a thought.

Emerson's depiction of the birth of will and freedom as the enactment of thought is situated in the antihumanist critique of 1841 and the revaluation effected on it by the doctrine of fate. One can explore it, then, by thinking again about the doctrine of fate in relation to the method of nature. The method of nature dictated the disposal of Man in the play of nature's appearing as an obeying or commanding will. Will succumbed to the play of nature, was desubstantialized by a force it could not trace to its cause. The doctrine of fate revalues this play of appearing, affirming it as nature's destiny. But the revaluation does not effect the essential structure of nature in relation to Man. Man remains disposed in the power of nature's fluctuations, and, more importantly, remains disposed either as that which obeys or that which is given to command a situation. What has changed is Emerson's evaluation of Man and will. These were severed from thought during the transitional period, again, only because they were taken to name the possibility of principial value, and thought, as the vehicle of nature's irresolution and acausality, was seen as subverting that possibility. The fatal revaluation of the method of nature has the primary effect of setting aside the assumption that nature's activity is for Man, even subversively so—recognizing that Man is a function of nature's destiny—and thus renewing the possibility of self-evident presence, but now as nature's destiny outside the demands, essentially humanist, for causal responsibility.

It is Man then that is finally most revalued by the doctrine of fate; Man comes to consist in no more than a fatal capacity. Freedom resides in being the will that gathers together nature's destinal presence. But the roles of obedience and command, implied for Man in the method of nature, are not revalued by Emerson in order to reinvigorate the humanist faith in Man but to affirm will's fatality. To be sure, when fate arrives as a thought, it dictates Man in the role of the commanding will in a situation, as the voice and eyes of nature's presence, as the legislator of nature. "He who sees through a design, presides over it, and must will that which must be" (*C* 6:31). Will is reconciled with thought through the doctrine of fate by being detached from the universalist pretensions of humanism, by being read back into nature as a function of its destiny. Emerson asserts the necessity of will in nature, which is to say simply the fact of the gathering of nature in ordered, though transient, structures. Indeed, he views nature as consisting of the lateral growth, intersection, and proliferation of such gatherings. What is important to him in the second half of "Fate" is that it is sometimes given to thought to see through nature's order and identify with the will that renders nature coherent, and that Man at those moments finds himself identified with the gathering will and partakes of its commanding vision. As early as 1841 Emerson had seen that such moments of freedom and power could not be forged by the individual. Man's will always misses in its efforts to articulate nature. All interpretations reflect the interests of the individual and not the value of nature. The energy that gathers together and presences nature is not Man's. But only with the doctrine of fate does he explicitly acknowledge that it is the destiny of nature to rely and that this destiny is realized through the event of thought and the will it generates. The doctrine of fate enunciates nature's destiny to presence and precisely thereby recovers the relation between thought and will.

Will becomes for Emerson the sheer, pragmatic articulation of law—a finite law of a specific circumstance—given in thought. Indeed, will is nothing but the occasion or occurrence of the practical articulation of the law of nature. Freedom occurs when Man is given a commanding view of the law of nature and thus arises as the will that articulates it, when Man, then, is the will that gathers nature together in a unity under a single law. The discussion in "Fate" makes clear that most of human existence consists in obeying powers more capacious than our own. But when thought comes, it comes as the recognition of the law of an event, and as such it comes as the will that binds nature together. It comes, in short, as the will that commands an event. Emersonian freedom in its final form is the fatal occurrence of such will. As such, it distinguishes us from our condition under blind obedience to fate.

> It distances those who share it from those who share it not. Those who share it not are flocks and herds. It dates from itself; not from former men or better men, gospel, or constitution, or college, or custom. Where it shines Nature is no longer intrusive, but all things make a musical or pictorial impression. The world of men show like a comedy without laughter: populations, interests, government, history; 'tis all toy figures in a toy house. (*C* 6:30–31)

Thought introduces into the workings of fate a moment of vision, an apprehension of nature's "thisness" that has a comic and joyous effect. It brings freedom, which arrives as thought and will and sets one apart from blind conduct. Pragmatic agency is born out of the event of thought, a clarity of vision, that in being given fatally gives will, a self-sustained event that lays out the sense of the circumstance before us as the will that articulates its law.

Emerson's emphasis in the description of thought as an event is on the emancipatory effect of this destiny, on the manner in which an event of thought dissociates us from the kind of blind conduct I described at the beginning of this section. One can rightly understand this effect in terms of the appearance of the law of the event, which suggests the individual's inhabitation, fatally, of the paradigmatic posture of human freedom, that of overlooking the unity and order of the scene of nature. Certainly this is what Emerson has in mind. But the fatal emergence of thought reflects destinal emancipation in a second and more important sense as well, inasmuch as it both compares to and differs from the emergence of unifying will described in the "Reality" section of "Experience." It is useful for that reason to compare what Emerson says here about thought to his discussion in "Reality."

The event of thought, like the description of Reality, signals conceptual or *formal* freedom; but this is, in one sense at least, no emancipation at all, inasmuch as it is embedded in the fate of nature's self-destructive activity. It is more important then that the event of thought indicates emancipation in a second sense by enabling a posture from which *to affirm* the conceptual event, a freedom unavailable during the transitional phase, principally, as I have shown, because of the totalizing scope of the discourse of humanism still evident in the method of nature. The description thus reveals an important shift that takes place from "Reality" to "Fate" in Emerson's tone and attitude toward the emergence of thought and freedom.

Clearly, the occurrence of thought bears substantial relation to the surprising appearance of a unifying will described in "Reality." As I have shown, it is precisely will that is generated by virtue of the event of thought. As in "Reality," a unifying will is engendered coincident with the emergence of a new thought. But whereas in "Experience" Emerson had declared this the principle of reality, here he explicitly distances the event from reality by noting the comic nature of the unity of thought. The event of thought reveals the unity of an order that refers to nothing, that moves in a field distinct from the principial constructions of reality, that derives from no cause, is driven by no telos, and is, thus, fundamentally irresponsible. Its law is the coherent sense of the event, limited to the power of radically finite relations, a coherent body, or constellation, of forces, which appeal to no concept of metaphysical depth, and thus allow no subversion comparable to the reduction of Reality to a kind of illusion seen in "Experience." It should not need to be said, then, Emerson describes no metaphysical vision. His conception is utterly divorced from the premises of traditional philosophy. The event presences a moment of natural sense and a pragmatic realism then, but in no respect places nature in a referential relation to thought. Put otherwise, there is nothing behind an event to which it refers, not even a nostalgic attitude that would dispose it as an ironic illusion. But if from the perspective of metaphysics, an event is therefore merely a surface phenomenon, then from the perspective of fate, which in *Conduct of Life* replaces the humanist point of view, the opposition of surface and depth is moot, and the implied criticism is beside the point. An event is the showing forth of the relations that inhere among things, understood as the destiny of nature to become practical power and pragmatic reality. The destiny of nature is fatal will, it manifests power as against the illusions of "Experience."

Emerson's description of freedom is not of a principle of reality that will not hold, but of a comic unity that precisely does hold sway, pragmatically and effectively, in our vision of the world, until such time as a more powerful organizing thought overtakes us. The change in tone between "Experience" and "Fate," which derives I would say from the distinction Emerson draws between fate and nature, signifies an affirmation of freedom as pragmatic and powerful. It implies a release to the formulation given by fate to thought, a release to it as purely given, as utterly fatal, implying no depth or reality. Freedom, that is to say, inheres in a release *from* the anxiety over thought's possible reality and a subsequent release *to* its effective power to organize the world. The role of the medium of clear vision, a role undercut in the transitional works, is retrieved here in the sense that, as an event, freedom is justified by virtue of the distinction drawn between fate and nature. As a fatal event, freedom is released from the subversive dynamic of nature's concealment. By identifying the fatality of thought as distinct from the transitional conception of the speciousness of thought and action, Emerson establishes the posture from which he can justify and affirm the event of thought as emancipatory both conceptually and pragmatically: the event of thought presents the world as the power of will's articulation, the law of nature active as what we may do, neither real nor illusory, neither profound nor superficial, but effective. The event of freedom is simply unfounded but found pragmatic power.

Concretely considered, release to the effectiveness of the order given by thought, and the consequent affirmation of it as the content of conduct, consists in *becoming* the will that is implicated in the thought and, moreover, becoming it with *no remainder*, with no suggestion that the order given in thought is anything but effective. To treat thought as so radically pragmatic, as utterly used up in, and as, the will that enacts it, is to treat it as comic, successful, affirmative, for no remainder looks on at the spectacle to remark its illusoriness and lament its meaninglessness. Given this understanding, one can view events as the fatal production of the means for the exteriorization of nature's law. The value of the operation of will is its capacity to bring nature's law to presence, to show unity and direction in nature, as against the mere profusion of sense and circumstance, and thus to meliorate nature. It would be more correct, however, to reverse this formulation: the exteriorization of nature's organization occurs in and through a finite event of will. In either formulation, the value of the event (will, the presence of nature's organization) resides in the manifestation of nature as effective power—as the sheer exteriority of will—in the contextual exercise of effectively purposive power.

The explanation I am offering has two consequences for the significance of will and Man. First, it suggests that will has value as the activity of reason understood as the work of power in nature. Once again, no universality is attributed to an act of will, no deduction from the fact of practical power to a separable practitioner. Emerson characterizes the activity of will as finite in scope, and equally, then, he conceives of reason as a limited *instrument*. Simply, it is the fatal capacity of will to articulate the organization of an event. His characterization of the appearance of will accords with this explanation: "When a strong will appears, it usually results from a certain unity of organization, as if the whole energy of body and mind flowed in one direction. All great force is real and elemental. There is no manufacturing a strong will" (*C* 6:32). Will is fatal and emerges as the desire to enact the organization given through thought. To this extent the event is tool-like; it arrives as an instrument to accomplish work, to meliorate nature, and it is the function of Man's presence in nature to *become* this tool. Nature remains organized around its preeminent medium of presentation: Man's will as a becoming tool. But for reflective consciousness the progressive organization of nature comes as partial and sporadic events of unity amid the repetition of thought that makes up most of our experience.

The second consequence of my explanation of will can be drawn from these remarks. Emerson's acknowledgment of fate allows him to affirm unequivocally the identity of will and Man. The nostalgia for humanist Man still present in "Experience" barred this affirmation, as I have made clear. In "Experience" Emerson locates the emergence of will and the potential identity of Man and will, but the affirmation of that identity is withheld from him due to the illusory foundation of nature, the slippage of nature out of the grasp of Man's will, which has the effect of implicating a wider field of human efficacy than will can account for and thus subverting the power of will. The delimitation of nature within fate entails the identity of Man as will but does so through a diminution of Man to the radically finite will that enacts a fatal thought. To be sure, in a sense this is no longer what Emerson had meant by Man; that is, it is no longer the universal center and purpose of nature. But in another sense it is precisely what Man has always meant to Emerson: the power to articulate nature's order. Nature itself, however, is reduced to the fatal, circumstantial terms of the event of thought. Within the limits of nature's circumstantial presence, freedom is the event of Man that articulates and enacts nature's law and unity. Emerson regains the concept of freedom by redefining nature as disjunctive, sporadic, fatal—that is, the destiny to presence, the inevitability of will.

ANARCHIC SENSES OF ENDING

Emerson's theorizing comes to completion in "Fate" with the determination of will as the fatal event of nature, the occurrence of Man as the radically finite site of nature. The remaining essays in *Conduct of Life* apply the doctrine of fate, predicting the society and culture it entails. In conclusion I wish to remark the continuity and unity of Emerson's development, a continuity I have emphasized throughout the preceding five chapters. Emerson's thought ends in "Fate" in much the same place it began. And it is therefore fitting that he turns again to the idea of self-reliance and the doctrine of compensation in these late essays. But if everything remains the same in one sense, then in another sense everything in his thought has changed. To my mind, it is this sameness amid profound change that makes the development of Emerson's thought interesting. It can be seen in his assertion that the book of nature is the book of fate. As the book of fate, nature exceeds Man, becomes for itself, engages *its* destiny. Yet it cannot be severed from Man. The single fact, the essential thing, the One that stands at the center of Emerson's thought, first as Man, then as nature, and finally as fate, is nothing but the interaction of Man and nature, the powerful pragmatics of appearing *and* disappearing.

Emerson reaffirms that essential interaction, the fundamental dynamic of nature, in "Fate," when he writes of the event that gives nature's presence that it both gives and derives from the person. "The secret of the world is the tie between person and event. Person makes event, and event person" (*C* 6:42). But, he adds, "the copula is hidden" (*C* 6:43). It is not nature but identity in nature that now hides, and this cunning of identity bars the grounds for humanist self-recognition and recovery. Emerson does not doubt that Man and nature arise together. His inquiry, from *Nature* to "Fate," meditates on and reformulates this always interesting fact. He sees a fittingness between Man and nature that initially led him to assert the centrality and causality of will. The above statement suggests, however, why he no longer holds to that humanist principle. Our fate inheres in the fact that events are us, we are their root, but "we have not eyes sharp enough to descry the thread that ties cause and effect" (*C* 6:44).[2]

But to what degree has Emerson's thought actually changed? I have argued that the doctrine of fate sets aside the metaphysical problematic of teleology and turns, in a way that predicts a number of later thinkers—I've mentioned Nietzsche and Heidegger—to the non-metaphysical conception of thought as an event. Both Emerson's own vocabulary and, much more to the point, the development of his thought indicate that this is the case. And yet, doesn't the above statement reflect precisely the all-too-metaphysical desire to locate the cause of the world's appearance? Doesn't it indicate a desire, moreover, to locate that cause finally in Man, where it had been for Emerson since 1836? Isn't Emerson, then, as much a radical humanist in 1860 as he was in 1836? Isn't fate itself the illusion, and shouldn't we conclude, as one reader does, that the "truth, beauty, and goodness of necessity will always be obscured by the devastating illusion that fate is caprice. . . . the misperception . . . is to think one's fate is 'alien, because the copula are hidden'" (*sic*).[3]

These are, I think, good and viable questions. But I would say they are good questions, not because they refute Emerson's theory, demonstrating once again that he was indeed inconsistent, but because they suggest the extent to which his thought is situated in a moment of cultural and intellectual transition, and the extent to which it stands at the threshold of a new approach to the question of human being's relation to nature. These questions do not tend toward a refutation of Emerson's ideas, but rather enact the very thought he sought to articulate. They enact the problem of Man's superficiality and nature's irresolution. More than anything else, Emerson's assertion of the hidden tie between person and event grapples with the very issue of the passing of the metaphysical interpretation of Man and nature, which is to say,

---

2. Julie Ellison cites a strikingly similar statement from a draft of Emerson's first publication. "In an 1822 draft of 'Thoughts on the Religion of the Middle Ages,' he had written, 'Not percieving [*sic*] ourselves the connection which binds events, we are unable to discover how far a sublime uniformity may prevail'" (*Emerson's Romantic Style*, 39). Ellison traces the movement characteristic of Emerson's early humanism, by which "a year later, his vision of progress has sharpened into a vision of control" (39). But Emerson's repetition of the early sentiment here in "Fate" indicates the powerful continuity of the themes of fate and obedience in his work, and supports the contention that his humanist phenomenology represents only his first brief and finally inadequate response to those themes.

3. Hughes, *Emerson's Demanding Optimism*, 27.

the issue of the collapse of causal explanations of the relation of Man and nature. Emerson grapples with the problem of the role and value of Man when viewed outside the terms of a theory of action, and thus outside the system of causal relations that the metaphysical tradition shows leads back always to Man's efficacy in nature. I would characterize Emerson's doctrine of fate as a liminal appearance of a nonmetaphysical theory of value. It addresses the question of what the conduct of Man can be, and it indicates that fatal conduct will arise from the externalized historicity of the individual. The fatal revaluation of the method of nature consists in nothing but this externalization. This is implicit in the above citation, which says, as I have been urging throughout this chapter, that the individual's historicity does not belong to Man. As Man's, historicity is ambiguously prolific and subversive. It opens possibilities for Man, but it renders all his endeavors superficial, ideological. The revaluation carried out by the doctrine of fate makes Man's historicity an alien power, gives destiny over to nature and thereby enables Man as the functional will that presences nature.

Our question, then, should be what the externalization of historicity would mean, in concrete terms, for the behavior, the action and agency, of human beings. It would mean two things, I would suggest, only one of which can I say with certainty was apparent to Emerson. It means that fate now names the exteriority of nature as dehumanized will, as the history of the individual that is detached from him, a world of will that situates the individual, dictates him, and, in a sense, is the preparation that gives rise to Man. Accordingly, it means that human will is all exterior, finite, that it returns no authenticity to the individual but represents only the externality of performance in an essentially technological world. It may not have been apparent to Emerson, but the doctrine of fate can be seen in retrospect to anticipate a technocratic society. Many of Emerson's images in fact suggest a mechanistic vision of the world, a mathematical conception of nature and justice. If it is surely too much to say Emerson foresaw the advanced technocracy that characterizes contemporary America, then one can at least note the prescient technological vision these images convey.

The externality of historicity in the doctrine of fate has a second meaning, however, which I think Emerson was well aware of and, indeed, toward which I would say he intended his thought. The externality of will as fate releases will from its humanist obligations and frees it to the immediate articulation of nature. It gives will as an unprincipled articulation of nature, an anarchic presencing of nature. Nothing is withheld from the will's labor; though radically finite, it is complete and exhaustive. As such, it is an innocent expression of nature as the power of will. Here is the pure pragmatism that Emerson's early thought promised under the name of self-reliance; it is realized through the doctrine of fate under the same name. And here the continuity in Emerson's thought is most evident. Finally, it seems to me, Emerson's embrace of fatalism is best understood in terms of the project that informed his writings at least from the first series of essays on: the project of locating the virtue and dignity of the human being in *the innocent expression of power*.

Emerson had first sought innocence in terms of humanist self-reliance, which he described most characteristically under the figure of the self-reliant boy. He admired the reckless will of the boy who "looks on" the world from his position of "unaffected, unbiased, unbribable, unaffrighted innocence," who "is in the parlour what the pit is in the playhouse; independent, irresponsible . . . [and who] cumbers himself never about consequences, about interests, [but] gives an independent, genuine verdict" (*CW* 2:29). He admired the boy's innocence and creativity, and he conceived of human dignity in terms of that innocence no less in 1860 than in 1840. I shouldn't need to add, however, that there is a crucial difference between his early and late positions; it concerns the self-reliant boy's "neutrality" in the scene he observes and judges. Emerson came to realize that in a world defined by will, the assumption of such independence is a myth. The individual is always implicated in a structure of power relations. The critique of humanism in 1841 indicates that there is no such thing as a neutral perspective, that all perspectives, and equally all judgments issuing from them, are invested with their own interests and, moreover, are convicted to those interests. The pessimism of the transitional phase stems from the failure of innocence. And with it comes our guilt, our indebtedness—or better yet—the recognition *both* that our account of the world is indebted to the perspective and disposition in which we find ourselves and is in no way representative of the universal sense of the world, *and* that under the humanist scheme we stand always in debt to the responsibility and burden to articulate the value of the world and ourselves. I read the above citation as a response to this guilt, so that when Emerson writes that our eyes are not sharp enough to discern the copula, I no longer hear a metaphysical desire, a longing and lament that the First Cause exceeds our knowledge. Instead, I hear patient counseling that the debt to that ideal, to the myth of such eyes, is an unnecessary casting of thought as the Sisyphean labor of self-recovery. Emerson's fate turns him from this burden to the joyous uses of power. Through the doctrine of fate he recuperates human innocence and provides a directive for human dignity, finding both in the expression of power free of the insurmountable debt to hold the world accountable through one's actions, to gather the world together within the horizon of one's eye, indeed, the very burden of making the world account for itself by making oneself accountable. Emersonian freedom, in his final formulation of it, arises by turning from the accountability of Man and nature; it arises as the innocence of nature's power before the accusations of representational thought that would cheat it of its destiny, as the innocence of Man's power before the indictments of moral rectitude that would shackle and persecute its joy. It satisfies Emerson's earliest desire by releasing will and nature to the fluctuations and hierarchies of power, and thereby justifies Emerson's self-description as "a professor of the Joyous Science . . . an affirmer of the One Law, yet as one who should affirm it in music or dancing, a priest of the Soul yet one who would better love to celebrate it through the beauty of health & harmonious power."

Conclusion:
The Art of Power

Emerson's philosophical development began where Western metaphysics began, with the desire to know what is, to know the whence and whereto of nature that defines its Being. In a letter to his brother he cast this desire in terms of a "crack" in nature, and as in the metaphysical tradition, he soldered the crack by stuffing it full of spirit. But the crack didn't go away. It infiltrated spirit, and the perfect meld began to tremble, as Derrida puts it. What makes Emerson most interesting to me is that he didn't stop his inquiry at the point of this trembling, nor did he credit this *solution* of metaphysics as the end of philosophy. "[Not] *what*, but *how*," he said. The statement solicits a philosophical advance from the defining question of metaphysics. It seeks the practical orientation of thought that characterizes his final philosophical attitude, and suggests Emerson's turning from interior contemplation of the trembling of metaphysical apparatuses, the quivering of whatness, to an exterior glance: "[not] *what*, but *how*"; wisdom found and loved, not in being in the know but in practicing life, in behavior stretching from "the figure, movement and gesture of animated bodies [to] articulate speech" (*C* 6:163).[1] Emerson's philosophical development comes to completion by affirming the locus of nature's law in the sheer practice of the individual,

---

1. Cf. Hughes, *Emerson's Demanding Optimism*, 2ff.

one's eccentricities and one's entanglements. It is named by the doctrine of fate, which formulates an exterior or pragmatic path of thought that apprehends practice prior to its insinuation in an interior dialectic. And it concludes in a pious relation to the source, earned by the turn from what to how.

Emerson's remarks on metaphysics in "Natural History of Intellect" reflect this turn away from the necessarily interior pursuit of whatness. "Metaphysics," he says, "[is] a grammar to which, once read, we seldom return" (*C* 12:12). Metaphysics, properly understood, is a method then, a set of rules for thinking, and not a science that has its own content. But Emerson goes further than just describing the finitude of the method of metaphysics; he asserts it is misguided, disparaging as "somewhat mean, as spying," the inward direction of metaphysics, "this watching of the mind, in season and out of season, to see the mechanics of the thing" (*C* 12:13). In distinction he conceives of philosophy as a method of thinking that by precluding an inward direction takes it as its goal to accommodate the power of an idea, not to dispose of it. He writes, "My metaphysics are to the end of use," and means by this that his philosophy has as its goal rightly situating oneself with the power held in the informing ideas of one's world. Needless to say, he intends no reduction of the world to its cost-value. Rather, his remarks entail a manner of thought sensitive to the full play of tones and hues in our world, recognizing, tallying, and carrying along the range of our susceptibility to the world. In the following lines Emerson describes this kind of thought directed toward an object and gives a sense of the operation of pragmatic philosophy.

> I wish to know the laws of this wonderful power, that I may domesticate it. I observe with curiosity its risings and settings, illumination and eclipse; its obstructions and its provocations, that I may learn to live with it wisely, court its aid, catch sight of its splendor, feel its approach, hear and save its oracles and obey them. (*C* 12:13)

The doctrine of fate frees what is given to thought from relation to what is withheld in thought, and allows an idea to stand apart as sovereign and whole. As the description makes clear, thought's goal is to do justice to the scope of the idea, to draw out its eloquence by tracking its contours, by knowing how it works, not what it is. In Emerson's still-phenomenological imagery, this means by marking what it illuminates and what it casts into darkness. Perhaps more concretely, it means thinking through the richness and capacity of an idea and knowing its utility in relation to other ideas. Emerson readily notes this is a poetic conception of thought. Indeed, it is no more than a description of the apprehension of the work of eloquence. And because it is motivated by the poet's imperative to do justice to the wholeness and power of an idea, this manner of thought saves and obeys what is given in thought, demarcating what is withheld only as the limit of an idea's power. It preserves the integrity of the idea, both for a history of intellect (such as the topic of this work suggests) and, more importantly, for the individual. The goal Emerson attributes to a thoughtful posture in the world is to dwell with the eloquence of ideas that inhere in our contemporary practice, to draw out and mark their power, and by so doing to preserve the integrity of our practice. This requires, paradoxically, that we be responsible to the irresponsible manifestation of our lives, that we concede the susceptibility that drives our behavior and by dwelling thoughtfully with it bear witness to its legacy for us.

"Fate" sets the theoretical foundation for *Conduct of Life* precisely by externalizing and rendering systematic Emerson's insight that wisdom derives from the reduction of learning to practice. The methodology it identifies consists in unprincipled and uncritical obedience to the practice of life. This sense of uncritical obedience is evident already in the early characterization of self-reliance as that which "relies because it works and is." In that description Emerson reveals the same impatience one sees later with a critical distance that would speak in poor external ways of reliance, and already hints at his recognition of the power of gathering—of reliance in the Latin sense of *religare*—carried in our practice. But whereas this led him in the early period to conclude that individual will stands as the principle and cause of the unity of our experience, the doctrine of fate acknowledges that experience accounts for itself, writes itself, in what we do. It casts the individual as a reader, then, but, distinct from the earlier writings, it casts him as a reader who refuses to warrant the informing power of his eye, releasing it, instead, to serve as monitor and index of the text. By 1860 Emerson concludes that the adequacy of an interpretation of the law of nature requires, not a critical gesture of detachment and command, but rather absolute fidelity to the fatal line of practice, wherein, moreover, resides the path of thought.

The practical turn of "Fate" presses Emerson's philosophy to the frontier of politics and raises questions about its nature, about what relation there is between politics and practice, and, equally, about the distance, if any, there should be between everyday practices and the arena of politics. The doctrine of fate suggests a political theory that refuses artificially defined boundaries of political discourse, and minimally recognizes the political significance of a wide field of behavior beyond institutional power. It directs attention to a field of political value that is important precisely because it eludes institutional representation, a nomadic power that Emerson calls "a *plus* condition of mind and body" and that he says is "rarely found in the right state for an article of commerce, but oftener in the supersaturate or excess which makes it dangerous and destructive" (*C* 6:72). Such descriptions suggest an extension of the politics of democracy beyond the institutional limits of the "citizen" to the mundanity and eccentricity of actions that make up people's behavior, the plurality of images evident in the fatal practice of language, no longer policed and obscured by the imperative to self-possessive articulations. The radical political promise of Emerson's early intuition, the revolution it predicted would be based on the unobstructed play of individual practice, is clarified under the doctrine of fate, and it appears to have a deep affinity with contemporary efforts to expand our understanding of what the political is. It is beyond the scope of this book to pursue these ideas, but it seems to me the long tradition that denies political viability to Emerson's thought, that casts it as "at bottom an anti-political stance," overemphasizes a single aspect of Emerson's *early* period and owes some response to the practical turn in his later thought.[2]

A response might begin by amending Stephen Whicher's characterization of Emerson's later works as "radically anarchic."[3] Emerson's final philosophy is radical and anarchic, indeed. But if it is not directed toward any specific mode of practice, least of all toward conformity with conventions, then it is equally true that the modernist privilege given to the act of emancipation from conventions, so evident in Emerson's early period, is absent in the later works. In its place is a more thoroughgoing anarchy built on the sovereignty of ideas and concepts, their freedom precisely to manifestation in the practice of life. Thought, in consequence, is retrieved from the interrogative probings and ideological intrusions that are the legacy of interiority and that demand conformity: to social conventions, on the one hand, but just as resolutely to a transgressive structure of thought and action, on the other. An exterior orientation of mind recuperates thought, as described in the citation above, for the affirmation and utilization of ideas.

---

2. Marr, *American Worlds since Emerson*, 3.
3. *Freedom and Fate*, 56.

Emerson's emphasis during the transitional period is on the voracious eloquence of ideological structures and the inability of nature to gain sovereignty from linguistic accounts that are inadequate to it. The pragmatics of thought turn away from this interior obsession with tracing an ideational genealogy of the individual's practices. It would be naive to think they cannot be, at least partially, traced, but at issue is the priority such a genealogy has. Or, to look at it from the other direction, at issue is the surprising eloquence of our practice and the justice of its capacity to overtake and compel our behavior. In his later works Emerson refuses the seduction of an ethics of transgression that incessantly limns dialectical oppositions, and earns, instead, a theory that gives methodological priority to moments of eloquence, showing that they essentially precede and are free of interrogations that seek to account for and dispose of them. And he thus earns the retrieval of thought as the medium of obedience and command, as the pragmatic knowledge of when to obey and when to command, as the art of power.

In this manner Emerson's final philosophy preserves the power of fate, the power of the practice of language, if we want to put it that way, and preserves it as a field of value distinct from language itself. Gertrude Reif Hughes wisely remarks, "The important thing is not to quibble over distinctions between truth and life, but to see that the Emersonian essay ends with power and to recognize as fully as possible the ramifications of that fact."[4] The most important ramification, to my mind, is that it preserves a content for philosophical discourse, articulating a method that wins thought back from the legacy of interior, metaphysical withdrawal, and the enfeebling narcissism that results from the imperative to command, dispose, and overcome the images of the world. The duty Emerson ultimately sets for the individual, his responsibility under this anarchic philosophy, is to accommodate himself in earnest discernment to the power of the images that make up his world. It seems clear, moreover, that Emerson concluded the individual's vision can be preserved and expressed only by giving up control over it and releasing the claim to grasp it.

The doctrine of fate expresses the risings and settings over the topography of Man's relation to nature; it expresses the illumination and eclipse of Emerson's single idea: self-reliance. Above all, it articulates the eloquent movement of that idea, revealing its necessity to reside in the exterior orientation of mind that commands obedience to the prac-

---

4. *Emerson's Demanding Optimism*, 7.

tice of life. But is the doctrine of fate itself necessary? The point I have tried to make in this book is that Emerson's writings, in tracing the movement in thought from interiority to a pragmatic vision, obey the "double force of reason and destiny," as he characterized the imperative of eloquence (*C* 7:92). Thus, if the greater cogency of an exterior direction of mind relative to the interior fascinations of humanism and antihumanism became evident to Emerson with the irresistibleness of a philosophical necessity, this can only be due to the power and value vested in his language. The most that can be said, then, is that the philosophical "reach" and necessity of the doctrine of fate reflects the earned compass of the figures and language Emerson used.

Index

abandonment, 27, 43–44, 46
affect, 150–59
alienation, 67, 78, 80
"American Scholar, The" (Emerson), 17, 32 n. 4; and humanist synthesis, 20, 41, 98; polarity, 57; and "Self-Reliance," 60, 63, 66
anarchy, 196, 202–4
Anaxagoras, 152
Anaximenes, 152
Anderson, Quentin, 65
antihumanism, 20–26, 91–98
Aristotle, 9, 88
authenticity. *See* humanist synthesis

Barzilai, Shuli, 105 n. 10
Bentham, Jeremy, 65
Bercovitch, Sacvan, 5
Bible, 138
Bishop, Jonathan, 127 n. 5

Cameron, Sharon, 127 n. 5
Cascardi, Anthony J., 131 n. 10
Categorical Imperative, 32–33
Cavell, Stanley, 2 n. 2, 7 n. 11, 11, 17 n. 26, 32 n. 4, 36 n. 7, 61, 72 n. 7, 94, 101, 101 n. 9, 111, 117 n. 1, 131 n. 10, 177
"Circles" (Emerson), 17, 38–43, 45–46, 73, 86, 87; and "Experience," 116, 128; and humanist synthesis, 38–42; and "The Method of Nature," 94–97; phenomenological method of, 38, 41
cogito, 36 n. 7
Columbus, Christopher, 160, 165
"Compensation" (Emerson), 11, 19, 38; doctrine of, 46–58; and exteriority, 167; and labor, 72–74; and polarity, 56–57; pragmatism of, 46; and sensualism, 50–52; and the spirit of revenge, 47–54, 141; and "Surface," 141; temporality of, 49–51
compensation, doctrine of, 46–58
Confucius, 93
"Copernican revolution," 124
Copernicus, Nicolaus, 124
Cox, James M., 8 n. 14, 128
Cratylus, 113

Dante Alighieri, 138
deconstruction, 40, 162
Derrida, Jacques, 86 n. 1, 88, 89, 108, 109 n. 11, 199
Descartes, René, 6, 7, 28, 36 n. 7
Dewey, John, 124, 125
doctrine of the farm, 69–73

Edmundson, Mark, 49 n. 16
Ellison, Julie, 3–4 n. 4, 5 n. 7, 6 n. 8, 7, 10, 15 n. 23, 33 n. 5, 195 n. 2

eloquence: and affect, 151–53; and "Experience," 131, 151–53; fatality of, 170 n. 3; and *Nature*, 15; and reason, 3–4, 3 n. 4, 4 n. 5, 18, 151–53, 201–4

Emerson, Ellen Tucker, 127

Emerson, Ralph Waldo: on anarchy, 196–204; and "the end of philosophy," 86–89; and modernism, 6–8, 18, 28–30; and philosophy, 2–3, 8–10; and pious exteriority, 167–70. *See also* eloquence; event; humanist synthesis, the; obedience; phenomenological method; pragmatism
WORKS: *Address*, to the Harvard Divinity School, 63; *Conduct of Life*, 4, 135, 141, 150, 161, 171, 194, 201; "Eloquence," 7 n. 13, 25; *Essays: First Series*, 1, 12; *Essays: Second Series*, 178; "History," 110; "Human Culture," 66–70; "Illusions," 167; "Intellect," 118; "Lectures on the Times," 22, 130; "Montaigne, or the Skeptic," 36; "Natural History of Intellect," 167, 169, 200; "Nature," 107; "Poet, The," 107–12, 144; "Poetry and Imagination," 106; "Power," 80, 181, 183; "Spiritual Laws," 43; "Transcendentalist, The," 111; "Wealth," 80, 183. *See also* "American Scholar, The"; "Circles"; "Compensation"; "Experience"; "Fate"; "Man, the Reformer"; "Method of Nature, The"; *Nature*; "Self-Reliance"

Emerson, Waldo, 127

epistemological dualism, 9–21, 98

ereignis. *See* event

event: and Descartes, 170; in "Experience," 146–51; fatality of, 176, 180; in "Fate," 186–94

"Experience" (Emerson), 3, 17 n. 26, 22, 24, 86 n. 1, 115–63 ("Illusion," 118–23, 126–31, "Succession," 123–26, "Temperament," 131–34, "Surface," 136–43, "Surprise," 143–45, "Reality," 145–55, "Subject, or the One," 155–61), 167, 171–77 passim, 183; and affect, 119, 151–53, 158–59; antihumanism of, 115; and Waldo Emerson, 126–27; on event, 146–51; and exteriority, 138–41; and "Fate," 188, 191, 192, 193; grief, 127–31; and Heraclitus, 117–19; and Kant, 124–25; and "The Method of Nature," 93, 95, 100, 105, 107, 111–13; and phenomenological method, 115–18; and "The Poet," 107, 109, 111; pragmatism of, 139, 142, 145; structure of, 119–23, 161–63; and teleology, 122, 139–40

"Fate" (Emerson), 15 n. 24, 24, 171–94, 201; and anarchy, 196–98; on conduct, 182–94; distinct from nature, 175–81; on event, 186–94; and "Experience," 113, 149–50, 163, 188–94; and piety, 169; pragmatism of, 190–93, 197

Francis, Richard Lee, 95

Fritz-Piggott, Jill, 109 n. 11

Furet, François, 6 n. 10

Galilei, Galileo, 124

Gifford Lectures, 124

Gilmore, Michael T., 42 n 13

Goodman, Russell B., 2 n. 2, 117 n. 1

Hegel, G.W.F., 14, 28, 29, 69, 125

Heidegger, Martin, 10 n. 19, 49, 72 n. 7, 88, 166, 170, 186, 195

Heraclitus, 93, 117, 117 n. 1, 118, 119, 122, 131

Hill, David W., 127 n. 6

Homer, 138

Hughes, Gertrude Reif, 3 n. 4, 7 n. 12, 131 n. 9, 170 n. 3, 203

humanist synthesis: and antihumanism, 20, 22, 92, 99–100, 115; and "Circles," 38–42; in "Man, the Reformer," 64–66; and "The Method of Nature," 92, 99–100; in *Nature*, 8, 12–19; and phenomenological method, 8–19; scope of, 5–6, 17–18, 17 n. 26; in "Self-Reliance," 31–34, 38, 45, 58

innocence, 35–38, 57, 61–62, 182, 197–98

irony, 5, 39 n. 9, 168, 178–79

Joyous Science, the, 11–12, 19, 22–25

Kant, Immanuel, 15, 28, 29, 31–34, 60, 124–25

Kepler, Johann, 160

Knox, John, 65

Kristeva, Julia, 104, 105 n. 10

Kronick, Joseph, 109 n. 11

labor, 69–73

Lacan, Jacques, 104

Last Judgment, 46, 47, 50, 54, 138, 141
logos, 42, 61, 89, 93
Lopez, Michael, 95

"Man, the Reformer" (Emerson), 12, 17, 18, 63–83, 91, 92; criticism of trade, 73–75; and "Human Culture," 68–70; and humanist synthesis, 64–83; on labor 69–73; on phenomenology and culture, 68–79; and politics, 79–83; and the pragmatic maxim, 70; and "Self-Reliance," 64–66
Marr, David, 31, 33 n. 6
Marx, Karl, 69
Mecca, 148–49
Mencius, 153
Menu, 93
"Method of Nature, The" (Emerson), 42, 91–114; antihumanism of, 5, 19–23, 86–87, 92–104; and "Circles," 94–97; criticism of, 94–96; and "Experience," 115–16, 119, 126–27, 143–44, 157; and "Fate," 171, 173, 178–80, 186; and Heraclitus, 92–93; and "Man, the Reformer," 91–92, 97–98; and memory, 93–94; and metaphoricity, 109–13; on obedience, 1–2, 87; and phenomenological method, 98–99, 115–16, 119, 157; and "The Poet," 107–11; on the temporality of nature, 104–7; on thought and teleology, 101–3
Michael, John, 2 n. 2, 14 n. 22, 41 n. 12
Milton, John, 37, 138
modernity, 6–7, 18, 28–30
moral utopianism, 33
mourning, 127–31

Nature (Emerson), 1, 3, 38, 58, 92, 100, 121, 128, 160, 169, 194; and Descartes, 7, 28; and epistemology, 12–15; and Hegel, 14, 28–29; and humanist synthesis, 6–12; "Idealism" and "Spirit," 6, 12–18; and modern philosophy, 28–30; phenomenological method of, 8–12; practical teleology of, 18; and the sublime, 15
Nietzsche, Friedrich, 10 n. 19, 94, 141, 170, 195; and "Compensation," 49–53

obedience: and antihumanism, 24–26, 87–89; and eloquence, 3, 8; fatality of, 6, 8, 24–26; in "Fate," 185, 189; in "The Method of Nature," 1–2, 87; and practice, 1–8, 24–26, 201

Packer, B. L., 5 n. 7, 6 n. 8, 7 n. 13, 9, 12 n. 20
Paradise Lost (Milton), 37
Paul, Sherman, 8 n. 14, 46 n. 15, 94
Pease, Donald E., 8, 9 n. 16, 15 n. 24
phenomenological method: in "Circles," 38, 41; critique of, 19–20, 86 n. 1, 98–99, 115–19; of culture and labor, 68–79; and domesticity, 66, 78; and "Experience," 115–18; and humanist synthesis, 8–19; in "Man, the Reformer," 70–83; and "The Method of Nature," 96, 98–99, 119; in *Nature*, 8–18; and pragmatism, 70, 81; in "Self-Reliance," 34–38; as the site of politics, 75, 79–83
phusis, 42, 44, 53, 62
piety, 32, 33 n. 5, 169
Plato, 2, 109 n. 11, 125
Poirier, Richard, 40, 42
polarity, 56–57
Porte, Joel, 41 n. 11, 42 n. 13
Porter, David, 93 n. 1
practical imperative, 31–34, 42
pragmatism, 25; and "Compensation," 46; and event, 186–92; and exteriority, 139, 142, 169–70; in "Fate," 184–85, 190–93, 197; in "Human Culture," 70; and humanist synthesis, 64, 70, 81–83, and innocence of power, 197–98; in "Man, the Reformer," 81–83; and phenomenology, 70, 81; in "Surface," 139–45; and thought, 200
Ptolemaic system, 124

Rand, Nicholas, 10 n. 19
rationalism, 28
ressentiment, 141
Ricoeur, Paul, 9 n. 16
Robinson, David, 66 n. 2, 95, 95 n. 6

Sealts, Merton M., 6 n. 9, 12 n. 20
"Self-Reliance" (Emerson), 10, 17 n. 26, 18, 31–62, 36 n. 7, 106; and Categorical Imperative, 32–34; and "Circles," 38–42; and "Compensation," 45–60; and humanist synthesis, 31–34; and innocence, 35–38; and "Man, the Reformer," 64, 73, 77, 82; phenomenological method of, 36–45;

and skepticism, 36–38; and speech, 43–45; transcendentalism of, 60–62
Shakespeare, William, 138
skepticism, 35–38
Smith, David L., 109 n. 11
Society of the Adelphi, 1
Socrates, 93
solipsism, 37
speech, 42–45
spirit of revenge, 47–53, 141
Steele, Jeffrey, 3 n. 4, 39 n. 9
sublime, 7, 15
Swedenborg, Emanuel, 65

Tanner, Tony, 8 n. 14, 36
Thales, 152
Thus Spoke Zarathustra (Nietzsche), 49

transcendental pragmatics, 3 n. 4
transcendentalism, 16, 34, 39, 60–62
Transfiguration, 138
Trismegisti, 93

Van Leer, David, 2 n. 2
Very, Jones, 6 n. 8

Waterville College, 1, 8
Wesley, John, 65
West, Cornel, 2 n. 2, 177
Whicher, Stephen, 5, 94, 101, 127 n. 5, 202

Yoder, R. A., 92, 93 n. 1, 120, 126, 127, 127 n. 5

Zoroaster, 93, 104, 152

www.ingramcontent.com/pod-product-compliance
Lightning Source LLC
Chambersburg PA
CBHW031550300426
44111CB00006BA/251